Lister's Gr

MW01675219

Harold Bindloss

Alpha Editions

This edition published in 2022

ISBN : 9789356891074

Design and Setting By
Alpha Editions
www.alphaedis.com
Email - info@alphaedis.com

Contents

PART I
BARBARA'S REBELLION

CHAPTER I

CARTWRIGHT MEDDLES

Dinner was over, and Cartwright occupied a chair on the lawn in front of the Canadian summer hotel. Automatic sprinklers threw sparkling showers across the rough, parched grass, the lake shimmered, smooth as oil, in the sunset, and a sweet, resinous smell drifted from the pines that rolled down to the water's edge. The straight trunks stood out against a background of luminous red and green, and here and there a slanting beam touched a branch with fire.

Natural beauty had not much charm for Cartwright, who was satisfied to loaf and enjoy the cool of the evening. He had, as usual, dined well, his cigar was good, and he meant to give Mrs. Cartwright half an hour. Clara expected this, and, although he was sometimes bored, he indulged her when he could. Besides, it was too soon for cards. The lights had not begun to spring up in the wooden hotel, and for the most part the guests were boating on the lake. When he had finished his cigar it would be time to join the party in the smoking-room. Cartwright was something of a gambler and liked the American games. They gave one scope for bluffing, and although his antagonists declared his luck was good, he knew his nerve was better. In fact, since he lost his money by a reckless plunge, he had to some extent lived by bluff. Yet some people trusted Tom Cartwright.

Mrs. Cartwright did so. She was a large, dull woman, but had kept a touch of the beauty that had marked her when she was young. She was kind, conventional, and generally anxious to take the proper line. Cartwright was twelve years older, and since she was a widow and had three children when she married him, her friends declared her money accounted for much, and a lawyer relation carefully guarded, against Cartwright's using her fortune.

Yet, in a sense, Cartwright was not an adventurer, although his ventures in finance and shipping were numerous. He sprang from an old Liverpool family whose prosperity diminished when steamers replaced sailing ships. His father had waited long before he resigned himself to the change, but was not altogether too late, and Cartwright was now managing owner of the Independent Freighters Line. The company's business had brought him to Montreal, and when it was transacted he had taken Mrs. Cartwright and her family to the hotel by the Ontario lake.

Cartwright's hair and mustache were white; his face was fleshy and red. He was fastidious about his clothes, and his tailor cleverly hid the bulkiness of his figure. As a rule, his look was fierce and commanding, but now and then his small keen eyes twinkled. Although Cartwright was clever, he was, in some respects, primitive. He had long indulged his appetites, and wore the stamp of what is sometimes called good living.

The managing owner of the Independent Freighters needed cleverness, since the company was small and often embarrassed for money. For the most part, it ran its ships in opposition to the regular liners. When the *Conference* forced up freights Cartwright quietly canvassed the merchants and offered to carry their goods at something under the standard rate, if the shippers would engage to fill up his boat. As a rule, secrecy was important, but sometimes, when cargo was scarce, Cartwright let his plans be known and allowed the *Conference* to buy him off. Although his skill in the delicate negotiations was marked, the company paid small dividends and he had enemies among the shareholders. Now, however, he was satisfied. *Oreana* had sailed for Montreal, loaded to the limit the law allowed, and he had booked her return cargo before the *Conference* knew he was cutting rates.

Mrs. Cartwright talked, but she talked much and Cartwright hardly listened, and looked across the lake. A canoe drifted out from behind a neighboring point, and its varnished side shone in the fading light. Then a man dipped the paddle, and the ripple at the bow got longer and broke the reflections of the pines. A girl, sitting at the stern, put her hands in the water, and when she flung the sparkling drops at her companion her laugh came across the lake. Cartwright's look got keen and he began to note his wife's remarks.

"Do you imply Barbara's getting fond of the fellow?" he asked.

"I am afraid of something like that," Mrs. Cartwright admitted. "In a way, one hesitates to meddle; sometimes meddling does harm, and, of course, if Barbara really loved the young man—" She paused and gave Cartwright a sentimental smile. "After all, I married for love, and a number of my friends did not approve."

Cartwright grunted. He had married Clara because she was rich, but it was something to his credit that she had not suspected this. Clara was dull, and her dullness often amused him.

"If you think it necessary, I won't hesitate about meddling," he remarked. "Shillito's a beggarly sawmill clerk."

"He said he was *treasurer* for an important lumber company. Barbara's very young and romantic, and although she has not known him long—"

"She has known him for about two weeks," Cartwright rejoined. "Perhaps it's long enough. Shillito's what Canadians call a looker and Barbara's a romantic fool. I've no doubt he's found out she'll inherit some money; it's possible she's told him. Now I come to think about it, she was off somewhere all the afternoon, and it looks as if she had promised the fellow the evening."

He indicated the canoe and was satisfied when Mrs. Cartwright agreed, since he refused to wear spectacles and own his sight was going. Although Clara was generous, he could not use her money, and, indeed, did not mean to do so, but he was extravagant and his managing owner's post was not secure. When one had powerful antagonists, one did not admit that one was getting old.

"I doubt if Shillito's character is all one could wish,'" Mrs. Cartwright resumed. "Character's very important, don't you think? Mrs. Grant—the woman with the big hat—knows something about him and she said he was *fierce.* I think she meant he was wild. Then she hinted he spent money he ought not to spend. But isn't a treasurer's pay good?"

Cartwright smiled, for he was patient to his wife. "It depends upon the company. A treasurer is sometimes a book-keeping clerk. However, the trouble is, Barbara's as wild as a hawk, though I don't know where she got her wildness. Her brother and sister are tame enough."

"Sometimes I'm bothered about Barbara," Mrs. Cartwright agreed. "She's rash and obstinate; not like the others. I don't know if they're tame, but they had never given me much anxiety. One can trust them to do all they ought."

Cartwright said nothing. As a rule, Clara's son and elder daughter annoyed him. Mortimer Hyslop was a calculating prig; Grace was finicking and bound by ridiculous rules. She was pale and inanimate; there was no blood in her. But Cartwright was fond of the younger girl. Barbara was frankly flesh and blood; he liked her flashes of temper and her pluck.

When the canoe came to the landing he got up. "Leave the thing to me," he said. "I'll talk to Shillito."

He went off, but when he reached the steps to the veranda in front of the hotel he stopped. His gout bothered him. At the top Mortimer Hyslop was smoking a cigarette. The young man was thin and looked bored; his summer clothes were a study in harmonious colors, and he had delicate hands like a woman's. When he saw Cartwright stop he asked: "Can I help you up, sir?"

Cartwright's face got red. He hated an offer of help that drew attention to his infirmity, and thought Mortimer knew.

"No, thanks! I'm not a cripple yet. Have you seen Shillito?"

"You'll probably find him in the smoking room. The card party has gone in and he's a gambler."

"So am I!"

Mortimer shrugged, and Cartwright wondered whether the fellow meant to imply that his gambling was not important since he had married a rich wife. The young man, however, hesitated and looked thoughtful.

"I don't know your object for wanting Shillito, but if my supposition's near the mark, might I state that I approve? In fact, I'd begun to wonder whether something ought not to be done. The fellow's plausible. Not our sort, of course; but when a girl's romantic and obstinate—"

Cartwright stopped him. "Exactly! Well, I'm the head of the house and imagine you can leave the thing to me. Perhaps it doesn't matter if your sister is obstinate. I'm going to talk to Shillito."

He crossed the veranda, and Mortimer returned to his chair and cigarette. He did not approve his step-father, but admitted that Cartwright could be trusted to handle a matter like this. Mortimer's fastidiousness was sometimes a handicap, but Cartwright had none.

Cartwright entered the smoking-room and crossed the floor to a table, at which two or three men stood as if waiting for somebody. One was young and tall. His thin face was finely molded, his eyes and hair were very black, and his figure was marked by an agile grace.

He looked up sharply as Cartwright advanced.

"I want you for a few minutes," Cartwright said roughly, as if he gave an order.

Shillito frowned, but went with him to the back veranda. Although the night was warm and an electric light burned under the roof, nobody was about. Cartwright signed the other to sit down.

"I expect your holiday's nearly up, and the hotel car meets the train in the morning," he remarked.

"What about it?" Shillito asked. "I'm not going yet."

"You're going to-morrow," said Cartwright grimly.

Shillito smiled and gave him an insolent look, but his smile vanished. Cartwright's white mustache bristled, his face was red, and his eyes were very steady. It was not for nothing the old ship-owner had fronted disappointed investors and forced his will on shareholders' meetings. Shillito saw the fellow was dangerous.

"I'll call you," he said, using a gambler's phrase.

"Very well," said Cartwright. "I think my cards are good, and if I can't win on one suit, I'll try another. To begin with, the hotel proprietor sent for me. He stated the house was new and beginning to pay, and he was anxious about its character. People must be amused, but he was running a summer hotel, not a gambling den. The play was too high, and young fools got into trouble; two or three days since one got broke. Well, he wanted me to use my influence, and I said I would."

"He asked you to keep the stakes in bounds? It's a good joke!"

"Not at all," said Cartwright dryly. "I like an exciting game, so long as it is straight, and when I lose I pay. I do lose, and if I come out fifty dollars ahead when I leave, I'll be satisfied. How much have you cleared?"

Shillito said nothing, and Cartwright went on: "My antagonists are old card-players who know the game; but when you broke Forman he was drunk and the other two were not quite sober. You play against young fools and *your luck's too good.* If you force me to tell all I think and something that I know. I imagine you'll get a straight hint to quit."

"You talked about another plan," Shillito remarked.

"On the whole, I think the plan I've indicated will work. If it does not and you speak to any member of Mrs. Cartwright's family, I'll thrash you on the veranda when people are about. I won't state my grounds for doing so; they ought to be obvious."

Shillito looked at the other hand. Cartwright's eyes were bloodshot, his face was going purple, and he thrust out his heavy chin. Shillito thought he meant all he said, and his threat carried weight. The old fellow was, of course, not a match for the vigorous young man, but Shillito saw he had the power to do him an injury that was not altogether physical. He pondered for a few moments, and then got up.

"I'll pull out," he said with a coolness that cost him much.

Cartwright nodded. "There's another thing. If you write to Miss Hyslop, your letters will be burned."

He went back to the smoking-room, and playing with his usual boldness, won twenty dollars. Then he joined Mrs. Cartwright on the front veranda and remarked: "Shillito won't bother us. He goes in the morning."

Mrs. Cartwright gave him a grateful smile. She had long known that when she asked her husband's help difficulties were removed. Now he had removed Shillito, and she was satisfied but imagined he was not. Cartwright knitted his white brows and drew hard at his cigar.

"You had better watch Barbara until the fellow starts," he resumed. "Then I think you and the girls might join the Vernons at their fishing camp. Vernon would like it, and he's a useful friend; besides, it's possible Shillito's obstinate. Your letters needn't follow you; have them sent to me at Montreal, which will cover your tracks. I must go back in a few days."

Mrs. Cartwright weighed the suggestion. Vernon was a Winnipeg merchant, and his wife had urged her to join the party at the fishing camp in the woods. The journey was long, but Mrs. Cartwright rather liked the plan. Shillito would not find them, and Mrs. Vernon had two sons.

"Can't you come with us?" she asked. "Mortimer is going to Detroit."

"Sorry I can't," said Cartwright firmly. "I don't want to leave you, but business calls."

He was relieved when Mrs. Cartwright let it go. Clara was a good sort and seldom argued. He had loafed about with her family for two weeks and had had enough. Moreover, business did call. If the *Conference* found out before his boat arrived that he had engaged *Oreana's* return load, they might see the shippers and make trouble. Anyhow, they would use some effort to get the cargo for their boats. Sometimes one promised regular customers a drawback on standard rates.

"I'll write to Mrs. Vernon in the morning," Mrs. Cartwright remarked.

"Telegraph" said Cartwright, who did not lose time when he had made a plan. "When the lines are not engaged after business hours, you can send a night-letter; a long message at less than the proper charge."

Mrs. Cartwright looked pleased. Although she was rich and sometimes generous, she liked small economies.

"After all, writing a letter's tiresome," she said. "Telegrams are easy. Will you get me a form?"

CHAPTER II

IN THE DARK

In the morning Cartwright told the porter to take his chair to the beach and sat down in a shady spot. He had not seen Barbara at breakfast and was rather sorry for her, but she had not known Shillito long, and although she might be angry for a time, her hurt could not be deep. Lighting his pipe, he watched the path that led between the pines to the water.

By and by a girl came out of the shadow, and going to the small landing-stage, looked at her wrist-watch. Cartwright imagined she did not see him and studied her with some amusement. Barbara looked impatient. People did not often keep her waiting, and she had not inherited her mother's placidity. She had a touch of youthful beauty, and although she was impulsive and rather raw, Cartwright thought her charm would be marked when she met the proper people and, so to speak, got toned down.

Cartwright meant her to meet the proper people, because he was fond of Barbara. She had grace, and although her figure was slender and girlish, she carried herself well. Her brown eyes were steady, her small mouth was firm, and as a rule her color was delicate white and pink. Now it was high, and Cartwright knew she was angry. She wore boating clothes and had obviously meant to go on the lake. The trouble was, her companion had not arrived.

"Hallo!" said Cartwright. "Are you waiting for somebody?"

Barbara advanced and sat down on a rocky ledge.

"No," she said, "I'm not waiting *now*."

Cartwright smiled. He knew Barbara's temper, and his line was to keep her resentment warm.

"You mean, you have given him up and won't go if he does arrive? Well, when a young man doesn't keep his appointment, it's the proper plan."

She blushed, but tried to smile. "I don't know if you're clever or not just now, although you sometimes do see things the others miss. I really was a little annoyed."

"I've lived a long time," said Cartwright. "However, perhaps it's important I haven't forgotten I was young. I think your brother and sister never were very young. They were soberer than me when I knew them first."

"Mortimer *is* a stick," Barbara agreed. "He and Grace have a calm superiority that makes one savage now and then. I like human people, who sometimes let themselves go—"

She stopped, and Cartwright noted her wandering glance that searched the beach and the path to the hotel. He knew whom she expected, and thought it would give her some satisfaction to quarrel with the fellow. Cartwright did not mean to soothe her.

"Mr. Shillito ought to have sent his apologies when he found he could not come," he said.

Barbara's glance got fixed, and Cartwright knew he had blundered.

"Oh!" she said, "now I begin to see! Mother kept me by her all the evening; but mother's not very clever and Mortimer's too fastidious to meddle, unless he gets a dignified part. Of course, the plot was yours!"

Cartwright nodded. Sometimes he used tact, but he was sometimes brutally frank.

"You had better try to console yourself with the Wheeler boys; they're straight young fellows. Shillito is gone. He went by the car this morning and it's unlikely he'll come back."

"You sent him off?" said Barbara, and her eyes sparkled. "Well, I'm not a child and you're not my father really. Why did you meddle?"

"For one thing, he's not your sort. Then I'm a meddlesome old fellow and rather fond of you. To see you entangled by a man like Shillito would hurt. Let him go. If you want to try your powers, you'll find a number of honest young fellows on whom you can experiment. The boys one meets in this country are a pretty good sample."

"There's a rude vein in you," Barbara declared. "One sees it sometimes, although you're sometimes kind. Anyhow, I won't be bullied and controlled; I'm not a shareholder in the Cartwright line. I don't know if it's important, but why don't you like Mr. Shillito?"

Cartwright's eyes twinkled. In a sense, he could justify his getting rid of Shillito, but he knew Barbara and doubted if she could be persuaded. Still she was not a fool, and he would give her something to think about.

"It's possible my views are not important," he agreed. "All the same, when I told the man he had better go he saw the force of my arguments. He went, and I think his going is significant. Since I'd sooner not quarrel, I'll leave you to weigh this."

He went off, but Barbara stopped and brooded. She was angry and humiliated, but perhaps the worst was she had a vague notion Cartwright might be justified. It was very strange Shillito had gone. All the same, she did not mean to submit. Her mother's placid conventionality had long irritated her; one got tired of galling rules and criticism. She was not going to be molded into a calculating prude like Grace, or a prig like Mortimer. They did not know the ridiculous good-form they cultivated was out of date. In fact, she had had enough and meant to rebel.

Then she began to think about Shillito. His carelessness was strangely intriguing; he stood for adventure and all the romance she had known. Besides, he was a handsome fellow; she liked his reckless twinkle and his coolness where coolness was needed. For all that, she would not acknowledge him her lover; Barbara did not know if she really wanted a lover yet. She imagined Cartwright had got near the mark when he said she wanted to try her power. Cartwright was keen, although Barbara sensed something in him that was fierce and primitive.

Perhaps nobody else could have bullied Shillito; Mortimer certainly could not, but Barbara refused to speculate about the means Cartwright had used.

Shillito ought not to have gone without seeing her; this was where it hurt. She was entitled to be angry—and then she started, for a page boy came quietly out of the shade.

"A note, miss," he said with a grin. "I was to give it you when nobody was around."

Barbara's heart beat, but she gave the boy a quarter and opened the envelope. The note was short and not romantic. Shillito stated he had grounds for imagining it might not reach her, but if it did, he begged she would give him her address when she left the hotel. He told her where to write, and added if she could find a way to get his letters he had much to say.

His coolness annoyed Barbara, but he had excited her curiosity and she was intrigued. Moreover, Cartwright had tried to meddle and she wanted to feel she was cleverer than he. Then Shillito was entitled to defend himself, and to find the way he talked about would not be difficult. Barbara knitted her brows and began to think.

At lunch Mrs. Cartwright told her they were going to join the Vernons in the woods and she acquiesced. Two or three days afterwards they started, and at the station she gave Cartwright her hand with a smiling glance, but Cartwright knew his step-daughter and was not altogether satisfied. Barbara did not sulk; when one tried to baffle her she fought.

The Vernons' camp was like others Winnipeg people pitch in the lonely woods that roll west from Fort William to the plains. It is a rugged country pierced by angry rivers and dotted by lakes, but a gasolene launch brought up supplies, the tents were large and double-roofed, and for a few weeks one could play at pioneering without its hardships. The Vernons were hospitable, the young men and women given to healthy sport, and Mrs. Cartwright, watching Barbara fish and paddle on the lake, banished her doubts. For herself she did not miss much; the people were nice, and the cooking was really good.

When two weeks had gone, Grace and Barbara sat one evening among the stones by a lake. The evening was calm, the sun was setting, and the shadow of the pines stretched across the tranquil water. Now and then the reflections trembled and a languid ripple broke against the driftwood on the beach. In the distance a loon called, but when its wild cry died away all was very quiet.

Grace looked across the lake and frowned. She was a tall girl, and although she had walked for some distance in the woods, her clothes were hardly crumpled. Her face was finely molded, but rather colorless; her hands were very white, while Barbara's were brown. Her dress and voice indicated cultivated taste; but the taste was negative, as if Grace had banished carefully all that jarred and then had stopped. It was characteristic that she was tranquil, although she had grounds for disturbance. They were some distance from camp and it would soon be dark, but nothing broke the gleaming surface of the lake. The boat that ought to have met them had not arrived.

"I suppose this is the spot where Harry Vernon agreed to land and take us on board?" she said.

"It's like the spot. I understand we must watch out for a point opposite an island with big trees."

"Watch out?" Grace remarked.

"Watch out is good Canadian," Barbara rejoined. "I'm studying the language and find it expressive and plain. When our new friends talk you know what they mean. Besides, I'd better learn their idioms, because I might stop in Canada if somebody urged me."

Grace gave her a quiet look. Barbara meant to annoy her, or perhaps did not want to admit she had mistaken the spot. Now Grace came to think about it, the plan that the young men should meet them and paddle them down the lake was Barbara's.

"I don't see why we didn't go with Harry and the other, as he suggested," she said.

"Then, you're rather dull. They didn't really want us; they wanted to fish. To know when people might be bored is useful."

"But there are a number of bays and islands. They may go somewhere else," Grace insisted.

"Oh well, it ought to amuse Harry and Winter to look for us, and if they're annoyed, they deserve some punishment. If they had urged us very much to go, I would have gone. Anyhow, you needn't bother. There's a short way back to camp by the old loggers' trail."

Grace said nothing. She thought Barbara's carelessness was forced; Barbara was sometimes moody. Perhaps she felt Shillito's going more than she was willing to own. For all that, the fellow was gone, and Barbara would, no doubt, presently be consoled.

"If mother could see things!" Barbara resumed. "Sometimes one feels one wants a guide, but all one gets is a ridiculous platitude from her old-fashioned code. One has puzzles one can't solve by out-of-date rules. However, since she doesn't see, there's no use in bothering."

"I'm your elder sister, but you don't give me your confidence."

Barbara's mood changed and her laugh was touched by scorn. "You are worse than mother. She's kind, but can't see; you don't want to see. I'd sooner trust my step-father. He's a very human old ruffian. I wish I had a real girl friend, but you tactfully freeze off all the girls I like. It's strange how many people there are whom virtuous folks don't approve."

Grace missed the note of appeal in her sister's bitterness. She did not see the girl as disturbed by doubts and looked in perplexity for a guiding light. Afterwards, when understanding was too late, Grace partly understood.

"Mr. Cartwright is not a ruffian." she said coldly.

"I suppose you're taking the proper line, and you'd be rather noble, only you're not sincere. You don't like Cartwright and know he doesn't like you. All the same, it's not important. We were talking about getting home, and since the boys have not come for us we had better start."

The loon had flown away and nothing broke the surface of the lake; the shadows had got longer and driven back the light. Thin mist drifted about the islands, the green glow behind the trunks was fading, and it would soon be dark.

"In winter, the big timber wolves prowl about the woods," Barbara remarked. "Horrible, savage brutes! I expect you saw the heads at the packer's house. Still, one understands they stay North until the frost begins."

She got up, and when they set off Grace looked regretfully across the lake, for she would sooner have gone home on board the fishing bateau. She was puzzled. The bays on the lake were numerous, and islands dotted the winding reaches, but it was strange the young men had gone to the wrong spot. They knew the lake and had told Barbara where to meet them. In the meantime, however, the important thing was to get home.

Darkness crept across the woods, and as she stumbled along the uneven trail Grace got disturbed. She felt the daunting loneliness, the quiet jarred her nerve. The pines looked ghostly in the gloom. They were ragged and strangely stiff, it looked as if their branches never moved, and the dark gaps between the trunks were somehow forbidding.

Grace did not like Canada. Her cultivation was artificial, but Canada was primitive and stern. In the towns, one found inventions that lightened labor, and brought to the reach of all a physical comfort that in England only the rich enjoyed, but the contrasts were sharp. One left one's hotel, with its very modern furniture, noisy elevators and telephones, and plunged into the wilderness where all was as it had been from the beginning. Grace shrank from primitive rudeness and hated adventure. Living by rule she distrusted all she did not know. She thought it strange that Barbara, who feared nothing, let her go in front.

They came to a pool. All round, the black tops of the pines cut the sky; the water was dark and sullen in the gloom. The trail followed its edge and when a loon's wild cry rang across the woods Grace stopped. She knew the cry of the lonely bird that haunts the Canadian wilds, but it had a strange note, like mocking laughter. Grace disliked the loon when its voice first disturbed her sleep at the fishing camp; she hated it afterwards.

"Go on!" said Barbara sharply.

For a moment or two Grace stood still. She did not want to stop, but something in Barbara's voice indicated strain. If Barbara were startled, it was strange. Then, not far off, a branch cracked and the pine-spray rustled as if they were gently pushed aside.

"Oh!" Grace cried, "something is creeping through the bush!"

"Then don't stop," said Barbara. "Perhaps it's a wolf!"

Grace clutched her dress and ran. At first, she thought she heard Barbara behind, but she owned she had not her sister's pluck and fear gave her speed. She must get as far as possible from the pool before she stopped. Besides, she imagined something broke through the undergrowth near the trail, but her heart beat and she could not hear properly.

At length her breath got labored and she was forced to stop. All was quiet and the quiet was daunting. Barbara was not about and when Grace called did not reply. Grace tried to brace herself. Perhaps she ought to go back, but she could not; she shrank from the terror that haunted the dark. Then she began to argue that to go back was illogical. If Barbara had lost her way, she could not help. It was better to push on to the camp and send men who knew the woods to look for her sister. She set off, and presently saw with keen relief the light of a fire reflected on calm water.

CHAPTER III

BARBARA VANISHES

Grace's arrival was greeted by a shout, and when she stopped in front of the dining-tent a group of curious people surrounded her. The double roof of the big tent was extended horizontally, and a lamp hanging from a pole gave a brilliant light. Grace would sooner the light had been dim, for she was hot and her clothes were torn and wet with dew. Besides, she must tell her tale and admit that she had not played a heroic part.

"Where's Barbara?" Mrs. Cartwright asked.

"I don't know. Harry Vernon did not meet us and we started home by the loggers' trail. I lost Barbara by the pool. Something in the bush tried to creep up to us; a wolf, I think—"

"Oh, shucks!" remarked a frank Winnipeg girl who did not like Miss Hyslop. "In summer, you can't find a wolf south of Broken Range. Looks as if you were scared for nothing, but I can't see why Barbara didn't beat you at hitting up the pace."

Others asked questions, and when Grace got breath she tried to satisfy their curiosity. Some of the group looked thoughtful and Mrs. Vernon said:

"Nothing can have hurt Barbara, and if she has lost her way, she cannot wander far, because she must be in the loop between the river and the lake. But Harry did go to meet you, and when he found you had not come back went off again with Bob. I expect they'll soon arrive with Barbara."

They waited for half-an-hour, and then, when the splash of paddles stole out of the dark, ran down to the beach. Presently a double-ended bateau crossed the beam of light and grounded. A young man helped Barbara out and gave her his arm.

"You mustn't bother, Harry. I can walk all right," she said.

"Get hold," said Vernon. "You're not going to walk. If you're obstinate, I'll carry you."

Barbara leaned upon his arm, but her color was high and her look strained when he helped her across the stones. Harry Vernon was a tall, thin, wiry Canadian, with a quiet face. When he got to the tent he opened the curtain, and beckoning Mrs. Cartwright, pushed Barbara inside.

"You'll give her some supper, ma'am, and I'll chase the others off," he said. "The little girl's tired and mustn't be disturbed."

Barbara gave him a grateful look and the blood came to his sunburned skin.

"I am a little tired," she declared, and added, too quietly for Mrs. Cartwright to hear: "You're a white man."

Vernon pulled the curtain across, and joining the others, lighted a cigarette.

"The girls stopped at False Point, two miles short of the spot we fixed," he said. "I reckon Bob's directions were not plain enough. Since we didn't come along, they started back by the loggers' trail, while we went to look for them by the other track. At the pool, they thought they heard a wolf. That's so, Miss Hyslop?"

"Yes," said Grace. "I ran away and thought I heard Barbara following. But what happened afterwards?"

"She fell. Hurt her foot, had to stop, and then couldn't make good time. We found her limping along, and shoved through the bush for the river, so she needn't walk. Well, I think that's all."

It was plausible, but Grace was not altogether satisfied. Moreover, she imagined Vernon was not, and noted that Mrs. Vernon gave him a thoughtful glance. All the same, there was nothing to be said, and she went to her tent.

At daybreak Vernon left the camp, and when he reached the pool walked round its edge and then sat down and lighted his pipe. A few yards in front, a number of faint marks were printed on a belt of sand. By and by he heard steps, and frowned when Winter came out from an opening in the row of trunks. They were friends, and Bob was a very good sort, but Vernon would sooner he had stopped away.

"Hallo!" he said. "Why have you come along?"

"I lost my hunting-knife," Winter replied. "It was hooked to my belt and I thought the clip let go when we helped Miss Hyslop over the big log. A bully knife; I wanted to find the thing." He paused and smiled when he resumed: "I reckon you pulled out of camp to meditate?"

Vernon hesitated. Had Winter stopped a few yards off, he would have begun some banter and drawn him away from the pool. Bob was a woodsman and his eyes were keen. The sun was, however, rising behind the pines and a beam of light touched the sand. There was no use in trying to hide the marks. In fact, Vernon imagined Bob had seen them.

"No," he said. "I thought I'd try to trail the wolf Miss Hyslop talked about."

"Looks as if you'd found some tracks," Winter remarked. "Well, they're not a wolf's." He sat down opposite Vernon. "A man's! I saw another at a soft spot. He followed the girls from the lake and stopped for some time. I allow I reckoned on something like that."

Vernon made an experiment. "Might have been a packer going to a logging camp, or perhaps an Indian."

"Shucks!" said Winter, although he gave Vernon a sympathetic smile. "There are no Indians about the lake and packers' boots don't make marks like those. A city boot and a city man! A fellow who's wise to the bush lifts his feet. Anyhow, I reckon he doesn't belong to your crowd."

"A sure thing!" Vernon agreed. "I can fix where all the boys were. Besides, if somebody in our lot had wanted to talk to Miss Hyslop, he wouldn't have hung around in the woods. My mother's pretty fastidious about her guests. Well, I'll own up the thing bothers me."

Winter nodded. Harry was frank and honest, and Bob imagined he had felt Barbara Hyslop's charm. He was sorry for Harry. The thing was awkward.

"What are you going to do about it?" he asked.

"To begin with, I'm going to hide these tracks. After all, I don't see much light. I suppose I ought to tell my mother and put Mrs. Cartwright wise; but I won't. Spying on a girl and telling is mean. All the same, I'm surely bothered. In a sense, my mother's accountable for her guests and the girl's nice. I'd like it if I could talk to the man."

"Nothing doing there; he'll watch out. Well, we'll hide up his tracks and look for my knife. D'you think Grace Hyslop knew the job was put up?"

"I don't," said Vernon dryly. "I reckon she was puzzled, but that's all. You couldn't persuade Miss Hyslop her sister liked adventures in the dark. Anyhow, the thing's done with. We have got to let it go."

They went off and Winter pondered. Harry had got something of a knock. Perhaps he was taking the proper line; anyhow, it was the line Harry would take, but Bob doubted. The girl was very young and the man who met her in the dark was obviously a wastrel.

When they returned for breakfast Barbara had joined the others and wore soft Indian moccasins. Bob looked at Harry and understood his frown. Harry had played up when he helped her home, but he, no doubt, thought the game ought to stop. Bob wondered whether Barbara knew, because she turned her head when Harry advanced.

After breakfast, Mrs. Vernon, carrying a small bottle, joined Mrs. Cartwright's party under the pines outside the tent. The dew was drying and the water shone like a mirror, but it was cool in the shade. Barbara occupied a camp-chair and rested her foot on a stone, Mrs. Cartwright knitted, and Grace studied a philosophical book. Her rule was to cultivate her mind for a fixed time every day. Harry Vernon strolled up to the group and Mrs. Cartwright put down her knitting.

"You're kind, but the child's obstinate and won't let me see her foot," she said to Mrs. Vernon.

"It's comfortable now," Barbara remarked. "When something that hurt you stops hurting I think it's better to leave it alone. Besides, one doesn't want to bother people."

"You won't bother me, and I'll fix your foot in two or three minutes so it won't hurt again," Mrs. Vernon declared. "The elixir's famous and I haven't known it to miss. I always carry some when we camp in the woods." She turned to her son. "Tell Barbara how soon I cured you when you hurt your arm."

"You want to burn Miss Hyslop with the elixir?"

"It doesn't burn much. You said you hardly felt it, and soon after I rubbed your arm the pain was gone."

Harry glanced at Barbara and saw she was embarrassed, although her mouth was firm. Since she did not mean to let Mrs. Vernon examine her supposititious injury, his business was to help, and he laughed.

"Miss Hyslop's skin is not like my tough hide. You certainly fixed my arm, but it was a drastic cure, and I think Miss Hyslop ought to refuse. I try to indulge you, like a dutiful son, but you are not her mother."

"I am her mother and she will not indulge me," Mrs. Cartwright remarked with languid grievance, and Barbara gave Harry a quick, searching glance. His face was inscrutable, but she wondered how much he knew. She felt shabby and ashamed.

When Mrs. Vernon went off with the elixir, Harry sat down.

"If you could bring Mr. Cartwright out, I might persuade my father to come along," he said. "The old man likes Cartwright; declares he's a sport."

"He is a ship-owner." Grace remarked. "I think he used to shoot, but it's some time since."

Harry looked at Barbara and his eyes twinkled. "American English isn't Oxford English, but your people are beginning to use it and Miss Barbara learns fast. All the same, running the Independent Freighters is quite a sporting proposition, and I imagine Mr. Cartwright generally makes good.

The old man and I would back him to put over an awkward deal every time."

"My husband is a good business man," Mrs. Cartwright agreed. "But you belong to Winnipeg and I understand his business is at Montreal."

"The steamship *Conference* understood something like that, until Cartwright put them wise. You see, we Western people grow the wheat that goes down the lakes, and when the *Conference* got to know an Independent boat was coming out they went round and offered Montreal shippers and brokers a drawback on the rates. That is, if the shippers gave them all their stuff, they'd meet their bills for a rebate some time afterwards. Bully for the shippers, but it left the Western men, who raised the wheat, in the cold. Well, while the *Conference* got after him at Montreal, Cartwright came West and booked all the grain he could load before it started off. When the *Conference* got wise, the cargo was in the Independent freighter's hold. Cartwright's surely a business man."

Barbara laughed and Mrs. Cartwright languidly agreed, but Grace frowned. Although she did not approve Cartwright, he was the head of her house, and to know his clever tricks were something of a joke hurt her dignity. Harry saw her frown.

"Anyhow, Cartwright's promise stands," he resumed. "If he ran his boat across half empty, he'd make good. You can trust him."

He went off and Barbara mused unhappily. She thought Harry had talked to help her over an awkward moment, and she was grateful but disturbed. It looked as if he knew something and he might know much. All the same, when he talked about her step-father she agreed. Cartwright was bold and clever, and, although he was sometimes not very scrupulous, people did trust him. Barbara wished she had his cleverness and his talent for removing obstacles. There were obstacles in her path and the path was dark. Yet she had promised to take it and must make good. She tried to banish her doubts and began to talk.

After lunch she allowed one of the party to help her on board a canoe. The afternoon was calm, and the light breeze that now and then sighed in the pine-tops hardly ruffled the shining water. In the evening, when the straight trunks cut against a blaze of gold and green, they sat by a smudge fire that kept off the mosquitoes and sang to an accompaniment of banjos and mandolins. Barbara sang with the others, but it cost her an effort. The tranquil day was nearly done and she felt it was the last tranquillity she might know for long. Her companions were frank and kind, Canadians, but her sort, and she was going to make a bold plunge with another who was not. Yet she knew one could not rebel for nothing, and she had pluck. The light faded behind the trees, a loon's wild cry rang across the dark water, and the party went to bed.

In the morning Grace awoke Mrs. Cartwright quietly.

"Barbara is gone," she said.

"Ridiculous!" said Mrs. Cartwright.

"She is gone. Her clothes are not about; but we must be calm and not disturb the camp. Mrs. Vernon ought to know, but nobody else. You see, it's important—"

Mrs. Cartwright saw, and a few minutes afterwards her hostess knew.

"It's plain I must give Harry my confidence, to some extent," Mrs. Vernon said, and went to look for her son.

She found him going off for a swim, and when she told her tale he frowned.

"In a way, perhaps, I'm accountable, but we'll talk about this again," he said. "Get Mrs. Cartwright on board the launch and come along yourself. As soon as Bob's inside his clothes we'll start."

"But Bob—" Mrs. Vernon began.

"Bob *knows*, and I'll need a partner. If Miss Hyslop didn't leave the settlement on the night express, she'll be hitting the trail through the woods for the United States. You must hustle."

Mrs. Vernon left him, and a few minutes afterwards the fast motor launch swung out from the landing and sped down river with a white wave at her bows. Grace watched the boat vanish behind a wooded point and then went to her tent. She was horribly angry and shocked. Barbara had cheated her and disgraced them all.

CHAPTER IV

THE GIRL ON THE PLATFORM

The Vancouver express was running in the dark through the woods west of Fort William. After the rain of early summer, wash-outs that undermine the track are numerous and the express had been delayed. Now, however, the road was good and the engineer drove his big locomotive with throttle wide open. Black smoke blew about the rocking cars, cinders rattled on the roofs, and showers of sparks sped past the windows. The wheels roared on shaking trestles and now and then awoke an echoing clang of steel, for the company was doubling the track and replacing the wooden bridges by metal.

This was George Lister's business, and he lounged in a corner of a smoking-compartment, and rather drowsily studied some calculations. He was bound West from Montreal, and in the morning would resume his labors at a construction camp. There was much to be done and the construction bosses who had sent for him were getting impatient.

Lister's thoughts wandered from the figures. He liked his occupation and admitted that he had been lucky, but began to see he had gone as far as he could expect to go. The trouble was, he had not enjoyed the scientific training that distinguished the men who got important posts. His mechanical career began in the engine-room of a wheat-boat on the lakes, and he had entered the railroad company's service when shipping was bad and steamers were laid up. Although he had studied for a term or two at McGill University, he knew his drawbacks. Sometimes promotion was given for merit, but for the most part the men who made progress came from technical colleges and famous engineering works.

An accident in the ranges on the Pacific slope, when a mountain locomotive jumped the track and plunged down a precipitous hillside, gave Lister his first chance. He got the locomotive back to the line, and being rewarded by a better post, stubbornly pushed himself nearer the front. Now, however, it looked as if he must stop. Rules were not often relaxed in favor of men who had no highly-placed friends. Yet Lister wondered.

Not long since, a gentleman whose word carried some weight at the company's office had visited the construction camp with his indulged daughter. The girl was clever, adventurous, and interested by pioneer work, and Lister had helped her to some thrills she obviously enjoyed. She had, with his guidance, driven a locomotive across a shaking, half-braced bridge, fired a heavy blasting shot, and caught big gray trout from his canoe. Although Lister used some reserve, their friendship ripened, and when she left she hinted she had some power she might be willing to use on his behalf.

All the same, Lister was proud. The girl belonged to a circle he could not enter, and if he got promotion, it must be by his merits. He was not the man to get forward by intrigue and the clever use of a woman's influence; he had no talent for that kind of thing. He let it go, and tried to concentrate on his calculations.

By and by the colored porter stopped to tell him his berth was fixed and the passengers were going to bed. Lister nodded, put up his papers, and then lighted a cigarette. The smoking-compartment was hot, the light the rocking lamp threw about had hurt his eyes, and he thought he would go out on the platform for a few minutes.

He went. The draught that swept the gap between the cars was bracing and cool. There was a moon, he saw water shine and dark pines stream past. The snorting of the locomotive broke in a measured beat through the roll of wheels; the rocks threw back confused echoes about the clanging cars. Then the gleam among the trees got wider and Lister knew they were nearing a trestle that crossed an arm of a lake. In fact, he had wondered whether he would be sent to pull down the bridge and rebuild it with steel.

He sat down on the little box-seat, with his back against the door. The platform had not the new guards the company was then fitting; there was an opening in the rails, and one could go down the steps when the train was running. The moonlight touched the back of the car in front, but Lister was in the gloom, and when the vestibule door opposite opened he was annoyed. If somebody wanted to go through the train, he must get up.

A girl came out of the other car and seizing the rails looked down. She was in the light, and Lister remarked that she did not wear traveling clothes; he thought her small, knitted cap, short dress, and loose jacket indicated that she had come from a summer camp. Then she turned her head and he saw her face was rather white and her look was strained. It was obvious that something had disturbed her.

The girl did not see him, and while he wondered whether he ought to get up she put her foot on the step and leaned out, as if she weighed the possibility of jumping off. She swung back when the cars lurched round a curve, and the measured roll of wheels changed to a sharp, broken din. The train was running on to the trestle and Lister saw the water shine below the platform. He got up, and moving quietly, seized the girl's arm and pulled her from the rails.

"A jolt might throw you off," he said.

She looked up with a start and the blood came to her skin, but she gave him a quick, searching glance. Lister was athletic, his face was bronzed by frost and sun, and his look was frank. She lowered her eyes and her color faded.

"Does the train stop soon?" she asked.

"If the engineer's lucky, we won't stop until he makes the next water-tank, and it's some distance."

She turned with a quick, nervous movement and glanced at the door. Lister imagined she was afraid somebody might come out.

"Could one persuade or bribe the conductor to pull up?"

Lister hesitated. He knew the train gang and was a railroad boss, but the company was spending a large sum in order to cut down the time-schedule and somebody must account for all delay.

"I think not. You see, unless there's a washout or the track is blocked, nothing is allowed to stop the Vancouver express."

The girl glanced at the door again and then gave him an appealing look.

"But I must get off! I oughtn't to have come on board. I want to go East, towards Montreal, and not to Winnipeg."

Although he was not romantic, Lister was moved. She was very young and her distress was obvious. Somehow he felt her grounds for wanting to leave the train were good. Indeed, he rather thought she had meant to jump off had they not run on to the bridge. Yet for him to stop the express would be ridiculous; the conductor and engineer would pay for his meddling. With quiet firmness he pulled the girl farther from the opening of the rails.

"We stop long before we get to Winnipeg," he said soothingly. "Then it's possible we'll be held up by a blocked track. Wash-outs are pretty numerous on this piece of line. However, if we do stop and you get down, you'll be left in the woods."

"Oh!" she said, "that's not important! All I want is to get off."

"Very well," said Lister. "If we are held up, I'll look for you. But I don't know if the jolting platform is very safe. Hadn't you better go back to your car?"

She gave him a quick glance and he thought she braced herself.

"I'm not going back. I can't. It's impossible!"

Lister was curious, but hesitated about trying to satisfy his curiosity. The girl was afraid of somebody, and, seeing no other help, she trusted him.

"Then, you had better come with me and I'll find you a berth where you won't be disturbed," he said.

She followed him with a confidence he thought moving, and when they met the conductor he took the man aside.

"That's all right," said the other. "Nobody's going to bother her while I'm about."

Lister returned to the smoking-compartment, but the adventure had given him a pleasant thrill and he did not feel sleepy. He got out his calculations and tried to interest himself until a man entered the car. The fellow was rather handsome and his clothes were good, but Lister thought he looked perplexed. He gave Lister a keen glance and went on through the car. Some minutes afterwards, he came back, frowning savagely, stopped in front of Lister, as if he meant to speak, hesitated, and went out by the vestibule.

It was plain the fellow had gone to look for the girl and had not found her. The conductor had seen to that. Lister smiled, but admitted that the thing was puzzling. The man was older than the girl, although he was not old enough to be her father. If he were her husband, she would not have run away from him, and it did not look as if he were her lover. Lister saw no light, but since it was obvious she feared the man he resolved, if possible, to help her to escape.

Some time afterwards, the whistle pierced the roll of wheels, and Lister, going to the platform, saw a big electric head-lamp shine like a star. The cars were slowing and he imagined the operator had tried to run a construction train across the section before the express came up. They would probably stop for a minute at the intersection of the main and side tracks. Hurrying through the train, Lister found the conductor, who look him to a curtained berth, and the girl got down. She was dressed and wore her knitted cap.

"If you are resolved to go, I may be able to help you off," Lister said.

"I must go," she replied, and although Lister remarked that her hands trembled as she smoothed her crumpled dress, her voice was steady.

"Very well," he said. "Come along."

When he opened the vestibule door the train was stopping and the beam from a standing locomotive's head-lamp flooded the track with dazzling light. For a moment the girl hesitated, but when Lister went down the steps she gave him her hand and jumped. Lister felt her tremble and was himself conscious of some excitement. He did not know if he was rash or not, but since she meant to go, speed was important, because the man from whom she wanted to escape might see them on the line. He went to the waiting engine in front of a long row of ballast cars, on which a big gravel plough loomed faintly in the dark.

"Who's on board?" he asked.

A man he knew looked out from the cab window.

"Hallo, Mr. Lister! I'm on board with Jake. We're going to Malcolm cut for gravel. Washout's mixed things; operator reckoned he could rush us through—"

"Then you'll stop and get water at the tank," Lister interrupted. "Will you make it before the East-bound comes along?"

"We ought to make it half-an-hour ahead. Wires all right that way. Nothing's on the road."

Lister turned to the girl. "If you're going East you must buy a new ticket at Malcolm. Have you money?"

"I have some—" she said and stopped, and Lister imagined she had not until then thought about money and had not much.

"You'll take this lady to Malcolm, Roberts, and put her down where she can get to the station," he said to the engineer. "Nobody will see you have a passenger, but if the agent's curious, I'll fix the thing with him."

It was breaking rules, but the man knew Lister, and Lister knew he could be trusted. He took some bills from his wallet, and as he helped the girl up the steps pushed the paper into her hand.

She turned to the cab door, and Lister imagined she was hardly conscious of the money he had given her. Her color was high but her look indicated keen relief.

"Oh!" she said, "I owe you much! You don't know all you have done. I will not forget—"

Somebody waved a lantern, a whistle shrieked, and the locomotive bell began to toll. Lister jumped back and seized the rails above the platform steps as the car lurched forward. They moved faster, the beam of the head-lamp faded, and the train rolled on into the dark.

CHAPTER V

SHILLITO GETS AWAY

When the train started Lister did not go to his berth. His curiosity was excited and he wondered whether he had been rash. Now he came to think about it, the girl was attractive, and perhaps this to some extent accounted for his willingness to help. Moreover she was young, and it was possible her relations had put her in the man's control. If so, his meddling could not be justified.

After a time he heard the whistle, and imagined the train was going to stop at a small station to which mails were brought from some mining camps. The neighboring country was rugged and lonely, but a trail ran south through the woods to the American frontier. When the cars stopped he pushed down the window and looked out.

Small trees grew along the track and the light from the cars touched their branches. The line was checkered by illuminated patches and belts of gloom. Lister heard somebody open the baggage car and then saw a man run along the line beside the train. Another jumped off a platform and they met not far from Lister's window. The man who got down was the fellow who had gone through the car looking for the girl. The locomotive pump throbbed noisily and Lister could not hear their talk, but he thought they argued.

The one who came up the line looked impatient and put his hand on his companion's arm, as if to urge him away. The other stepped back, and his gesture implied that he refused to go. The train was long, the passengers were asleep, and the men, no doubt, imagined nobody saw them. Lister thought the fellow who got down did not know the girl was gone and did not mean to leave the train without her. The light touched the men's faces, and it was obvious that one was angry and the other disturbed. The scene intrigued Lister. It was like watching an act in a cinema play of which one did not know the plot.

After a minute or two a lantern flashed up the track, the bell tolled, and the nearer man jumped back on the step. Lister heard a vestibule door shut and then the throb of wheels began. The fellow on the line frowned and threw out his hands angrily. From the movement of his lips Lister thought he swore, but the car rolled past him and he melted into the dark.

Lister went to his berth, but did not undress. Much of the night had gone, he would reach his camp soon after daybreak, and the train would only stop long enough for him to jump off. He could sleep in his clothes for an hour or two. A slackening of the roll of wheels wakened him and he got out of his berth, but the big lamps were burning and when he went to the door he saw dawn had not come. It was obvious they had not reached the construction camp. Lister shivered, and was returning to his berth when the conductor opened the door.

"Our luck's surely not good to-night," he said. "They're pulling us up at Maple. If it's not a washout, somebody will get fired."

He went off, grumbling, but when the train stopped came back with a trooper of the North-West Mounted Police.

"Where's the guy you told me to watch out for?" he asked.

Lister said he did not know and offered to go with them and help find the man. It looked as if he were going to see the end of the play.

When they opened a vestibule door a man came out of the car in front and stopped, as if he were dazzled by the beam from the conductor's lifted lamp.

"That's the fellow," Lister shouted.

He thought the other saw the trooper's uniform, because he stepped back quickly. The door, however, was shut. When he let go the handle the spring-bolt had engaged.

"Nothing doing that way!" said the trooper. "My partner's coming along behind you; you're corraled all right. I've a warrant for you, Louis Shillito."

The North-West Police work in couples and the situation was plain. One trooper had begun his search at the front of the train, the other at the back, and Shillito, hearing the first turn the passengers out of their berths, had tried to steal away and met the other. His face got strangely white, but Lister thought it was rather with rage than fear. His lips drew back in a snarl, and the veins swelled on his forehead. He occupied the center of the illuminated circle thrown by the conductor's lamp, and his savage gaze was fixed. Lister saw he was not looking at the policeman but at him.

"Blast you!" Shillito shouted. "If you hadn't butted in—"

"Cut it out!" said the trooper. "Hands up; we've got you! Don't make trouble."

Shillito's hand went behind him. It was possible he felt for the door knob, but the trooper meant to run no risks. Although he had put down his rifle and taken out his handcuffs, he jumped forward, across the platform, and Shillito bent sideways to avoid his spring. The fellow was athletic and his quick side-movement indicated he was something of a boxer; the policeman was embarrassed by his handcuffs and young. Shillito seized him and threw him against the rails, close to the gap where the steps went down. The trooper gasped, his grasp got slack, and his body slipped along the rails. It looked as if Shillito would throw him down the steps, and Lister jumped.

He saw Shillito's hand go up and next moment got a heavy blow. For all that, he seized the man and held on, though blood ran into his eyes and he felt dizzy. Shillito struggled like a savage animal and Lister imagined the trooper did not help much. He got his arms round his antagonist and tried to pull him down; Shillito was trying to reach the opening in the rails. After a moment or two, Lister felt his muscles getting slack, lurched forward, and saw nothing in front. He plunged out from the gap, struck a step with his foot, and somebody fell on him. Then he thought he heard a rifle-shot, and knew nothing more.

By and by somebody pulled him to his feet and he saw the conductor holding his arm. A group of excited passengers stood round them in the light that shone from the train and some others ran along the edge of the woods. The trooper and Shillito were gone.

Lister's head hurt, he felt shaky, and when he wiped his face his hand was wet with blood.

"My head's cut. S'pose I hit something when I fell," he said.

"Shillito socked it to you pretty good," the conductor replied, and waved his lamp. "All aboard!" he shouted, and pushed Lister up the steps.

When they reached the platform the car jolted and Lister sat down, with his back against the door.

"My legs won't hold me," he said in an apologetic voice. "Did Shillito get off?"

"Knocked out the trooper and made the bush; the other fellow was way back along the train," the conductor replied. "They want him for embezzlement and will soon get on his trail, but the wash-out's broke the wires and I reckon he'll cross the frontier ahead. Now you come along and I'll try to fix your cut."

Lister went, and soon after a porter helped him into his berth. His head hurt and he felt very dull and slack, but he slept and when he woke bright sunshine streamed into the standing car and he saw the train had stopped at

Winnipeg. Soon afterwards the conductor and one of the station officials put him into an automobile.

"If the reporters get after you, remember you're not to talk about the girl," he said to the conductor.

The other nodded, and signed the driver to start. The car rolled off and stopped at the house of a doctor who dressed the cut on Lister's head and ordered him a week's rest. Lister went to a hotel, and in the morning found a romantic narrative of Shillito's escape in the newspaper, but was relieved to note that nothing was said about the girl. The report, however, stated that a passenger who tried to help the police had got badly hurt and Shillito had vanished in the woods. The police had not found his trail and it was possible he would reach the American frontier.

Lister thought the thing was done with, and when a letter arrived from the construction office, telling him to stay until he felt able to resume his work, resigned himself to rather dreary idleness. For some days his head ached and he could not go out; the other guests were engaged in the city and there was nobody to whom he could talk. He got badly bored, and it was a relief when one afternoon the gentleman he had met at the construction camp arrived with his daughter. For all that, Lister was surprised. Duveen was a man of some importance, Miss Duveen was a fashionable young lady, and Lister had imagined they had forgotten him. He took his guests to a corner of the spacious rotunda where a throbbing electric fan blew away the flies, and Duveen gave him a cigarette.

"The *Record* did not give your name, but we soon found out who was the plucky passenger," he said with a friendly smile. "Ruth thought she'd like to see you, and since I wasn't engaged this afternoon we came along."

"I did want to come, but I really think you proposed the visit," Ruth remarked.

"Oh, well," said Duveen, "I don't know if it's important, but perhaps we oughtn't to make Mr. Lister talk."

Lister declared he wanted to talk, and Duveen said presently, "I don't see why you butted in."

For a moment or two Lister hesitated. He was resolved to say nothing about the girl; it was obvious she would not like her adventure known, but he must be cautious. Duveen was clever, and he thought Miss Duveen gave him a curious glance.

"The trooper was young and I sympathized with his keenness. Looked as if it was his first important job and he meant to make good."

"A romantic impulse?" Duveen remarked, and laughed. "Well, when one is young, I expect it's hard to stand off while a fight's going on. All the same, it's strange you didn't sympathize with the fellow who was corraled. That's youth's natural instinct, although I allow it's not often justified."

"The trooper was corraled. He'd put down his rifle and Shillito had a gun; I reckon it was the sharp butt of a heavy automatic that cut my head. Then I didn't like the fellow; he'd come through the train before and looked a smart crook."

"He is a crook and got away with a big wad of the lumber firm's money. However, you were rash to jump for a man with a pistol. You didn't know he'd use the butt. All the same, you look brighter than we thought and can take a rest. I expect the construction office won't rush you back until you're fit."

"I want to get back. Loafing round the hotel is dreary and my job's not getting on. Although I'm ordered to lie off, this won't count for much. I'll be made accountable for getting behind."

Duveen said nothing for a moment or two, but he looked thoughtful, and Lister imagined Miss Duveen studied him quietly. He did not belong to the Duveens' circle; he was ruder. In fact, it was rather strange to see these people sitting with him, engaged in friendly talk, although, now he thought about it, Miss Duveen had not said much.

She was a pretty girl and Lister liked her fashionable dress. Somehow Ruth Duveen harmonized with the tall pillars and rich ornamentation of the rotunda. One felt she belonged to spacious rooms. Duveen's clothes were in quiet taste, he wore a big diamond, and looked commanding. One felt this was a man whose word carried weight.

"You're something of a hustler," he remarked with a smile. "For all that, you got a nasty knock, and your quitting for a time is justified. Well, if you feel lonesome, come along and dine at our hotel. Then we'll go and see the American opera. I'm told the show is good."

Lister made some excuses, but Duveen would not be refused.

"When we stopped at your camp you made things smooth for us. You gave Ruth some thrills, showed her the romance of track-grading, and generally helped her to a good time. Anyhow, the thing is fixed. We'll send the car for you."

They went off soon afterwards, and Lister mused and smoked. He had hardly expected to meet the Duveens again and wondered whether he owed the visit to Ruth or her father; he had remarked at the camp that she was generally indulged. Well, it was plain Duveen could help him and Lister was ambitious, but he frowned and pulled himself up. He was not going to intrigue for promotion and use a girl's friendship in order to force his chiefs to see his merits. Things like that were done, but not by him; it demanded qualities he did not think were his. Moreover he did not know if Ruth Duveen was his friend. She was attractive, but he imagined she was clever. All the same, if he could get the doctor to fix his bandage so as to make it inconspicuous he would dine with the Duveens.

CHAPTER VI

WINNIPEG BEACH

Lister went to the opera with his hosts and was moved by the music and the feeling that he was one of a careless, pleasure-seeking crowd. For the most part, his life had been strenuous and the crowds he knew were rude. His home was a bare shack, sometimes built on the wind-swept alkali plains, and sometimes in the tangled woods. From daybreak until dusk fell, hoarse shouts, the clank of rails, the beat of heavy hammers filled his ears, and often the uproar did not stop at dark. When a soft muskeg swallowed the new track, he must watch, by the flaring blast-lamps, noisy ploughs throw showers of gravel from the ballast cars.

Labor and concentration had left their mark. Lister's muscles were hard, but his body and face were thin. He looked fine-drawn and alert; his talk was direct and quick. As a rule, his skin was brown, but now the brown was gone, and the lines on his face were deeper. His injury accounted for something and he felt the reaction from a strain he had hardly noted while it must be borne. Although he had not altogether hidden his bandage and his clothes were not the latest fashion, Ruth Duveen was satisfied. Somehow he looked a finer type than the business men in the neighboring stalls. One felt the man's clean virility and got a hint of force.

Lister was highly strung. The music stirred his imagination, and when the curtain went down the light and glitter, the perfume that drifted about, the women's dress, and the society of his attractive companion gave him a curious thrill. He began to see he had missed much; ambitions that had forced him to struggle for scope to use fresh efforts took another turn. Life was not all labor. Ruth Duveen had enlightened him.

He studied her. She had grace and charm; it was much to enjoy, for one evening, the society of a girl like this. Duveen went off between the acts to meet his friends, but Ruth stopped and talked. Her smile was gracious and Lister let himself go. He told her about adventures on the track and asked about her life in the cities. Perhaps it was strange, but she did not look bored, and when the curtain went down for the last time he felt a pang. The evening was gone and in a day or two he must resume his labor in the wilds. Lister did not cheat himself; he knew the strange, romantic excitement he had indulged would not be his again. When they went down the passage Ruth gave him a smiling glance and saw his mouth was firm.

"You look rather tired," she said. "Have we tired you?"

Lister turned and his eyes were thoughtful. She had stopped to fasten her cloak, and the people pushing by forced her to his side. An electric lamp burned overhead and her beauty moved him. He noted the heavy coils of her dark hair, her delicate color, and the grace of her form.

"I'm not at all tired," he said. "I feel remarkably braced and keen, as if I'd waked up from sleep. In fact, I think I have awakened."

Ruth laughed. She saw he was not smiling and his graveness gave her a sense of power. He had owned, with typical frankness, that she had moved him.

"Sometimes to wake up suddenly gives one a jolt," she said. "However, you will soon get calm again in the woods."

He sensed something provocative and challenging in her voice, but he would not play up.

"I wonder—" he said quietly. "In a way, the proper line's to go to sleep again."

"Sometimes one dreams! I expect you dream about locomotives breaking through trestles and dump-cars plunging into muskegs?"

He laughed. "They're things I know, and safe to dream about. All the same, I rather expect I'll be haunted by lights and music, pretty dresses and faces—"

He stopped, and Ruth remarked: "If these have charm, there are no very obvious grounds for your going without. You can command a locomotive and Winnipeg's not very far from your camp. But we're stopping the people, and I can't fix this clasp."

She moved, and the opera cloak fell back from her arm, which was uncovered but for the filmy sleeve that reached a little below the shoulder. He noted its fine curves and the silky smoothness of her skin. Although he fastened the clasp with a workman's firm touch, he thrilled. Then the crowd forced them on and they found Duveen waiting by the car. When they stopped at Lister's hotel Ruth said, "We are going to Winnipeg Beach, Saturday. Would you like to come?"

Duveen nodded. "A happy thought! I've got to talk to some business people who make Ruth tired. If you come along, I needn't bother about her."

"That's how one's father argues!" Ruth exclaimed.

Lister hesitated. "I was told to lie off because I was hurt. If I'm fit to enjoy an excursion, I'm fit to work."

"You're too scrupulous, young man. Have a good time when it's possible, or you'll be sorry afterwards. I reckon you're justified to take all the company will give."

"It was caution, not scruples. Suppose I meet one of the railroad chiefs?"

"I'll fix him," Duveen rejoined. "Your bosses won't get after you when you belong to my party. Anyhow, we'll look out for you."

The car rolled off, and Lister, going to the rotunda, lighted a cigarette and mused. Ruth Duveen had beauty, he liked her but must use caution, since he imagined the friendship she had given him was something of an indulged girl's caprice. Then he began to think about the girl he had met on board the train. Now he was able, undisturbed, to draw her picture, he saw she, too, had charm, but she was not at all like Ruth. The strange thing was, one did not note if she were beautiful or not. In a way, this did not matter; her pluck and firmness fixed one's interest.

Lister threw away his cigarette. He was poor and not romantic. The girl he had helped had vanished, and after their excursion he hardly expected to see Ruth again. Ruth was kind, but she would soon forget him when he was gone. He would go to Winnipeg Beach with her, and then return to the woods and let his job absorb him. In the meantime, his head had begun to ache and he went to bed.

The Saturday morning was typical of Winnipeg in summer. The fresh northwest breeze that sweeps the Manitoba plains had dropped. Dark thunder-clouds rolled about the sky, but the sun was hot and an enervating humidity brooded over the town. The perspiring crowd in Main Street moved slackly, the saloon bars were full, and the groups of holiday-makers flocking to the station wore a languid look.

Lister met his hosts in the marble waiting hall where a gold-framed panorama of Canadian scenery closes the view between the rows of stately pillars. Duveen had brought three or four keen-eyed, nervous business men, a rather imposing lady, and Ruth, and they got on board a local train soon after Lister arrived. Winnipeg Beach was then beginning to attract holiday-makers from the prairie town. One could row and fish in sheltered bays, and adventure on board a gasoline launch into the northern wilds. Boating, however, had no charm for Duveen's friends. The excursion was an opportunity for friendly business talk, and when lunch was over Ruth and Lister went out on the lawn in front of the hotel.

There was no wind. A few dark clouds floated motionless overhead, but outside their shadow the lake shone like glass, running back until it melted into faint reflections on the horizon. A varnished launch flashed in the sun and trailed a long white wake across the water.

"Do you want to stay and talk to Mrs. Knapp?" Ruth asked.

"I do not," said Lister. "Anyhow, I imagine Mrs. Knapp doesn't want to talk to me. I'm not a big-business man."

Ruth laughed. "Oh, well, when you speculate at the Board of Trade, a railroad engineer is not a useful friend. I suppose I ought to stay, but the things one ought to do are tiresome. Let's go on the lake."

Lister got a canoe, and fixing a cushion for Ruth, picked up the paddle.

"Where shall we go?"

"North, as far as you can. Let's get away from the boats and trippers and imagine we're back in the woods where you helped me catch the big gray trout."

"Then you liked it at the construction camp?" Lister remarked. "It was a pretty rude spot."

"For an indulged city girl?" Ruth said, smiling. "Well, perhaps I'd got all the satisfaction dinner parties and dances and the society at hotels can give. I knew the men who handle finance and work the wires behind the scenes, but I wanted to know the others who do the strenuous things and keep the country going. I came, and you helped me to understand the romance of the lakes and woods."

Lister did not remember if he had tried to do so and thought he had not. All the same, the girl was keen and interested. In summer, it was not hard to feel the lonely sheets of water and tangled bush were touched by romance. Then, perhaps, everybody felt at times a vague longing for the rude and primitive. But he was not a philosopher, and dipping the paddle, he drove the canoe across the tranquil lake.

In the meantime, he imagined Ruth studied him with quiet amusement, and wondered whether she thought he was not playing up. He did not mean to play up; the game was intricate, and, if he were rash, might cost him much. He had taken off his hat and jacket and effort had brought back the color to his skin. His thin face had the clean bronze tint of an Indian's; the soft shirt showed the fine-drawn lines of his athletic figure; but Lister was not conscious of this. He knew his drawbacks, but not all his advantages.

When he had gone some distance and the hotel and houses began to melt into the background, he stopped and let the canoe drift.

"How far shall we go?" he asked.

Ruth indicated a rocky point, cut off by the glimmering reflection, that seemed to float above the horizon.

"Let's see what is on the other side. Now and then one wants to know. Exploration's intriguing. Don't you think so?"

"Sometimes; in a practical sense. When a height of land cuts the landscape, I wonder whether one could find an easy down-grade for the track across the summit. That's about as far as my imagination goes."

"Oh, well," said Ruth, "exploration like that is useful and one doesn't run much risk. But risk and adventure appeal to some people."

Lister resumed paddling. The girl had charm and he was young; if he were not cautious, there might be some risk for him. He was not a clever philanderer, and Ruth and Duveen had been kind. By and by a puff of cool wind touched his hot skin and he looked round. A black cloud had rolled up and there were lines on the water.

"We may get a blow and some thunder," he remarked. "Shall we go back?"

"Not yet. We'll make the point first. If it does thunder, summer storms don't last."

He paddled harder and a small white wave lapped the canoe's bows. The sky was getting dark, and now the lines that streaked the lake were white, but the wind was astern and they were going fast. The glimmering reflections had vanished and the rocks ahead rose sharply from the leaden water. The point was some distance off, but Lister knew he must reach it soon.

A flash of forked lightning leaped from the sky and touched the lake, there was a long, rumbling peal, and then a humming noise began astern. Angry white ripples splashed about the canoe and lumps of hail beat Lister's head. Then, while the thunder rolled across the sky, the canoe swerved. It was blowing hard, the high bow and stern caught the wind, the strength was needed to hold her straight with the single paddle. If he brought her round, he could not paddle to windward, and to steer across the sea that would soon get up might be dangerous. They must make the point and land. He threw Ruth his jacket, for spray had begun to fly and the drops from the paddle blew on board.

"Put on the thing; I've got to work," he said.

In a few minutes his work was hard. Short, white waves rolled past, the canoe lurched and swerved, and Lister knew if she swung off across wind and sea she might capsize. He must keep her running and let the combers split against her pointed stern. The combers were getting large and their hissing tops surged by some height above the gunwale, but so long as he could keep her before them they would not come on board. When her bows went up she sheered, as if she meant to shoot across the hollow left by the sea that rolled by. He stopped her with a back-stroke and then drove hard ahead, for he must have speed to steer when the next sea came on. In the meantime, the lightning flickered about the lake and between the flashes all was nearly dark. The tops of the waves tossed against leaden cloud and he could hardly see the rocks for which he steered.

By and by, however, the point stood out close ahead. The trees on the summit bent in the wind; spray leaped about the bowlders where the white foam rolled. He must go round and find a landing to lee, but to go round he must cross the belt of breaking water, with the savage wind abeam. The canoe shipped some water, and riding in on a comber's crest, narrowly missed a rock that lifted its top for a moment out of the foam. Then Lister drove her in behind the point and helped Ruth to land on a gravel beach. Her eyes sparkled and he saw she had not been daunted.

"We're all right now, but we have got to stay until the storm blows out," he said.

They found shelter in a hollow of the cliff and sat among the driftwood while the rain that blotted out the lake drove overhead. The deluge did not reach them and the cold was going.

"You go back on Monday?" Ruth said at length.

Lister smiled with humorous resignation. "I must. The strange thing is, when I left my job before I was keen to get back. Now I'd rather stop and loaf."

"Then you were not bored at Winnipeg?"

"Not at all," Lister declared. "If it would give me a holiday like this, I'd get hurt again."

"I expect the woods get dreary. Then, perhaps, one doesn't make much progress by sticking to the track? Don't you want to get into the office where the big plans are made?"

"I don't know," said Lister thoughtfully. "On the track you're all right if you know your job; at headquarters you need qualities I don't know are mine. Anyhow, I'm not likely to get there, if I want or not."

Ruth gave him a curious glance. "Sometimes one's friends can help. Would you really like a headquarters post?"

Lister moved abruptly and his mouth got firm. Perhaps Ruth exaggerated her father's importance, but it was possible Duveen could get him promotion. All the same, Lister saw what his taking the job implied; he must give up his independence and be Duveen's man. Moreover, if the girl meant to help, she had some grounds for doing so. He thrilled and was tempted, but he thought hard. It looked as if she liked him and was perhaps willing to embark upon a sentimental adventure, but he thought this was all. She would not marry a poor man.

"No," he said, with a touch of awkwardness. "I reckon I had better stick to the track. To know where you properly belong is something, and if I took the other job, my chiefs would soon find me out."

"You're modest," Ruth remarked. "One likes modest people, but don't you think you're obstinate?"

"When the trail you hit goes uphill, obstinacy's useful."

"If you won't take help, you may be long reaching the top, but we'll let it go. The wind hasn't dropped much. How can we get back?"

"We must wait," Lister replied with a twinkle. "The trouble about an adventure is, when you start you're often forced to stay with it and put it over. That sometimes costs more than you reckon."

Ruth's eyes sparkled, but she forced a smile. "Logical people make me tired. But why do you imagine I haven't the pluck to pay?"

"I don't," said Lister. "I've no grounds to imagine anything like that. My business was to take care of you and I ought to have seen the storm was coming. Now I'm mad because I didn't watch out."

"Sometimes you're rather nice," Ruth remarked. "You know I made you go on. All the same, we must start as soon as possible."

Lister got up presently and launched the canoe. The thunder had gone, but the breeze was strong and angry white waves rolled up the lake. To drive the canoe to windward was heavy labor, and while she lurched slowly across the combers the sun got low. Lister's wet hands blistered and his arms ached, but he swung the paddle stubbornly, and at length the houses and hotel stood out from the beach. When they got near the landing Ruth looked ahead.

"The train's ready to pull out!" she exclaimed. "Can you make it?"

Lister tried. His face got dark with effort and his hands bled, but in a few minutes he ran the canoe aground. Ruth jumped out and they reached the station as the bell began to toll. Duveen waved to them from the track by the front of the train and then jumped on board, and Lister pushed Ruth up the steps of the last car. The car was second-class and crowded by returning holiday-makers, but the conductor, who did not know Lister and Miss Duveen, declared all the train was full and they must stay where they were. When he went off and locked the vestibule Lister looked about.

All the seats and much of the central passage were occupied, for the most part by young men and women. Some were frankly lovers and did not look disturbed by the banter of their friends. Lister was embarrassed, for Ruth's sake, until he saw with some surprise that she studied the others with amused curiosity. Looking down he met her twinkling glance and thought it something like a challenge. His embarrassment got worse. One could not talk because of the noise and to shout was ridiculous. He must stand in a cramped pose and try not to fall against Ruth when the cars rocked. He admitted that his proper background was the rude construction camp, and it was something of a relief when they rolled into Winnipeg.

Duveen's car was at the station, and Ruth stopped for a moment before she got on board.

"You start on Monday and we will be out of town to-morrow. I wish you good luck."

Lister thanked her, and when she got into the car she gave him a curious smile. "I think I liked you better in the woods," she said, and the car rolled off.

CHAPTER VII

LISTER'S DISSATISFACTION

Soon after his return from Winnipeg, Lister stood one evening by a length of track planned to cut out an awkward curve. The new line ran into a muskeg that sucked down brush and logs and the loads of numerous gravel trains. Angry foremen declared one could not fill up the bog, and Lister knew the heads of the construction office grumbled about the delay. He was tired, for he had been strenuously occupied since morning, but could not persuade himself that the work had made much progress.

Small trees lay in tangled rows about the fresh gravel; farther back, the standing bush ran in a broken line against the fading light. In front, thin mist drifted across the muskeg where slender trunks rose from the quaking mud. Not far off a high, wooden trestle carried the rails across a ravine. The bridge would presently be rebuilt with steel, but in the meantime the frame was open and the gaps between the ties were wide.

It was getting dark and noisy blast-lamps threw up pillars of white fire. The line had sunk in the afternoon and it was necessary to lift the rails and fill up the subsidence before the next gravel train arrived. Lister was angry and puzzled, for he had pushed the road-bed across to near the other side, but the rails had not sunk in the new belt but in ground over which the trains had run.

By and by a man joined him and remarked: "The boys have got the ties up, but I reckon they won't fix the track for three or four hours. Looks as if the blamed muskeg was going to beat us."

"She can't beat us," Lister rejoined impatiently. "The trouble is, hauling the stuff she swallows runs up construction costs, and that counts against us. Did you leave Willis with the gang?"

The other laughed. "I did not. He was tired. Wanted something at the office and allowed he'd stop and take a smoke."

"Hustle him out when you go along, Kemp. I'd sooner our chiefs down East had kept that young man. The job's not soft enough for him. However, I s'pose he lighted the lamp across the bridge?"

"Willis has friends," Kemp remarked meaningly, and indicated a reflection behind the trees. "The lamp's burning."

Lister glanced at the trembling light. "I expect it's good enough for the engineer, but the flame's not steady. Willis hasn't bothered to get the pressure right. It's possible he didn't wait until she warmed the oil."

The powerful lamp had been carried across the bridge in order to warn the engineer of the gravel train, who on his last journey had run to the end of the line. The light could be seen for some distance up the track.

"I got after Hardie about making good time. We must dump his load in the soft spot before we stop," Lister resumed.

"He's coming now; climbing the height of land," said Kemp. "He'll let her go all out when he makes the top."

A measured throb rolled across the woods, and as the noise got louder the beat of the exhaust marked the progress of the train. The explosive snorts indicated that the locomotive labored up the last steep pitch, and Lister sat down by the rails. He was tired and would not be needed until the gravel plough threw the rattling ballast off the cars. After a few moments he looked up, for a man came out of the gloom.

"Hello, Willis! I s'pose you've been taking a quiet smoke?"

"That's so," said the other. "I've hustled round since sun-up and imagined the gang could get along for half an hour without my watching. You want to leave something to your foremen."

Lister said nothing. He did not choose his helpers, but tried to make the best use of those the bosses sent. Willis had some useful qualities, but he was slack, and got sulky if one drove him hard. The young man had come from the drawing-office of a famous bridge-building works.

In the meantime, the rumble of the gravel train grew to a pulsating roar. The locomotive had crossed the divide and was running furiously down grade. The roughly-ballasted track was uneven, but the engineer had been on board since daybreak and no doubt wanted to finish his job.

"She's in the rock cut now," Kemp remarked. "Hardie ought to throttle down when he runs out and sees the light."

Lister listened. The swelling note indicated that the train had left the cut, but it did not look as if the engineer was pulling up.

"She's coming along pretty fast," said Willis. "If he doesn't snub her soon, she'll jump the steel and take the muskeg."

Next moment Lister was on his feet. Hardie was driving too fast; Lister doubted if he could stop before the heavy train plunged through the broken track. The unsteady white flicker behind the trees had sunk and changed to smoky red. If looked as if the oil was not vaporizing properly and the lamp was going out. When the engineer saw the light it would be too late.

"Get the boys off the track. I'll try to fix the lamp," Lister shouted, and started for the bridge.

The errand was not his. Willis had lighted the lamp: moreover, one might have sent a workman, but when a job was urgent Lister went himself. The job was urgent and dangerous. Unless he made good speed, he would meet the train on the bridge and the cylinders of the locomotive projected beyond the edge.

The track was rough and fresh gravel rolled under his feet. Now and then he struck a cross-tie and nearly fell. It had got dark and among the trees the gloom was deep; one could not see the ties. Yet he must run, and his breath got labored and his heart thumped. He did not know where the train was, only that it was near. The woods throbbed with a savage din; the big cars, loaded with rattling gravel, clanged and roared as they plunged down grade.

Lister hardly thought he could stop the train. It looked as if he would be caught on the trestle, but he meant to go on. He did not argue about it; he was rather moved by instinctive stubbornness. At moments of strain one does not argue and logic has no appeal. Character counts for all, and Lister followed his bent. His job was urgent and must be carried out.

When he reached the bridge he saw white threads of water between the timbers of the open frame. The spacing of the ties was not regular, and if he stepped short, or too far, he would go through. Then, if he did not strike a brace, he would fall upon the rocks in the stream. All the same, he saw the blaze of the head-lamp pick out the trees across the ravine and sprang on to the bridge.

Somehow he hit the ties; perhaps by subconscious judgment, and perhaps by good luck. Then he felt loose gravel under his feet and thrilled with a strange fierce satisfaction. His breath was labored and his body wet by sweat, but the moving beam had not reached the lamp. He was going to make it.

When the black front of a gravel car leaped out of the gloom he jumped off the track. The locomotive pushed the cars, the train was long, and the lamp was but a few yards off. It had not gone out, although the flame had sunk to a faint red jet that would not be seen in the dust. His hands shook, but he gave the pump a few strokes and turned the valve wheel. The red jet got white and leaped higher and Lister, pumping hard, looked up the track. Big cars, rocking and banging, rushed past in a cloud of dust. Bits of gravel struck him and rattled against the lamp. The blurred, dark figures of men who sat upon the load cut against the fan-shaped beam, and in the background he saw a shower of leaping sparks.

But the other light was growing and Lister turned the wheel. Burning oil splashed around him, a pillar of fire rushed up, and when a whistle screamed he let go the valve and turned from the blinding dust. He was shaking, but the heavy snorting stopped. The engineer had seen the light and cut off steam.

When Lister looked round the train was gone. He had done what he had undertaken, and after waiting for a few moments he started back. Now he could go cautiously, he stopped and tried to brace himself at the end of the bridge. Although he had run across not long since, he shrank from the dark, forbidding gaps. For all that, he must get back, and feeling carefully for the ties, he reached the other side and was for some time engaged at the muskeg where two cars had overrun the broken rails. At length he went to the log shack he used for his office and sleeping-room, and soon after he lighted his pipe Kemp came in.

"You made it," Kemp remarked. "When you stopped me at the bridge I saw you'd get there."

Lister laughed. "Now you talk about it, I believe I did shout you to go back. Anyhow, you were some way behind. Did Willis come?"

"He did not. Willis was badly rattled and started for the muskeg. Thought he might get the track thrown across the hole, perhaps! I'm rather sorry for the kid. But what are you going to do about it?"

"Report we had two cars bogged and state the cost of labor. That's all, I think."

Kemp nodded. "Well, perhaps there's no use in talking about the lamp. Our business is to make good, using the tools we've got. All the same, if they want a man somewhere else, I guess I'd recommend Willis."

He smoked quietly for a time, and then resumed: "We don't get forward much. In fact, if the new Western irrigation company would take me on, I think I'd quit."

Lister pondered. Since his short stop at Winnipeg he had been conscious of a strange restlessness. He wanted something the woods could not give, and had begun to think life had more to offer than he had known. Besides, he was not making much progress.

"Since the double track is to be pushed on across the plains, the department will need a bigger staff and there ought to be a chance for some of us," he said. "Then there's the new work with the long bridges on the lake section that will carry higher pay. We're next on turn and have some claim. They ought to move us up."

"I doubt. We didn't come from a famous office, and it's not always enough to know your job."

"Somebody will get a better post, and if I'm lucky I'll stay. If not, I think I'll try the irrigation works."

"I feel like that," Kemp declared. "But suppose the irrigation people turn our application down?"

"Then I'll lie off for a time. Except when I went, to McGill with money I earned on a wheat barge, I haven't stopped work since I was a boy. Now I'm getting tired and think I'll pull out and go across to look at the Old Country. My father was an Englishman, and I have some money to burn."

"A good plan," Kemp agreed. "After a change you come back fresh with a stronger punch. Well, if we're not put on to the lake section, we'll try the irrigation scheme."

He got up and went off, but Lister sat on his bunk and smoked. The bunk was packed with swamp-grass on which his coarse Hudson's Bay blankets were laid, and the shack was bare. Ragged slickers and old overalls occupied the wall, long gum-boots a corner. A big box carried an iron wash-basin, and a small table some drawing instruments. Lister was not fastidious, and, as a rule, did not stop long enough at one spot to justify his making his shack comfortable. Besides, he found it necessary to concentrate on his work, and had not much time to think about refinements.

All the same, he felt the shack was dreary and his life was bleak. He had not felt this until he went to Winnipeg. On the whole, he had liked the struggle against physical obstacles. It was his proper job, but the struggle was stern and sometimes exhausting, and his reward was small. Now he wanted something different, and gave himself to vague and brooding discontent.

Ruth Duveen had broken his former tranquillity. In a sense, she had awakened him, and he imagined she had meant to do so. All the same, to think she loved him was ridiculous; she was rather experimenting with fresh material. Yet she was accountable for his discontent. She had helped him to see that while he labored in the woods he had missed much. He wanted the society of cultivated women and men with power and influence; to use control instead of carrying out orders; and to know something of refinement and beauty. After all, his father was a cultivated Englishman, although Lister imagined he had inherited qualities that helped him most from his Canadian mother. It was all he had inherited, except some debts he had laboriously paid.

He admitted that to realize his ambitions might be hard, but he meant to try. Canada was for the young and stubborn. If his chiefs did not promote him, he would make a plunge, and if his new plan did not work, he would go over and see the Old Country. Then he would come back, braced and refreshed, and try his luck again.

Putting down his pipe, he got into bed. He was tired and in the morning the gravel cars must be pulled out of the muskeg. The job was awkward, and while he thought about it he went to sleep.

CHAPTER VIII

THE TEST

A boisterous wind swept the high plain and round, white-edged clouds rolled across the sky. The grass that ran back from the horizon was parched, and in the distance a white streak of blowing dust marked a dried alkali lake. Dust of dark color drove along the row of wooden stores and houses that fronted the railroad track, across which three grain elevators rose like castles. The telegraph posts along the track melted into the level waste, and behind the spot where they vanished the tops of a larger group of elevators cut the edge of the plain.

The street was not paved, and the soil was deeply ploughed by wheels. The soil was the black gumbo in which the wheat plant thrives, but the town occupied the fringe of a dry belt and farming had not made much progress. Now, however, a company was going to irrigate the land with water from a river fed by the Rockies' snow. The town was square, and although it looked much smaller than real-estate agents' maps indicated, it was ornamented by four wooden churches, a Y.M.C.A. like a temple, and an ambitious public hall.

The Tecumseh Hotel occupied a corner lot at the end of the street and was not remarkably commodious or clean, but its charges were less than the Occidental's by the station, and Lister and Kemp were not fastidious. Some time had gone since they pulled the gravel cars out of the swamp and they had not been sent to the lake section. In consequence, they had applied to the irrigation company for a post, and having been called to meet the engineers and directors, imagined they were on the short list.

Lister lounged against the rails on the Tecumseh veranda. The boards were cracked and dirty; burned matches and cigar ends were scattered about, and a skeleton, gauze covered door that shut with a powerful spring kept some of the flies and mosquitoes out of the hotel.

"We'll know to-morrow," he remarked presently.

Kemp nodded. "I can't figure on our chances. Feel anxious about it?"

"Not much. In fact, I mean to use the thing to test my luck. If we're engaged, I'll stay in Canada; if they turn us down, I'll start for the Old Country."

"You have no particular plans, I reckon."

"No," said Lister, smiling. "I'm going to look about. I know our new Western towns, but I want to see old cities, churches, and cathedrals; the great jobs men made before they used concrete and steel. Then I'd like to study art and music and see the people my father talked about. Ours is a good country, but when it's all you know it gets monotonous." He indicated the row of wooden houses and lonely plain. "One wants more than the track and this."

"It's possible you may go across," said Kemp. "Looks as if the company's short list was pretty long. There's a gang of candidates in town, we have no pull on the directors, and I don't know if our advantages are very marked—" He stopped and laughed, for a man came round the corner. "Hello, Willis!" he exclaimed. "When did you arrive?"

"I came in on the last train. Got a notice to meet the Irrigation Board."

"Oh, well," said Kemp, "since the applicants are more numerous than the posts, I reckon another won't count. Do you expect they're going to take you on?"

"I expect my chance is as good as yours."

"I'll sell you my chance for ten dollars," Kemp rejoined.

"Nothing doing, at the price," said Willis, and went off.

Kemp laughed. Willis was marked by a superficial smartness his comrades sometimes found amusing and sometimes annoying. For the most part, they bore with him good-humoredly, but did not trust him when work that needed careful thought was done.

"The kid looks confident, but his applying for a job is something of a joke," Kemp remarked. "I'd put his value at fifty cents a day."

Lister agreed, and looked up the dusty street. The fronts of the small frame houses were cracked by the sun, and some were carried up to hide the roof and give the building a fictitious height. A Clover-leaf wagon stood in front of a store, the wheels crusted by dry mud, and the team fidgeted amidst a swarm of flies. Except for one or two railroad hands waiting by the caboose of a freight train, nobody was about. The town looked strangely dreary.

Yet Lister knew it stood for all the relief from labor in the stinging alkali dust one could get. One could loaf in a hard chair in front of the hotel, lose a dollar or two at the shabby pool-room, or go to a movie show and see pictures of frankly ridiculous Western melodrama. In the real West, the pictures were ridiculous, because romantic shootings-up did not happen. In fact, unless a stubborn labor dispute began, nothing broke the dull monotony of toilsome effort. Romance had vanished with the buffaloes. Lister admitted that he had not long felt the monotony. The trouble began when he stopped at Winnipeg.

"I think I'll go up the street," he said.

A rough plank sidewalk ran in front of the houses, and Lister imagined it was needed when the spring thaw and summer thunder-storms softened the gumbo soil. Opposite the Occidental he stopped, for Duveen occupied a chair on the veranda. While Lister hesitated Duveen beckoned him to come up.

"It's hot and dusty. Will you take a drink?" he said.

Lister refused with thanks and wondered whether Ruth was at the hotel. In a way, he would like to see her, but admitted that perhaps he had better not. When he asked if she was well Duveen said she had gone to Quebec, and gave Lister a cigar.

"It looks as if you had left the railroad," he remarked.

"I have not left yet," said Lister cautiously.

"Then, you won't go unless you get a better job? Did you know I had joined the Irrigation Board?"

Lister said he did not know, and got embarrassed when Duveen gave him a thoughtful glance. He wondered whether Ruth had talked to Duveen before she hinted he might get a better post.

"Perhaps I ought not to have come up. In fact, I hesitated—"

Duveen laughed. "So I remarked! You reckoned the Occidental stoop was pretty public and your talking to me might imply that you wanted my support? Well, I'll risk that. It's obvious you're on the short list. Do you want a post?"

For a moment or two Lister pondered. He did want a post; anyhow, he ought to try for it. On the whole he liked Duveen, and thought he might have liked Ruth better had she not been rich. All the same, Duveen was a shrewd manipulator of new industries and to take a post by his favor would be to own a debt, for which payment might be demanded. Yet Duveen had been kind and Lister hesitated.

"I asked for a post," he said. "If I'm engaged, I'll try to make good; but I must make good at the dam or on the ditch. Then I don't want to bother my friends. The company has my engineering record and must judge my usefulness by this. If they're not satisfied, I won't grumble much."

"You're an independent fellow, but I think I understand," Duveen rejoined with a twinkle. "A company director's duty *is* to judge an applicant for a post by his professional record. If you are appointed, you want us to appoint you because we believe you are the proper man?"

"Something like that," said Lister quietly.

Duveen nodded, and his glance rested for a moment on Lister's forehead.

"I see the mark you got on board the train hasn't altogether gone. Did you hear anything about the girl you helped?"

"I did not," said Lister, starting, for he had not imagined Duveen knew about the girl. "I have not seen her since she went off on the locomotive."

"Then she has not written to you since?"

"She could not write, because she doesn't know who I am, and I don't know her. We talked for a minute or two, that's all."

Duveen's face was inscrutable and Lister wondered whether he doubted his statement. He was annoyed because the other knew so much.

"Oh, well," said Duveen, "I expect you heard they didn't catch Shillito, and since he got across the frontier, it's possible the Canadian police won't see him again. But I must get ready for supper. Will you stay?"

Lister excused himself and went back to the Tecumseh, where the bill of fare was frugal and the serving rude. He imagined he had refused much more than a first-class supper, but was satisfied he had taken the proper line. For one thing, Duveen knew Ruth had given him her friendship and, since he knew his daughter, it was significant that he had not thought it necessary to meddle. Lister wondered whether he had meant to use him, and was glad he had kept his independence. If he got the post now, he would know he had rather misjudged Duveen, but he doubted. All the same, he liked the man.

After supper Kemp and he sat on the veranda and watched the green glow fade from the edge of the plain. They did not talk much, but by and by Kemp remarked: "I thought I saw you go into the Occidental."

"Duveen called me on to the stoop."

"Duveen?" Kemp exclaimed. "Then he's got his hand on the wires! If the Irrigation Company puts the undertaking over, a number of the dollars will go to Duveen's wad. If he's your friend, I expect you know he could get you the job."

"It's possible. All the same, I hinted I didn't want his help."

Kemp laughed. "You surprise me every time! I'm all for a square deal and down with scheming grafters and log-rollers, but I allow I hate them worst when they give another fellow the post I want."

"The thing's not fixed yet. The company's engineers are going to judge and our record's pretty good. They may engage us. We'll know to-morrow."

"Sure thing," Kemp remarked dryly. "I reckon we'll both pull out on the first train."

It began to get dark and Lister went off to bed. He must get water from a cistern in the roof and to carry the heavy jug was awkward when one could not see. At the Tecumseh the guests were expected to carry water for themselves, and Lister, groping along the shadowy passage with his load, thought his doing so had some significance. It was part of the price he must pay for freedom.

At the time fixed in the morning, he went to the Occidental and was shown into a room where a number of gentlemen occupied a table. One or two were smoking and the others talked in low voices, but when Lister came in and the secretary indicated a chair they turned as if to study him. Duveen sat next a man at the end of the table and gave Lister a nod. Somehow Lister thought he was amused.

Lister's heart beat. He felt this was ridiculous, because he had persuaded himself it did not matter whether he got the post or not. Now, however, when the moment to try his luck had come, he shrank from the plunge he had resolved to make if he were not engaged. After all, he knew and liked his occupation; to let it go and try fresh fields would be something of a wrench.

The gentlemen did not embarrass him. On the whole, they were urbane, and when the secretary gave the chairman his application one asked a few questions about the work he had done. Lister was able to answer satisfactorily, and another talked to him about the obstacles encountered when one excavated treacherous gravel and built a bank to stand angry floods. For all that, Lister was anxious. The others looked bored, as if they were politely playing a game. He thought they knew beforehand how the game would end, but he did not know. The inquiries that bored the urbane gentlemen had important consequences for him and the suspense was keen.

At length they let him go, and Duveen gave him a smile that Lister thought implied much. When he returned to the hotel Kemp remarked that he looked as if he needed a drink, and suggested that Lister go with him and get one.

"I need three or four drinks, but mean to go without," said Lister grimly. "I begin to understand how some men get the tanking habit."

He started off across the plain, and coming back too late for lunch, found Kemp on the veranda. Kemp looked as if he were trying to be philosophical, but found it hard.

"The secretary arrived not long since," he said. "A polite man! He didn't want to let us down too heavily."

"Ah!" said Lister. "The Irrigation people have no use for us?"

Kemp nodded. "Willis has got the best job; they've hired up two or three others, but we're left out."

"Willis!" exclaimed Lister, and joined in Kemp's laugh.

"After all, the money he's going to get is theirs," said Kemp. "In this country we're a curious lot. We let grafters and wire-pullers run us, and, when we start a big job, get away with much of the capital we want for machines; but somehow we make good. We shoulder a load we needn't carry and hit the pace up hot. If we got clean control, I reckon we'd never stop. However, there's not much use in philosophizing when you've lost your job, and the East-bound train goes out in a few minutes. You'd better pack your grip."

CHAPTER IX

BARBARA PLAYS A PART

Lister returned to the railroad camp and stayed until the company sent a man to fill his post. In the meantime, he wrote to some of his father's relations, whom he had not seen, and their reply was kind. They stated that while he was in England he must make their house his home. When his successor arrived he started for Montreal, and one afternoon sat under a tree in the square by the cathedral.

The afternoon was calm. A thunderstorm that wet the streets had gone, and an enervating damp heat brooded over the city. After the fresh winds that sweep the woods and plains, Lister felt the languid air made him slack and dull. His steamer did not sail until daybreak, and since he had gone up the mountain and seen the cathedral and Notre Dame, he did not know what to do. The bench he occupied was in the shade, and he smoked and looked about.

Cabs rolled up the street to the big hotel across the square, and behind the trees the huge block of the C.P.R. station cut the sky. One heard whistles, the rumble of heavy wheels, and the tolling of locomotive bells. Pigeons flew down from the cathedral dome and searched the damp gravel.

A group of foreign emigrants picnicked in the shade. Their clothes were old and greasy; they carried big shapeless bundles and looked tired and worn. Lister could not guess their nationality, but imagined they had known poverty and oppression in Eastern Europe. It was obvious they had recently disembarked from a crowded steerage and waited for an emigrant train. They were going West, to the land of promise, and Lister wished them luck. He and they were birds of passage and, with all old landmarks left behind, rested for a few hours on their journey.

He studied the group. The men looked dull and beaten; the women had no beauty and had grown coarse with toil. Their faces were pinched and their shoulders bent. Only the children, in spite of rags and dirt, struck a hopeful note. Yet the forlorn strangers had pluck; they had made a great adventure and might get their reward. Lister had seen others in the West, who had made good, breaking soil they owned and walking with the confident step of self-respecting men. On the plains, stubborn labor was rewarded, but one needed pluck to leave all one knew and break custom's familiar but heavy yoke.

By and by Lister remembered he wanted to take his relations a few typically Canadian presents. He had seen nothing that satisfied him at Winnipeg, and had better look about the shops at Montreal. Anyhow, it would amuse him for an hour or two. He got up, went along the path for a few yards, and then stopped.

Across the clanging of the locomotive bells and the roll of trolley cars at the bottom of the hill he heard sweet voices. The music was faint and somehow ethereal, as if it fell from a height. One lost it now and then. It came from the cathedral and Lister stopped and listened. He did not know what office was being sung, but the jaded emigrants knew, for a child got up and stood with bent head, holding a greasy cap, and a ragged woman's face got gentle as she signed herself with the cross. It looked as if the birds of passage had found a landmark in a foreign land. Lister was moved, and gave the child a coin before he went off.

He strolled east, past Notre Dame, towards the post office, about which the stately banks and imposing office blocks stand. This quarter of the city drew him, for one saw how constructive talent and imagination could be used, and he wondered whether England had new buildings like these. Sometimes one felt the Western towns were raw and vulgar, but one saw the bold Canadian genius at its best in Montreal.

After a time he stopped in front of a shop in a short side street. Indian embroidery work and enameled silver occupied the window, and although Lister was not an artist he had an eye for line and knew the things were good. The soft, stained deerskin was cleverly embroidered; he liked the warm colors of the enamel, and going in was shown a tray of spoons.

The shop, shut in by high buildings, was dark and smelt of aromatic wood and leather, but a beam from a window pierced the gloom and sparkled on the silver. This was emblazoned with the arms of the Provinces; the Ship, the Wheatsheaves, and the red Maple Leaf. Lister picked up the articles, and while he did so was vaguely conscious that a girl at the opposite counter studied him. He, however, did not look up until he had selected a few of the spoons, and then he started.

The light that touched the girl's face did not illuminate it all. Her profile was sharp as an old daguerreotype: he saw the flowing line from brow to chin, drawn with something of austere classic beauty, the arched lips and the faint indication of a gently-rounded cheek. The rest was in shadow, and the contrast of light and gloom was like a Rembrandt picture. Then the enameled spoons rattled as Lister put down the tray. He knew the picture. When he last saw the girl, her face was lighted like that by the blaze of a locomotive head-lamp.

"I'll take these things," he said, and crossed the floor.

The girl moved back, but he indicated a bundle of deerskin articles he thought her business was to sell. Her color was high; he noted the vivid white and pink against the dull background of stained leather.

"What does one do with those bags?" he asked.

"They're useful for keeping gloves and handkerchiefs," she replied. "The pattern is worked in sinews, but we have some with a neat colored embroidery." She paused and signed to a saleswoman farther on. "Will you bring this gentleman the Revillon goods?"

Lister's object for stopping her was not very plain, but he did not mean to let her go.

"Please don't bother. I expect to find something in this bundle," he said to the approaching saleswoman. Then he turned to the girl in front. "Let me look at the bag with the arrow-head pattern."

She gave him the bag, and although her glance was steady he knew she was embarrassed.

"If you will wrap it up, I'll keep this one," he resumed. "I expect you have not forgotten me. When I came into the shop I didn't imagine I should meet you, but if you'd sooner I went off, I'll go."

"I have not forgotten," she admitted, and her color faded and came back to her delicate skin.

"Very well! Since I sail to-night on the Allan boat, it's plain you needn't be afraid of my bothering you. All the same, we were partners in an adventure that ought to make us friends. Can't I meet you for a few minutes when you stop work?"

She hesitated, and then gave him a searching glance.

"Come to the fountain up the street in an hour. This is my early evening."

Lister went off with the bag and spoons, and when he returned to the fountain saw her crossing the square in front. She was dressed like the shop-girls he had seen hurrying on board the street cars in the morning; her clothes were pretty and fashionable, but Lister thought the material was cheap. He felt she ought not to wear things like that. While she advanced he studied her. She was attractive, in a way he had hardly remarked on board the train. One rather noted her quick, resolute movements, the sparkle in her eyes, and her keen vitality. Lister began to think he had unconsciously noted much.

"I'm going to take you to supper, and you can send me off when you like afterwards," he said and started across the square. A famous restaurant was not far off.

"No," she said, as if she knew where he was going. "If I go with you, it must be the tea-rooms I and my friends use." She gave him a rather hard smile and added: "There's no use in my going where I don't belong."

Lister said nothing, but while they walked across the town she talked with a brightness he thought forced, and when they stopped at a small tea-room in a side street he frowned. He was persuaded she did not belong there. She was playing a part, perhaps not very cleverly since he had found her out. She wanted him to think her a shop-girl enjoying an evening's adventure; her talk and careless laugh hinted at this, but Lister was not cheated.

They went in. The room was small and its ornamentation unusual. Imitation vines crawled about light wooden arches, cutting up the floor space into quiet corners. The room was rather dark, but pink lamps shone among the leaves and the soft light touched the tables and clusters of artificial grapes. Lister thought the plan was well carried out, for the grapes were the small red Muskokas that grow in Canada. When he picked up the menu card he understood why girls from the stores and offices used the place.

Lister ordered the best supper the French-Canadian landlady could serve, and then began to talk while he helped his companion. The corner they occupied was secluded and he owned that to sup with an attractive girl had a romantic charm. He noted that she frankly enjoyed the food and he liked her light, quick laugh and the sparkle in her eyes. Her thin summer clothes hinted at a slender, finely-lined form, and her careless pose was graceful.

He wondered whether she felt her meeting him was something of an adventure, but he was persuaded she was playing a part. Her frankness was not bold, the little, French-Canadian gestures were obviously borrowed, and some of the colloquialisms she used were out of date. Except for these, her talk was cultivated. For a time Lister tried to play up, and then resolved to see if he could break her reserve.

"It looks as if you made Malcolm all right on board the gravel train," he remarked.

She gave him a quick glance and colored. "Yes, I made it and got the East-bound express. The engineer was kind. I expect you told him he must help?"

"When I put you on board the locomotive I knew Roberts would see you out. He's a sober fellow and has two girls as old as you."

"You don't know how old I am," she said with an effort for carelessness.

"Anyhow, it's plain you are young enough to be rash," Lister rejoined.

She put down her cup and her glance was soft. He saw she was not acting.

"I don't think I really was rash—not *then*. It's something to know when you can trust people, and I did know."

Lister was embarrassed, but her gentleness had charm. He did not want her to resume her other manner. Then he was tempted to make an experiment.

"You know Shillito got away?"

Her lips trembled and the blood came to her skin, but she fronted him bravely and he felt ashamed.

"Yes," she said. "I think I would sooner he had been caught! But why did you begin to talk about Shillito?"

"Perhaps I oughtn't; I'm sorry."

She studied him and he thought she pondered, although it was possible she wanted to recover her calm.

"Unless you are very dull, you know something," she resumed with an effort. "Well, I was rash, but just before I saw you on the platform I found out all I'd risked. I think I was desperate; I meant to jump off the train, only it was going fast and water shone under the bridge. Then you pushed me from the step and I felt I must make another plunge and try to get your help. Now I'm glad I did so. But that's all."

Lister understood that the thing was done with. She would tell him nothing more, and he was sorry he had indulged his curiosity.

"Oh, well," he said, "there's not much risk of my bothering you about the fellow again. I start for England in a few hours."

Her glance got wistful. She moved her plate and her hand trembled.

"You are English?" he resumed.

"I met you first on board a Canadian train and now you find me helping at a Montreal store. Isn't this enough? Why do you try to find out where I come from?"

"I'm sorry. All the same, you're not a Canadian."

"I am a Canadian now," she rejoined, and then added, as if she were resolved to talk about something else, "There's a mark on your forehead, like a deep cut. You hadn't got it when I saw you on the platform."

"No," said Lister. "I fell down some steps not long afterwards."

She looked at him sharply and then exclaimed: "Oh! the newspapers said there was a struggle on the train! Somebody helped the police and got hurt. It was you. Shillito knew you had meddled. You got the cut for me!"

"We agreed we wouldn't talk about Shillito. I got the cut because I didn't want to see a young police trooper knocked out. People who meddle do get hurt now and then. Anyhow, it's some time since and I think we'll let it go. Suppose you tell me about Montreal and your job at the store?"

She roused herself and began to talk. Lister thought it cost her something, but she sketched her working companions with skill and humor. She used their accent and their French-Canadian gestures. Lister laughed and led her on, although he got a hint of strain. The girl was not happy and he had noted her wistful look when she talked about England. At length she got up, and stopping at the door for a moment gave him her hand.

"Thank you. I wish you *bon voyage*," she said.

"Can't we go somewhere else? Is there nothing doing at the theaters?" Lister asked.

"No," she said resolutely; "I'm going home. Anyhow, I'm going where I live."

Lister let her go, but waited, watching her while she went up the street. Somehow she looked forlorn and he felt pitiful. He remembered that he did not know her name, which he had wanted to ask but durst not.

When he returned to his hotel he stopped at the desk and gave the clerk a cigarette. As a rule, a Canadian hotel clerk knows something about everybody of importance in the town.

"I bought some *souvenirs* at a curiosity depot," he said, and told the other where the shop was. "Although they charged me pretty high, the things looked good."

"You haven't got stung," the clerk remarked. "The folks are French-Canadians but they like a square deal. If you put up the money, they put up the goods."

"The shop hands looked smart and bright. If you study the sales people, you can sometimes tell how a store is run."

"That's so. Those girls don't want to grumble. They're treated all right."

"Oh, well," said Lister, "since I don't know much about enameled goods and deerskin truck, I'm glad I've not got stung."

When he went off the other smiled, for a hotel clerk is not often cheated, and he thought he saw where Lister's remarks led. Lister, however, was strangely satisfied. It was something to know the storekeepers were honest and kind to the people they employed.

CHAPTER X

VERNON'S CURIOSITY

Silky blue lines streaked the long undulations that ran back to the horizon and the *Flaminian* rolled with a measured swing. When her bows went down the shining swell broke with a dull roar and rainbows flickered in the spray about her forecastle; then, while the long deck got level, one heard the beat of engines and the grinding of screws. A wake like an angry torrent foamed astern, and in the distance, where the dingy smoke-cloud melted, the crags of Labrador ran in faint, broken line. Ahead an ice-floe glittered in the sun. The liner had left Belle Isle Strait and was steaming towards Greenland on the northern Atlantic course.

Harry Vernon occupied a chair on the saloon-deck and read the *Montreal Star* which had been sent on board at Rimouski. The light reflected by the white boats and deck was strong; he was not much interested, and put down the newspaper when Lister joined him. They had met on the journey from Winnipeg to Montreal, and on boarding the *Flaminian* Lister was given the second berth in Vernon's room. Vernon liked Lister.

"Take a smoke," he said, indicating a packet of cigarettes. "Nothing fresh in the newspapers. They've caught the fellow Porteous; he was trying to steal across to Detroit."

Lister sat down and lighted a cigarette. Porteous was a clerk who had not long since gone off with a large sum of his employer's money.

"Canada is getting a popular hunting ground for smart crooks. It looks as if our business men were easily robbed."

"There are two kinds of business men; one lot makes things, the other buys and sells. Some of the first are pretty good manufacturers, but stop at that. They concentrate on manufacturing and hire a specialist to look after finance."

"But if the specialist's a crook, can't you spot him when he gets to work?"

"As a rule, the men who get stung know all about machines and material but nothing about book-keeping," Vernon replied. "A bright accountant could rob one or two I've met when he was asleep. For example, there was Shillito. His employers were big and prosperous lumber people; clever men at their job, but Shillito gambled with their money for some time before they got on his track. I expect you read about him in the newspapers?"

Lister smiled and, pushing back his cap, touched his forehead.

"I know something about Shillito. That's his mark!"

"Then you were the man he knocked out!" Vernon exclaimed. "But he hasn't got your money. Why did you help the police?"

"It isn't very obvious. Somehow, I didn't like the fellow. Then, you see, the girl—"

"The girl? What had a girl to do with it?"

Lister frowned. He had not meant to talk about the girl and was angry because he had done so, but did not see how he could withdraw his careless statement. Moreover Vernon looked interested, and it was important that both were typical Canadians. The young Canadian is not subtle; as a rule, his talk is direct, and at awkward moments he is generally marked by a frank gravity. Vernon was grave now and Lister thought he pondered. He had not known Vernon long, but he felt one could trust him.

"I met a girl on board the train," he said. "She was keen about getting away from Shillito."

"Why did she want to get away?"

"I don't know. Looked as if she was afraid of him. When I first saw her she was on the car platform and I reckoned she was bracing herself to jump off. Since we were running across a trestle, I pulled her from the steps. That's how the thing began."

"But it didn't stop just then?"

"It stopped soon afterwards," Lister replied. "She wanted to get off and go East; the train was bound West, but we were held up at a side-track, and I put her on board a gravel train locomotive."

"Then she went East!" said Vernon thoughtfully, and studied the other.

Lister sat with his head thrown back and the sun on his brown face. His look was calm and frank; his careless pose brought out the lines of his thin but muscular figure. Vernon felt he was honest; he knew Lister's type.

"She went off on board our construction locomotive," Lister replied.

"But I don't see yet! Why did you meddle? Why did she give you her confidence?"

"She didn't give me her confidence," Lister said, and smiled. "She wanted to get away and I helped. That's all. It's obvious I wasn't out for a romantic adventure, because I put her off the train."

Vernon nodded. Lister's argument was sound; besides, he did not look like a philanderer.

"Then you don't know who she is?"

"I don't know. She didn't put me wise and my business was not to bother her."

"What was she like? Did you guess her age? How was she dressed?"

Lister lighted a fresh cigarette. Vernon's keenness rather puzzled him, but he thought he had told the fellow enough. In fact, he doubted if the girl would approve his frankness. He was not going to state that he had met her at Montreal. Anyhow, not yet. If Vernon talked about the thing again and gave proper grounds for his curiosity, he might perhaps satisfy him.

"She was young," he answered vaguely. "Attractive, something of a looker, I think. I don't know much about women's clothes."

"Oh, well!" said Vernon. "You helped her off and Shillito found this out and got after you?"

"He got after me when he saw he was corraled," Lister replied, and narrated his struggle on the platform. He was now willing to tell Vernon all he wanted to know, but saw the other's interest was not keen and they presently began to talk about something else.

"What are you going to do in the Old Country?" Vernon asked.

"I have no plans. For a time, I guess I'll loaf and look about. Then I want to see my father's folks, whom I haven't met."

"Your father was English?"

"Why, yes," said Lister, smiling. "If you reckon up, you'll find a big proportion of the staunchest Canadians' parents came from the Old Country. In fact, I sometimes feel Canada belongs to us and the boys of the sourdough stock. Between us we have given the country its stamp and made it a land for white men; but we'll soon be forced to make good our claim. If we're slack, we'll be snowed under by folks from Eastern Europe whose rules and habits are not ours."

Vernon nodded. "It's a problem we have got to solve. But are you going back to the railroad when you have looked about?"

"I'm going back some time, but, now I have pulled out, I want to see all I can. I'd like to look at Europe, Egypt and India."

"Wandering around costs something," Vernon remarked.

"That is so. My wad's small, but if I've not had enough when it's used up, I'll look for a job. If nothing else is doing, I'll go to sea."

Vernon's smile was sympathetic and he looked ahead, over the dipping forecastle to the far horizon. The sea shone with reflected light and an iceberg glimmered against the blue. He felt the measured throb of engines and the ship leap forward. Vernon was a young Canadian and sprang from pioneering stock. The vague distance called; he felt the lure of going somewhere.

"If the thing was possible, I'd go with you," he said. "All the same, I'm tied to business and the old man can't pull his load alone. My job's to stick to the traces and help him along. But do you know much about the sea?"

"I was engineer on board a Pacific coasting boat and a wheat barge on the Lakes."

"Well," said Vernon thoughtfully, "I know an English shipping boss who might help you get a berth. I'd rather like you to meet him, but we'll talk about this again. Now let's join those fellows at deck-quoits."

Their friendship ripened, but it was not until the last day of the voyage Vernon said something more about the English ship-owner. *Flaminian* was steaming across the Irish Sea, with the high blue hills of Mourne astern and the Manx rocks ahead. Vernon lounged on the saloon-deck and his face was thoughtful as he looked across the shining water.

"We'll make Liverpool soon after dark, and if I can get the train I want, I'll pull out right then," he said. "You allowed you might try a run on board an English ship before you went back?"

"It's possible," said Lister. "Depends on how my wad holds out and on somebody's being willing to give me a post."

Vernon nodded. "That's where I'm leading." He stopped, and Lister wondered why he pondered. The thing did not seem worth the thought his companion gave it.

"I reckon you don't know Cartwright of the Independent Freighters, but he could put you wise about getting a ship," Vernon resumed. "I'm stopping for a week or two at his country house. The freighters are small boats, but Cartwright's worth knowing; in fact, to know him is something of an education. In the West we're pretty keen business men, and I've put across some smart deals at the Winnipeg Board of Trade, but I'll admit Cartwright would beat me every time. Where do you mean to locate?"

Lister said he was going to the neighborhood of a small country town in the North of England, and was puzzled by Vernon's start.

"That fixes it! The thing's strangely lucky. Cartwright's country house is not far off. You had better come along by my train. Soon after I arrive I'll get Mrs. Cartwright to ask you across."

"I mustn't bother your friends," said Lister. "Besides, I really don't know if I want to go to sea."

"All the same, you'll come over to Carrock. You ought to know Cartwright and I reckon he'll like to know you. I have a notion you and he would make a good team."

Lister wondered whether Vernon had an object for urging him to meet his friend, but this looked ridiculous.

"What's Cartwright like?" he asked carelessly.

"My notion is, Cartwright's unique. You imagine he's something of a highbrow Englishman, rather formal and polite, but he has an eye like a fish-hawk's and his orders go. Hair and mustache white; you don't know if his clothes are old or new, but you feel they're exactly what he ought to wear. That's Cartwright, so to speak, on top; but when you meet him you want to remember you're not up against a Canadian. We're a straight type. When we're tough, we're very tough all the time; when we're cultivated, you can see the polish shine. In the Old Country it's harder to fix where folks belong."

"You imply that you have got to know Cartwright before you fix him?"

Vernon laughed. "I haven't quite fixed him yet. At one time he's a sober gentleman of the stiff old school; at another he's as rough as the roughest hobo I've met in the West. I reckon he'd beat a business crook at the other's smartest trick, but if you're out for a straight deal, you'll find Cartwright straight."

He went off to change some money and Lister went to his cabin and began to pack his trunk. When he came up they had passed the Chicken Rock and a long bright beam touched the sea astern. In the East, water and sky faded to dusky blue, but presently a faint light began to blink as if it beckoned. The light got brighter and gradually drew abeam. The foaming wake glimmered lividly in the dark, the beat of screws seemed quicker, and Lister thought the ship was carried forward by a stream of tide.

Other lights began to blink. They stole out of the dark, got bright, and vanished, and Lister, leaning on the rails, felt they called him on. One knew them by their colors and measured flashes. They were beacons, burning on a well-ordered plan to guide the navigator, but he did not know the plan. In a sense, this was important, and he began to muse.

Now he would soon reach the Old Country, he felt he had made a momentous plunge. Adventure called, he knew Canada and wanted something fresh, but he wondered whether this was all. Perhaps the plunge had, so to speak, not been a thoughtless caprice. In a sense, things had led up to it and made it logical. For example, it might not have been for nothing he met the girl on the train and got hurt. His hurt had kept him at Winnipeg and stopping there had roused his discontent. Then he had met Vernon, who wanted him to know the English ship-owner. It was possible these things were like the flashes that leaped out of the dark. He would know where they pointed when the journey was over. Then Lister smiled and knocked out his pipe.

When he went on deck again some time afterwards the ship was steering for a gap between two rows of twinkling lights. They ran on, closing on each other, like electric lamps in a long street, and in front the sky shone with a dull red glow. It was the glimmer of a great port, they were entering the Mersey, and he went off to get up his luggage.

PART II
THE RECKONING

CHAPTER I

VERNON'S PLOT

Lister occupied the end of a slate-flag bench on the lawn at Carrock, Mrs. Cartwright's house in Rannerdale. Rannerdale slopes to a lake in the North Country, and the old house stands among trees and rocks in a sheltered hollow. The sun shone on its lichened front, where a creeper was going red; in the background birches with silver stems and leaves like showers of gold gleamed against somber firs. Across the lawn and winding road, the tranquil lake reflected bordering woods; and then long mountain slopes that faded from yellow and green to purple closed the view.

While Lister waited for the tea Mrs. Cartwright had given him to cool he felt the charm of house and dale was strong. Perhaps it owed something to the play of soft light and shade, for, as a rule, in Canada all was sharply cut. The English landscape had a strange elusive beauty that gripped one hard, and melted as the fleecy clouds rolled by. When the light came back color and line were as beautiful but not the same.

There was no grass in Canada like the sweep of smooth English turf, and Lister had not thought a house could give the sense of ancient calm one got at Carrock. Since his boyhood he had not known a home; his resting place had been a shack at a noisy construction camp, a room at a crowded cheap hotel, and a berth beside a steamer's rattling engines. Then the shining silver on the tea-table was something new; he marked its beauty of line, and the blue and gold and brown pattern on the delicate china he was almost afraid to touch. In fact, all at Carrock was marked by a strange refinement and quiet charm.

He liked his hosts. Mrs. Cartwright was large, rather fat, and placid, but he felt the house and all it stood for were hers by rightful inheritance. Her son and daughter were not like that. Lister thought they had cultivated their well-bred serenity and by doing so had cultivated out some virile qualities of human nature. Grace Hyslop had beauty, but not much charm; Lister thought her cold, and imagined her prejudices were strong and conventional. Mortimer's talk and manners were colorlessly correct. Lister did not know yet if Hyslop was a prig or not.

Cartwright was frankly puzzling. He looked like a sober country gentleman, and this was not the type Lister had thought to meet. His clothes were fastidiously good, his voice had a level, restrained note, but his eye was like a hawk's, as Vernon had said. Now and then one saw a twinkle of ironical amusement and some of his movements were quick and vigorous. Lister thought Cartwright's blood was red.

Vernon, lounging at the opposite end of the bench, talked about a day Hyslop and he had spent upon the rocks, and rather struck a foreign note. He had not Hyslop's graceful languidness; he looked alert and highly-strung. His thin face was too grave for Carrock and his glance too quick. Lister, listening to his remarks, was surprised to note that Hyslop was a bold mountaineer.

"Oh, well," he said, with a deprecatory smile, when Vernon stopped, "this small group of mountains is all the wild belt we have got, and you like to find a stranger keen about your favorite sport. Then your keenness was flattering. In your country, with its lonely woods and rivers running to the North, you have a field for strenuous sport and adventure."

"The woods pull," Vernon agreed. "All the same, I'm a business man. Betting at the Board of Trade is my proper job and I've got to be satisfied with a week at a fishing camp now and then. Adventure is for the pioneers, lumber men and railroad builders like my friend."

Lister looked up. He did not see why Vernon talked about him.

"My adventures don't count for much," he said. "Sometimes a car went into a muskeg and we had to hustle to dig her out. Sometimes the boys made trouble about their pay. Railroad building is often dull."

"I don't know if we're all modest in Canada, but my partner is," Vernon observed. "If you want a romantic tale, persuade him to tell you how he got the mark on his head."

"Oh shucks!" said Lister. "I had sooner you had cut that out." He turned to the others apologetically. "It was a dispute with a fellow on board a train who threw me down the steps. I don't want to bore you with the tale."

"The man was the famous crook, Shillito," Vernon remarked.

Cartwright lifted his head and looked at Vernon hard. Then he looked at Lister, who felt embarrassed and angry. He saw Grace and Mrs. Cartwright were curious and thought Hyslop's glance got keen.

"If it will not bother Mr. Lister, we would like to hear his narrative," said Cartwright quietly, but Lister got a hint of command.

He narrated his adventure on the train, and although he tried to rob the story of its romance, was surprised when he stopped for a moment. Vernon was carelessly lighting a cigarette, but Lister saw his carelessness was forced. When he got a light he crossed the grass, as if he meant to throw the match over the hedge. Lister thought Cartwright watched Harry with dry amusement. Mrs. Cartwright's look was obviously disturbed, but she had not altogether lost her calm. One felt her calm was part of her, but the Hyslops' was cultivated. Lister imagined it cost them something to use control.

"Go on," said Cartwright, rather sharply.

Lister resumed, but presently Cartwright stopped him.

"You imagined the girl was afraid of Shillito! What were your grounds?"

"She was disturbed and declared she must get off the train. I think she meant to jump off, although we were going fast. Then she asked me if the conductor could be bribed to stop."

"Perhaps we can take it for granted she wanted to get away from somebody. Why did you surmise the man was Shillito?"

"He came through the car afterwards, as if he tried to find the girl, and gave me a keen glance. When he came back I thought him angry and disappointed. By and by I had better grounds for imagining he suspected I had helped her."

Cartwright pondered, but Lister did not think he doubted. It rather looked as if he weighed something carefully. The lines on his face got deeper and his look was thoughtful.

"I understand the girl did not give you her name," he said. "What was she like? How was she dressed?"

Lister was rather surprised to find he could not answer satisfactorily. It was not the girl's physical qualities but her emotions he had marked. He remembered the pluck with which she had struggled against the fear she obviously felt, her impulsive trust when he offered help, and her relief when she got into the locomotive cab. Although he had studied her at Montreal, it was her effort to play a part that impressed him most.

"She was young, and I think attractive," he replied. "She wore a knitted cap and a kind of jersey a girl might use for boating. I thought she came from a summer camp."

Cartwright's face was inscrutable, but Lister saw the others' interest was keen. Mrs. Cartwright's eyes were fixed on him and he got a hint of suspense. Although Grace was very quiet, a touch of color had come to her skin, as if she felt humiliated. Mortimer's pose was stiff and his control over done. Then Cartwright turned to his step-daughter.

"Have you told Jones about the box of plants for Liverpool?"

Grace's look indicated that she did not want to go, but Cartwright's glance was insistent and she got up. Lister looked about and saw Vernon had not come back. He was studying the plants in a border across the lawn. When Grace had gone Cartwright asked:

"Can you remember the evening of the month and the time when you first saw the girl?"

Lister fixed the date and added: "It was nearly ten o'clock. The porter had just gone through the car and when he said my berth was ready I looked at my watch. He went to the next Pullman, and I thought he was getting busy late."

Cartwright nodded and Mortimer glanced at him sharply, but next moment looked imperturbable. Mrs. Cartwright's relief, however, was obvious. Her face had become animated and her hands trembled.

"Thank you," said Cartwright. "Go on."

Lister narrated his putting the girl on board the gravel train and Mrs. Cartwright interrupted.

"Do you know if she had money?"

"She had some. Enough to buy a ticket East."

"It's strange," said Mrs. Cartwright, and then exclaimed: "You mean you gave her some?"

"Oh, well," said Lister awkwardly, "I'd seen her look at her purse and frown, and as I helped her up the locomotive steps I pushed a few bills into her hand. I don't think she knew they were paper money. She was highly-strung and anxious to get off before Shillito came along."

Mrs. Cartwright gave him a look that moved him. Her eyes shone and he knew she was his friend.

"The poor girl was strangely lucky when she met you," she said.

Lister resumed his narrative, but it was plain the climax had passed. The others' interest was now polite, and he went on as fast as possible. He had begun to see a light and wanted to finish and get away. He did not, however, see that while he told his artless tale he had drawn his character. When he stopped Cartwright said:

"Then you did not know her name?"

"I don't know it yet," said Lister, as coolly as he could, but got embarrassed when he saw Cartwright's smile.

"You don't imagine Shillito rejoined her afterwards?"

"No," said Lister firmly, "I think it's impossible. The gravel train was going East, and when the police boarded the cars we had run some distance West." He stopped for a moment, because he saw he was very dull. If his supposition were correct, there was something the others ought to know. "Besides," he resumed, "I met her not long since at Montreal."

"At Montreal!" Mrs. Cartwright exclaimed.

"At a shop where they sold *souvenirs*," Lister replied. "I didn't expect to meet her; I went in to buy some enameled things. It was a pretty good shop and the hotel clerk declared the people were all right. She knew me and we went to a tea-room. She left me at the door, and I think that's all."

He got up. "I don't know if I have bored you, but I felt you wanted me to talk. Now I must get off, and I want to see Harry before I go."

"Mr. Vernon does not seem to be about," Cartwright remarked with some dryness. "I'll go to the gate with you."

Mrs. Cartwright gave Lister her hand and her glance was very kind. "You will come back? So long as you stop here I hope you will feel our house is open to you."

Hyslop got up, but Cartwright stopped him with a sign. He was quiet while they crossed the lawn, but when they reached the wood by the road he said, "I imagine you know we owe you much. After a time, your efforts to use some tact were rather obvious. Well, the girl you helped is my step-daughter."

"At the beginning, I did not know this," Lister declared.

"It was plain," said Cartwright, "Well, I agree with her mother—Barbara was very lucky when she met you, but since you look embarrassed, we'll let this go. Did she repay your loan?"

"She wanted to pay me," said Lister. "I refused."

"Why?" Cartwright asked, looking at him hard.

Lister hesitated, "For one thing, I didn't know the sum. Then I knew her wages were not high. You ought to see I couldn't take the money."

"You ought to have taken the money, for the girl's sake."

"Oh," said Lister, "I think she knew I didn't refuse because I wanted her to feel she owed me something."

"It's possible she did know," said Cartwright dryly. "You must try to remember the sum when you come again. Now I want the name of the shop at Montreal."

Lister told him and added: "You mean to write to Miss Hyslop?"

Cartwright smiled. "I'm going across as soon as possible to bring my step-daughter home."

CHAPTER II

BARBARA'S RETURN

When Lister had gone Cartwright returned to the tea-table and looked at Hyslop, who got up and went off. Hyslop did not altogether want to go but he had cultivated discretion, and it was plain his step-father meant to get rid of him. Then Cartwright gave his wife a sympathetic glance. Mrs. Cartwright was calm, but when she put some cups together her hand shook.

"Leave the things alone," said Cartwright in a soothing voice. "Vernon's plot was clever."

"Do you think Harry planned that Lister should tell us?"

"It looks like that," said Cartwright dryly. "He was keen about bringing his friend over, but was cautious enough to wait until the fellow began to know us. When he talked about Lister's adventures I wondered where he was leading. The other was puzzled, and didn't see until near the end."

"But why didn't Harry, himself, tell us all he knew?"

"Vernon's a good sort and more fastidious than one thinks; he saw he'd be forced to venture on rather awkward ground, and there was some doubt. He wanted us to weigh the story and judge if the clew he gave us ought to be followed. This was not Vernon's job, although I think he was satisfied."

"But you are satisfied?"

"Yes," said Cartwright "Lister's portrait of Barbara was lifelike and his own was pretty good. I think he drew himself and her better than he knew, and perhaps it's lucky we have to deal with fellows like these. A good Canadian is a fine type. However, we must bring Barbara back."

"Ah!" said Mrs. Cartwright, "I want her back! One must hide one's hurt, but to hide it is hard—" She pulled herself up and added: "Will you send a cablegram?"

"I think not. The girl is proud and as wild as a hawk. She thinks she has humiliated us, and if she's startled, she'll probably run away."

"You don't think she has humiliated us?" Mrs. Cartwright said in a hesitating voice.

Cartwright smiled. "It's plain that her escapade must not be talked about but we can trust these Canadians and I know Barbara. In a sense, Lister's narrative wasn't necessary. The girl is headstrong, but I was persuaded she would find the rascal out. Looks as if she did so soon after they got on board the cars, and I imagine Shillito had an awkward few moments; Barbara's temper is not mild. Then it's important that she was desperately anxious to escape from him. There's no more to be said."

Mrs. Cartwright gave him a grateful look. Her husband had never failed her and he had justified her trust again.

"If you don't send a cablegram, how shall we get Barbara back?"

"I'll go myself," said Cartwright "If she can't be persuaded, I'll bring her by force. It's lucky I can charge the cost to the office. The new wheat is coming down to Montreal, and the *Conference* people have a plan to get it all, but I expect to beat them and engage some cargo for our boats before the St. Lawrence freezes. However, since I'm going, I must get to work."

He started for the house and met his step-son at the porch. Mortimer looked thoughtful, and held an unlighted cigarette. Cartwright studied him with scornful amusement.

"Have you been speculating about the proper way of handling an awkward situation?"

"I have been talking to Grace," Hyslop replied in an even voice.

"I rather think Grace has been talking to you, but expect you agreed. You have, no doubt, decided the best plan is to leave your headstrong sister alone?"

"We did agree about something like that," said Hyslop coolly, although when Cartwright fixed his eyes on his he turned his head. "We thought if Barbara were given an allowance, she might, for example, stay with the Vernons. Grace's notion—"

Cartwright's mouth got hard and his mustache bristled. When he was moved his urbanity vanished and his talk was very blunt.

"We'll let Grace's notion go. My form is not my step-children's, but I try to moderate my remarks about women. We'll admit Grace is a woman, although I sometimes doubt. Anyhow, you are not a man; you haven't a drop of warm blood in your veins! You're a curled and scented fine lady's lap-dog pup!"

"I don't see much use in talking about my qualities, sir."

"You don't see," Cartwright agreed. "That's your drawback! You see nothing that's rude and human; you're afraid to look. All that's obvious is, Barbara must not come home to throw an awkward reflection on Grace's Puritanical virtue. People might find out something and talk? If anybody talks while I'm about, I'll ram the implication down his throat! You don't see, or perhaps you don't mind, the drawbacks to separating Barbara from her mother and banishing her from home? She's trustful, rash, and fiery, and not a statue like Grace. Anyhow, Barbara is coming back, and if you don't approve, I'll expect you to be resigned. Now get off before I let myself go!"

Hyslop went. One gained nothing by arguing with a brute like Cartwright, and since Mrs. Cartwright's infatuation for her husband could not be disturbed Hyslop knew he must acquiesce. Cartwright, rather braced by the encounter, went to the library and wrote some letters to Liverpool. A few days afterwards, he packed his trunk and was driven to the station in Mrs. Cartwright's car. Grace got up an hour earlier than usual in order to see him off, and when she brought his scarf and gloves Cartwright accepted her ministrations with politeness. Although he knew she disapproved of him, she thought her duty was to do things like this, and he played up.

When the throb of the car was getting faint she met Mortimer going to the lake. He stopped and looked up at the valley, which was streaked by a thin line of dust.

"For three or four weeks we'll be undisturbed," he said. "I admit I like Carrock better when my step-father is away."

"Barbara's coming back with him," Grace remarked. "In some ways, her return will be awkward, but perhaps she ought to come."

Mortimer gave her a surprised glance. "This was not your view!"

"Oh, well, I have been thinking. Barbara is rash and very young. In Canada, she would be free from all control, and one must not weigh drawbacks against one's duty. Perhaps Cartwright takes the proper line, although of course it costs him nothing. You didn't tell me what he said the other evening."

Mortimer shrugged. "As a rule, my step-father's remarks won't bear re-stating. He was a little franker than usual."

"He *is* coarse," said Grace. "One feels he gets coarser, as if his thoughts had begun to react on his body. There is a link, and, of course, with his habits—"

"I rather think you mean with his appetites. Cartwright does not often let himself go when he's at home, but when he is away he's another man."

Grace looked thoughtful. "One likes restraint. All the same, I sometimes think rude, primitive people have a vigor we have not. It's strange, but indulgence seems to go with force. One feels our friends are rather *bloodless*—I'm using Cartwright's phrase."

"Our Canadian friends are not bloodless. I expect you have remarked that Barbara's the type they like."

"She has an appeal for men like that," Grace agreed, and mused.

It was hard to own, but she began to see that when she thought Barbara ought to stop in Canada she was inspired by jealousy. Barbara's charm for men was strong and when she was about they left Grace alone. Still she had a vague perception that her sister's charm was not altogether physical. She herself had a classical beauty that did not mark the younger girl; it looked as if Barbara had attractive qualities that were not hers. Lister, for example, was not a brute like Cartwright, but it was plain that Barbara had attracted him. Grace approved his soberness and frank gravity; and then she pulled herself up. She must not be jealous about her sister.

"Cartwright's power is stronger because he does not use our money," Mortimer resumed. "I don't know if it was cleverness or scruples that urged him to refuse. All the same, if he were forced to ask mother's help, his influence would be less."

"But his needing help is not probable. He's managing owner of the line."

Mortimer smiled. "He gets a commission on the boat's earnings, but does not hold many shares. Then the fleet is small and the boats don't earn very much. Things are not going smoothly and some shareholders would like to put Cartwright off the Board. At the last meeting, one fellow talked about the need for fresh blood. However, I expect Cartwright's clever enough, to keep off the rocks, and when one can't get rid of a drawback one must submit."

Lighting a cigarette, he started for the lake and Grace returned thoughtfully to the house. Mortimer hated Cartwright and Grace admitted he had some grounds. Although her brother was indolent and philosophical, he did not forget. Rude disputes jarred him, but if by some chance he was able to injure the other, Grace thought he would do so. Grace, herself, strongly disapproved of Cartwright. All the same, he was her step-father and she had tried to cultivate her sense of duty. She was prejudiced, cold, and censorious, but she meant to be just and did not like Mortimer's bitterness.

Cartwright was occupied for some time at Montreal, and the birch leaves had fallen when he returned. The evening was dark, and chilly mist rolled down the dale, but a big fire burned in the hall at Carrock and tall lamps threw a cheerful light on the oak paneling. A flooded beck roared in the hollow of a ghyll across the lawn and its turmoil echoed about the hall. Mrs. Cartwright stood by the fire, Grace moved restlessly about, and Mortimer appeared to be absorbed by the morning's news.

"I wish you would sit down, mother," he said presently. "You can hear the car, you know, and the train is often late."

For a few minutes Mrs. Cartwright did not move, and then she started and fixed her eyes on the door. She heard an engine throb, there was a noise in the porch, and a cold wind blew into the room. Then the door opened and Cartwright entered, shaking the damp from his fur coat. He turned, beckoning somebody behind, and Barbara came out from the arch. Her face was flushed, her eyes were hard, and she stopped irresolutely. Mortimer advanced to take the coat she carried and Grace crossed the floor, but Barbara waited, as if she did not see them. Then her strained look vanished, for Mrs. Cartwright went forward with awkward speed and took her in her arms.

Cartwright saw his wife had forgotten him, and turning to the others with a commanding gesture, drove them and the servants from the hall. When they had gone he gave Mrs. Cartwright a smile.

"I've brought her back," he said. "Not altogether an easy job. Barbara's ridiculous, but she can fight."

He went off and Barbara clung to her mother. She was shaking and her breath came hard.

"You were ridiculous," said Mrs. Cartwright in a gentle voice. "I expect you were very obstinate. But he was kind?"

"He's a dear; I love him!" Barbara replied. "He understands everything. I think he ought to have stopped at Liverpool; the secretary met us and talked about some business, but if he hadn't come with me, I could not have borne—"

She stopped, and resting her head on Mrs. Cartwright's shoulder, began to cry. Mrs. Cartwright said nothing, but kissed and soothed her with loving gentleness.

When, some time afterwards, Barbara came down the stairs that occupied one side of the hall she was composed, but tea by the fire was something of a strain. It was plain that Grace's careless talk was forced and Mortimer's efforts to keep on safe ground were marked. Now and then Cartwright's eyes twinkled and Barbara thought she knew why he sometimes made a joke that jarred the others. When the meal was over he took them away.

"I imagine your sister understands Grace and you are willing to take her back and forget the pain she gave you," he said to Hyslop. "Your handling of the situation was tactful and correct, but you can leave her to her mother."

Mrs. Cartwright stopped with Barbara, who brought a footstool to the hearthrug, and sitting down leaned against her knee.

"I have been an obstinate, selfish, romantic fool!" she broke out.

Mrs. Cartwright touched her hair and smiled, for she felt comforted. This was the tempestuous Barbara she thought she had lost.

"My dear!" she said. "It's not important since you have come back."

"I oughtn't to have come back. If you had not sent father, I would not have come. He's determined, but he's gentle. You know he sympathizes."

"Although I wanted him to go, I did not send him," Mrs. Cartwright replied. "He went because he loves you, but we can talk about this again." She hesitated for a moment and went on: "It was not long, I think, before you found Shillito was a thief? Mr. Lister's story indicated this."

A wave of color came to Barbara's skin, but she looked up and her eyes flashed.

"At the beginning, I did not know he was a thief; I found out he was a cunning brute. Afterwards, when I read about his escape in the newspapers, I rather wished the trooper who shot at him had not missed—" She shook with horror and anger and it was a moment or two before she resumed: "I can't tell you all, mother. I was frightened, but anger gave me pluck. He said I must stick to him because I could not go back. I think I struck him, and then I ran away. People were going to their berths in the Pullman and he durst not use force. When I got to the car platform and was going to jump off I saw Mr. Lister—but he has told you—"

Mrs. Cartwright nodded, for she was satisfied.

"My dear," she said, "it's done with. Still I wonder why you were willing to leave us."

"Sometimes I wonder. To begin with, I have owned I was a fool; but things were dreary and I wanted a thrill. Then I had begun to feel nobody at home wanted me. Father and you were kind, but he seemed to think me an amusing, willful child. Grace always disapproved, and Mortimer sneered. They knew I was not their sort and very proper people are cruel if you won't obey their rules. I hated rules; Grace's correctness made me rebel. Then Louis came and declared I was all to him. He was handsome and romantic, and I was tired of restraint. I thought I loved him, but it was ridiculous, because I hate him now. Mortimer's a prig, but Louis is a brute!"

Mrs. Cartwright sighed. She liked tranquillity and the girl's passion jarred. She tried to soothe her, and presently Barbara asked in a level voice: "Where is Harry Vernon?"

"He went to town a few days since."

"When he knew I would soon arrive? His going is significant. I shall hate Harry next!"

"You must not be unjust. I imagine he thought to meet him would embarrass you."

"It would have embarrassed me, but Harry would not have known," Barbara declared. "If I have been a fool, I can pay. Still I ought to have stayed in Canada. Father's obstinate and I wanted to come home, but things will be harder than at Montreal."

Mrs. Cartwright kissed her. "My poor child, the hurt is not as deep as you think. We will try to help you to forget."

CHAPTER III

LISTER CLEARS THE GROUND

The sun was on the rocks and the lichen shone in rings of soft and varied color. Blue shadows filled the dale, which, from the side of the Buttress, looked profoundly deep. A row of young men and women followed a ledge that crossed the face of the steep crag; Mortimer Hyslop leading, a girl and Vernon a few yards behind, Lister and Barbara farther off.

Hyslop knew the rocks and was a good leader. He was cool and cautious and did not undertake a climb until he was satisfied about his companions' powers. The slanting edge looked dangerous, but was not, although one must be steady and there was an awkward corner. At the turning, the ledge got narrow, and one must seize a knob and then step lightly on a stone embedded in mossy soil.

When they reached the spot Hyslop stopped and told Vernon what to do; the girl immediately behind him was a clever mountaineer. They went round and Lister watched from a few yards off. For a moment or two each in turn, supported by one foot with body braced against the rock, grasped the knob and vanished round the corner. It was plain one must get a firm hold, but Lister thought this was all. He was used to the tall skeleton trestles that carried the rails across Canadian ravines.

After the others disappeared Lister seized the knob. He thought the stone he stood on moved and he cautiously took a heavier strain on his arm. He could get across, but he obeyed an impulse and gave the stone a push. It rolled out and, when he swung himself back to the ledge, plunged down and smashed upon the rocks below. For a few moments the echoes rolled about the crags, and then Hyslop shouted: "Are you all right? Can you get round?"

Lister said he thought not, and Hyslop replied that it did not matter. Barbara would take him up a grassy ridge and the others would meet them at the top. A rattle of nailed boots indicated that he was going off and Lister turned and glanced at Barbara. She had sat down on an inclined slab and her figure and face, in profile, cut against the sky. A yard or two beneath her, the sloping rock vanished at the top of a steep pitch and one saw nothing but the crags across the narrow dale. Yet Lister thought the girl was not disturbed.

"I expect I was clumsy," he apologized.

"Well," she said, "it looks like that!"

He gave her a quick glance and pondered. Although he had gone to Carrock since she came home, she had been strangely cold and, so to speak, aloof. He had imagined their meeting might embarrass her, but she was not embarrassed. In fact, she had met him as if he were a friend, but he had not seen her afterwards unless somebody was about. Now he meant to force her to be frank.

"I was clumsy," he resumed. "All the same, when I felt the stone begin to move I might have pulled myself across by my hands. I expect the block would have been firm enough to carry you."

"Yes, I know," said Barbara. "You didn't want me to get across!"

Lister studied her. He doubted if it was altogether exertion that had brought the blood to her skin and given her eyes the keen sparkle. Clinging to the rock, with the shadowy gulf below, she looked strangely alert and virile. Her figure cut against the sky; he noted its slenderness and finely-drawn lines. She was not angry, although he had admitted he pushed down the stone, but he felt as if something divided them and doubted if he could remove the obstacle.

"I wanted to talk and had found I could not get near you unless the others were about," he said. "It looked as if I had unconsciously given you some grounds for standing me off. Well, I suppose I did put your relations on your track."

"It wasn't that," said Barbara. "I imagine Harry Vernon helped you there. You were forced to tell your story."

"I was forced. All the same, I think Harry's plan was good."

"He went away a few days before I arrived!" Barbara remarked.

Lister thought he saw where she led and knitted his brows. He was on awkward ground and might say too much, but to say nothing might be worse.

"Harry's a good sort and I expect he pulled out because he imagined you'd sooner he did so," he said. "For all that, I reckon he ought to have stayed."

Although her color was vivid, Barbara gave him a searching glance. "In order to imply I had no grounds for embarrassment if I met him? Harry was at the camp in the woods."

"He knew you had no grounds for embarrassment," Lister declared. "I knew, and Harry's an older friend."

Barbara turned her head, and when she looked back Lister thought his boldness was justified. In a sense she had been very frank, although perhaps this situation made for frankness. They were alone on the face of the towering crag. All was very quiet but for the noise of falling water, and the only living object one could see was a buzzard hovering high up at a white cloud's edge. One could talk in the mountain solitude as one could not talk in a drawing-room. For all that, Lister felt he had not altogether broken the girl's reserve.

"One envies men like you who build railways and sail ships," she said, and now Lister wondered where she led. "You live a natural life, knowing bodily strain and primitive emotions. Sometimes you're exhausted and sometimes afraid. Your thought's fixed on the struggle; you're keenly occupied. Isn't it like that?"

"Something like that," Lister agreed. "Sometimes the strain gets monotonous."

"But it's often thrilling. Men and women need to be thrilled. People talk about the modern lust for excitement, but it isn't modern and I expect the instinct's sound. Civilization that gives us hot water before we get up and food we didn't grow is not all an advantage. Our bodies get soft and we're driven back on our emotions. Where we want action we get talk. Then one gets up against the rules; you mustn't be angry, you mustn't be sincere, you must use a dreary level calm."

Lister was puzzled and said nothing, but Barbara went on: "Perhaps some girls like this; others don't, and now and then rebel. We feel we're human, we want to live. Adventure calls us, as it calls you. We want to front life's shocks and storms; unsatisfied curiosity drives us on. Then perhaps romance comes and all the common longings of flesh and blood are transfigured."

She stopped, and Lister began to see a light. This was her apology for her rashness in Canada, all she would give, and he doubted if she had given as much to others. On the whole, he thought the apology good.

"Romance cheats one now and then," he remarked, and pulled himself up awkwardly, but Barbara was calm.

"I wonder whether it always cheats one!"

"I think not," he said. "Sometimes one must trust one's luck, and venture. All the same, philosophizing is not my habit, and when I didn't step lightly on the stone—"

"You mean, when you pushed the stone down?" Barbara interrupted.

"Oh, well. Anyhow, I didn't mean to philosophize. I wanted to find out why you kept away from me."

"Although you knew why I did so? You admitted you knew why Harry went off!"

"I see I've got to talk," said Lister. "Shillito was a cheat, but when you found him out you tried to jump off the train. You let me help because I think you trusted me."

"I did trust you. It's much to know my trust was justified. For one thing, it looks as if I wasn't altogether a fool."

"Afterwards, when I met you at Montreal, you were friendly, although you tried to persuade me you were a shop girl."

Barbara smiled. "I was a shop girl. Besides, you were a stranger, and it's sometimes easy to trust people one does not expect to see again."

"My plan's to trust the people I like all the time," Lister replied. "When I found you on the car platform I knew I ought to help, I saw you meant to escape from something mean. Then at Montreal it was plain you were trying in make good because you were proud and would not go back. I liked that, although I thought you were not logical. Well, I told your story because Vernon bluffed me, but if I'd known your step-father as I know him now, I'd have told the tale before."

"Then, it was in order that I might understand this you sent the stone down the crag?"

"I think it was," said Lister. "I hope I have, so to speak, cleared the ground."

Barbara gave him a puzzling smile. "You're rather obvious, but it's important you mean to be nice. However, I expect the others are waiting for us and we must join them, although we won't go by the grass ridge," She indicated the slope of cracked rock in front. "The hold is pretty good. Do you think you can get up?"

Lister doubted. He was athletic and steady, but the climb looked awkward for a beginner.

"If you are going, I'll try."

"You imagine you can go where I can go?"

"Something like that," Lister admitted. "If I'm beaten, you're accountable and will have to help."

He was satisfied by Barbara's frank laugh. Her mood was changeable. Not long since he had, with awkward sympathy, thought her a proud humiliated woman; now she was marked by the humor of a careless girl. He could, however, play up to her later mood, and when they set off he began to joke.

The rock slanted, and cracks and breaks gave a firm hold, but there was not a crack wherever one was needed and the pitch was steep. Then in places the slabs were slippery with wet lichen and Lister's ordinary walking boots could get no grip. His jokes stopped and the sweat began to dew his face. His breath got hard and he felt his heart beat. It was obvious that climbing needed study.

For all that, he went on and found a strange delight in watching Barbara. Her clothes harmonized with the soft colors of lichen and stone; her movements were confident and light. He got no sense of effort; her pose was seldom strained and the lines of her limbs and body flowed in easy curves. He thought she rather flitted than labored up the rock. Practice no doubt accounted for much, but something was due to temperament. Barbara did not hesitate; she trusted her luck and went ahead.

At length she stopped, pressed against the stone in the hollow of a gully, while Lister crept obliquely across a long wet slab. He looked up and saw her face, finely colored after effort, against a background of green and gold. The berries on a small mountain-ash in a cranny harmonized with the carmine of her skin. She looked down and smiled with careless amusement.

Then Lister's foot slipped and he could get no hold for his hands. His smooth boots drew a greasy line across the wet slab as he slid down. Perhaps the risk was not very daunting, but he knew he must not roll down far. At the bottom of the slab he brought up with his foot braced against a knob, and he saw Barbara coming after him. When she stopped her glance was apologetic.

"I forgot you hadn't proper boots. Give me your hand and try again."

"No, thanks," said Lister. "Do you think I'm going to let you pull me up?"

"Why not?" she asked with a twinkle.

"To begin with, I'm obstinate and don't mean to be beaten by a bit of greasy rock. Then I expect I'm heavier than you think."

"You're ridiculously proud. It would hurt to let a girl help," Barbara rejoined. "After all, you're a conventionalist, and I rather thought you were not."

"Anyhow, I'm going up myself," Lister declared.

He got up, but his clothes gathered some slime from the rock and his skin was stained by soil and moss. Barbara looked at him with a twinkle.

"Your obstinacy cost you something," she remarked. "If you're tired, you had better stop and smoke."

Lister lighted a cigarette. She had been rather keen about rejoining the others, but he thought she had forgotten. Barbara's carelessness gave her charm. Perhaps he ought to go on, but he meant to take the extra few minutes luck had given him.

"I'm really sorry I forgot about your boots and brought you up the rock," she said.

"I wonder why you did bring me up?"

"Oh, well, a number of the men I know have a comfortable feeling of superiority. Of course, nice men don't make you feel this, but it's there. One likes to give such pride a jolt."

"I think I see. If it's some comfort, I'll own you can beat me going up awkward rocks. But where does this take us?"

Barbara smiled. "It takes us some distance. When you admit a girl's your equal, friendship's easier. You know, one reason Mortimer and I can't agree is, his feeling of superiority is horribly strong."

"Couldn't you take him up an awkward gully and get him stuck?"

"No," said Barbara, in a regretful voice. "He's really a good cragsman and knows exactly how far he can go. When he starts an awkward climb he reckons up all the obstacles and is ready to get round them when they come. The plan's good. People like Mortimer don't get stuck."

"It's possible, but I expect they miss something now and then. There isn't much thrill in knowing you are safe."

"Sometimes you play up rather well," Barbara remarked.

"I'm not playing up. I'm preaching my code. I'm not as sober and cautious as you perhaps think."

"For example?"

"You'll probably get bored, but in Canada I turned down a pretty good job because it was monotonous. I wanted something fresh, and thought I'd go across and see the Old Country. Well, I'm here and all's charming, but I don't know how I'll get back when my wad runs out."

"Ah," said Barbara, "you mean your money will soon be gone? But you have relations. Somebody would help."

"It's possible, but I would refuse," Lister rejoined. "You're not adventuring much when another meets the bill. When my wallet's empty I'll pull out and take any old job. The chances are I'll go to sea."

Barbara gave him an approving glance. She had known but one other adventurer and he was a rogue. Lister was honest and she thought he would go far. She liked his rashness, but if he found it hard to get on board ship, she imagined she could help. All the same, she would not talk about this yet.

"We really must go," she said, and they started up a gully where holes and wedged stones helped them up like steps.

When they left the gully they saw a group of people on the neighboring summit of the hill and for a moment Lister stopped.

"We have had a glorious climb," he said, "Now it's over, I hope you're not going to stand me off again."

Barbara gave him a curious smile. "One can't stop on the mountains long. We're going down to the every-day level and all looks different there."

The others began to wave to them, and crossing a belt of boggy grass they joined the group. When they returned to Carrock, Cartwright was not about and Mrs. Cartwright said he had got a telegram calling him to Liverpool.

CHAPTER IV

A DISSATISFIED SHAREHOLDER

Cartwright had read the morning's letters and the *Journal of Commerce*, and finding nothing important, turned his revolving chair to the fire. He had been forced to wait for a train at a draughty station, and his feet were cold. His office occupied an upper floor of an old-fashioned building near the docks. Fog from the river rolled up the street and the windows were grimed by soot, but Cartwright had not turned on the electric light. The fire snapped cheerfully, and he lighted his pipe and looked about.

The furniture was shabby, the carpet was getting threadbare, and some of the glass in the partition that cut off the clerks' office was cracked. Cartwright had thought about modernizing and decorating the rooms, but to do the thing properly would cost five hundred pounds, and money was scarce. Besides, a number of the merchants who shipped goods by his boats were conservative and rather approved his keeping the parsimonious rules of the old school.

The house was old and had been at one time rich and powerful. Cartwright's father, however, had used sailing ships too long, and Cartwright's speculations and extravagance when he took control had not mended its fortunes. Then had come a number of lean years when few shipping companies earned a dividend and the line's capital steadily melted. Now the shareholders were not numerous and the ships were small.

Cartwright glanced at the pictures in tarnished gold frames. *Oreana*, drawn plunging across an Atlantic comber, was the best of the fleet, but her engineer had for some time demanded new boilers. Since the reserve fund was low and other boats needed expensive repairs, Cartwright resolved to wait. He had bought *Melphomene*, above the fireplace, very cheap; but her engines were clumsy compounds and she cost much to coal. Still she was fast, and now and then got a paying load by reaching a port where freights were high before the *Conference* found out that Cartwright meant to cut the rates.

Titania, with the white deckhouse and shade-deck, carried a good load on a light draught, and sometimes picked up a profitable cargo in shallow African lagoons. When he glanced at her picture Cartwright's look got thoughtful. She was one of two sister ships, launched at a famous yard, and Cartwright had wanted both, but the builders demanded terms of payment he could not meet, and another company had bought the vessel. She was wrecked soon afterwards, and now lay buried in the sand by an African river bar. The salvage company had given up their efforts to float her, but Cartwright imagined she could be floated if one were willing to run a risk. But no one, it seemed was willing. On the failure of the salvage company the underwriters had put the steamer into the hands of Messrs. Bull and Morse, a firm of Ship Brokers and Marine Auctioneers, but at the public auction no bids whatever had been made. Subsequently advertisements appeared in the shipping papers inviting offers for the ship as she lay and for the salvage of the cargo. These had run for several weeks, but without result. Cartwright had cut them out. Now and then he looked at them and speculated about the undertaking.

By and by the bookkeeper came in and filed some letters. Gavin's hair was going white, and he had been with Cartwright's since he was a boy. He was fat, red-faced, and humorous, although his humor was not refined. Gavin liked to be thought something of a sport, but Cartwright knew he was staunch.

"You imagine Mrs. Seaton will look me up this morning?" Cartwright said presently.

"Yes, sir. She called and demanded to see you. In fact, I think she doubted when I told her you hadn't come back from the North. She said the shareholders' meeting would be soon and she expected you to give a bigger dividend; the Blue Funnel people had paid five per cent. If you didn't return before long, she might run up to Carrock. So I sent the telegram."

Cartwright nodded. He trusted his bookkeeper, who had grounds for imagining it was not altogether desirable Mrs. Seaton should arrive at Carrock.

"Have you heard anything from Manners while I was away?"

"Nothing direct, sir. His nephew, Hatton, came round with a tender for the bunker coal, and implied that he ought to get the job. Then I had a notion Mrs. Seaton, so to speak, was *primed.* Looked as if somebody had got at her; her arguments about the dividend were rather good."

"It's possible," said Cartwright dryly. "If she comes, you can show her in. But what about the wine?"

"I don't know if it will see you out. There's not a great deal left, and last time—"

Cartwright's eyes twinkled. "Exactly! Send for another bottle and see you get the proper stuff. Some of the biscuits, too; you know the kind. Rather a bother, but perhaps the best plan!"

"Safer than going out to lunch," Gavin remarked. "Then, in the office, you're on your own ground. That counts."

"Gives you moral support and handicaps an antagonist who's not a business man?" Cartwright suggested. "Well, perhaps it does so, but I see some drawbacks. Anyhow, get the wine."

Gavin went off and Cartwright mused by the fire. The morning was raw and foggy, and if he went out, the damp might get at his throat; moreover, Gavin would reply to his letters. Cartwright had begun to feel it was time to let others work while he looked on. His control counted for less than he had thought; things went without much guidance and it was enough to give them a push in the proper direction now and then. To rouse himself for an effort was getting harder and he would have been satisfied to rest, had not his pride, and, to some extent, his step-children's antagonism, prevented his doing so. He needed money and would not use his wife's.

One must pay for old extravagances, and the bills were coming in; Mrs. Seaton's expected call was an example. Ellen was a widow, but before she married Seaton, Cartwright knew she counted him her lover. They were alike in temperament; rash, strong-willed, and greedy for all that gave life a thrill. In fact, Ellen was a stimulating comrade, but not the kind of girl one married. Cartwright married Clara and knew Mrs. Seaton bore him a lasting grudge.

Since Seaton was a merchant whose investments in Liverpool were numerous, it was perhaps not strange he left his widow shares that gave her some control of the Cartwright line. Although she was not poor, she was greedy and extravagant. In fact, Cartwright imagined greed was now her ruling passion.

By and by he heard steps in the passage behind the partition and thought he knew the tap of high-heeled shoes. Then he heard a laugh and Gavin's voice. Ellen was using her charm on his bookkeeper and the old sport would play up. The door opened, the room smelt of violets, and Mrs. Seaton came in. She was tall and her furs gave her large figure a touch of dignity. Her color was sharply white and red, and in the rather dim light her skin was like a girl's. Cartwright knew Ellen was younger than he, but not very much.

"You look hipped and rather slack, Tom," she said when he got up and Gavin fetched a chair.

"I feel the cold and damp," Cartwright replied. "Then managing a tramp-steamship line when freights are low is a wearing job."

Mrs. Seaton took off her coat. "Your office is shabby and climbing all those stairs is a pull. Why don't you launch out, get a lift, and modernize things?"

"My trouble is to keep the boats supplied with coal and stores. Besides, you see, I don't often use my office for a drawing-room."

"You're very cautious," Mrs. Seaton remarked with a laugh. "You start to get on guard before I begin my attack."

"Oh, well," said Cartwright, smiling, "I know your power. But would you like a cigarette?"

She took the curiously-decorated box he gave her and broke the seal. "Since you don't smoke these things, Tom, you were rather nice to remember."

"You had better take the box," said Cartwright. "I sent for a few when *Titania* went to the Levant. One understands they're hard to get in England. But I have something else you like. If you will wait a moment—"

He rang a bell and Gavin entered, carrying two small glasses, a bottle, and some biscuits. When he went out, Cartwright turned the bottle so Mrs. Seaton could see the label.

"Climbing our stairs is a fag," he said, and filled the glasses.

Mrs. Seaton smiled and took hers. Cartwright saw her rings sparkle and the gleam of her regular, white teeth. The reflection from the grate touched her hair and it shone a smooth golden-brown. He admitted with amusement that Ellen was nearly as attractive as he had thought her thirty years since.

"This is like old times, Tom," she said. "I remember evenings when you brought me sandwiches and iced cup at a dance—but I don't think you were ever remarkably romantic."

Cartwright remembered an evening when they sat under a shaded lamp in a quiet corner of a supper room, listening to music that somehow fired one's blood. But perhaps it was the iced cup he had generously drunk. All the same he had not been a fool, though he was tempted. He knew something about Ellen then, but he knew her better now. Perhaps it was typical that she had promptly put the box of Eastern cigarettes in her muff.

"Managing ships is not a romantic occupation," he rejoined.

"Anyway, your welcome's kind and I feel shabby because I'm forced to bother you. But suppose some of your customers arrive?"

"We shall not be disturbed," said Cartwright, smiling. "Gavin knows his job."

"Very well. Do you expect to declare a better dividend at the shareholders' meeting?"

"I do not. If I'm lucky, I may keep the dividend where it is, but I don't know yet."

"Two per cent. is really nothing," Mrs. Seaton remarked. "I've been forced to study economy and you know how I hate to pinch. Besides, I know an investment that would give me eight per cent."

"Then, if you're satisfied the venture is not risky, you ought to buy the shares."

"I want to buy, but it's a small, private company and the people stipulate I must take a large block. I have not enough money."

Cartwright doubted, but her plan was obvious. "When trade is slack, one ought to be careful about investing in a private company that pays eight per cent," he said. "After all, it might be prudent to be satisfied with a small profit."

"But I'm not satisfied and your dividend is remarkably small! Are you really unable to make it larger?"

"One can't pay dividends out of capital. Anyhow, one can't keep it up for long!"

"Then, as I mean to make a plunge, I must sell some of the investments that don't earn me much. My shares in the line carry a good number of votes and, if people grumble at the meeting, would give you some control. Will you buy them, Tom?"

Cartwright knitted his brows. He thought her hint about the shares giving him useful power was significant. In fact, it looked as if somebody had put Ellen on his track. He wondered whether Manners.... But she must not think him disturbed.

"What is your price?" he asked.

"My price?" she said with a puzzled look he thought well done. "Of course, I want the sum the shares stand for."

"I'm sorry it's impossible. Just now the shares of very few shipping companies are worth their face value. For example, five-pound shares in a good line were not long since offered at two pounds ten."

Mrs. Seaton looked disturbed. "That's dreadful!" she exclaimed. "But I'm not rich enough to bear a heavy loss, and if you bought my lot, the voting power would enable you to break the grumblers' opposition. They're worth more to you than anybody else. Can't you help me?"

Cartwright gave her a smiling glance, although he was bothered. Ellen was not a fool and he noted her insistence on the value of the shares to him. Where this led was obvious. He had one or two powerful antagonists and knew of plots to force his retirement. Ellen had given him his choice; he must promise a larger dividend or buy her shares at something over their market price. This, of course, was impossible, but he imagined she did not know how poor he was.

"I can't buy," he said. "I must trust my luck and fighting power. Although we have had stormy meetings and rates are bad, the line is running yet."

"If you haven't enough money, why don't you ask your wife? She's rich and hasn't risked much of her capital in the line."

"That is so," Cartwright agreed. Ellen meant to be nasty but he must be cool. "Although my wife is rich, I don't use her money."

"You're not logical, and sometimes your fastidiousness isn't very marked. However, it looks as if you didn't marry because Clara was rich. She was romantic before she began to get fat."

Cartwright's face got red. He had had enough and saw Ellen was getting savage. She had not forgotten that, in a sense, he ought to have married her, and since he would not buy her shares, she would, no doubt, help his antagonists. Crossing the floor, he poked the fire noisily.

"Shall I give you some more wine?" he asked, and while he was occupied with the glasses the telephone bell rang behind the partition. A few moments afterwards Gavin came in.

"Moreton has rung up, sir. If you can give him five minutes, he'll come across. He says it's important."

Mrs. Seaton put on her coat. "I mustn't stop when an important customer is coming." Then she laughed and gave Cartwright her hand. "You are very obstinate, Tom, but I know your pluck."

She went off. Gavin took away the wine, and Cartwright opened the window. The smell of violets vanished, but when he sat down again he pondered. He knew Mrs. Seaton, and thought she meant to hint his pluck might soon be needed. When Ellen smiled like that she was plotting something.

CHAPTER V

CARTWRIGHT'S SCRUPLES

The drawing-room at Mrs. Cartwright's house on the Cheshire side of the Mersey was large and old-fashioned. Cartwright thought the stiff, thick curtains and Victorian walnut furniture ugly, but Mrs. Cartwright liked the things and he was satisfied. Clara herself frankly belonged to the old school. She was conventional and often dull, but she had a placid dignity that did not mark all the up-to-date women Cartwright knew. Moreover, the house was comfortable. One got there by the Mersey tunnel and it was only a few minutes' walk from the station. For all that, the encroaching town had not yet reached the neighborhood, and the windows commanded a pleasant view of clean rolling country and the blue Welsh hills.

Cartwright felt the house was a snug harbor where he could rest when he was too old and battered to front the storms that had for some time been gathering, and sitting by the fire one evening, he speculated about the rocks and shoals ahead. All the same, the time to run for shelter was not yet; he thought he could ride out another gale.

An arch with heavy molding occupied the middle of the spacious room. The folding doors had been removed and curtains partly screened the arch. On the other side, a group of young men and women stood about the piano. On Cartwright's side the lights were low. He had dined well and liked to loaf after dinner. Besides, he felt dull; his gout bothered him and he had been forced to run for his train. He had begun to find out one could not do that kind of thing. Mrs. Cartwright sat opposite, knitting quietly, and her smooth, rhythmic movements were soothing. Clara was never abrupt and jerky.

"I got a letter from Stormont's by the afternoon post," she said. "They have been repaid the mortgage, and there's something about a foreign bond, drawn for redemption. They want to talk about a new investment."

Stormont, Wilmot and Stormont were her lawyers, and Cartwright nodded. "The money ought to be earning interest and you can safely buy stock Stormont's approve. Their judgment's sound."

"For all that, I think I'd like to choose for myself. Suppose I bought some shares in the line? I have a number, but it's really not large and I have felt I'm not supporting the house as I ought."

Cartwright knitted his brows. Clara did not know much about business, but she was sometimes shrewder than one thought. He wondered whether Mortimer had been talking. If the pup had talked, the thing was ominous, because it implied that others knew the difficulties Cartwright might have to meet.

"Do you imagine the house needs supporting?" he asked carelessly.

Mrs. Cartwright hesitated. "I really know nothing about it; but don't people grumble when you can't pay them much and their shares go down? Perhaps if the family owned a good part of the capital, you could take a firmer line."

It was plain that Clara had been pondering. Mortimer *had* talked and somebody who was not Cartwright's friend had informed him. Cartwright was tempted to let his wife do as she wanted: Clara owned shares in the line that he had let her buy when freights were good and she had afterwards refused to sell. Now, however, freights were very bad and the company was nearer the rocks than he hoped the shareholders knew. Cartwright imagined he could yet mend its fortunes, if he were left alone, but the job was awkward and opposition might be dangerous. To command a solid block of votes would certainly help.

For all that, there was a risk Clara ought not to run. His antagonists were getting stronger, and if they meddled and baffled him, the company would fail. Its bankruptcy would not ruin his wife, but she would feel the loss of her money, and he was not going to use Clara for a shield against Ellen Seaton's attacks. The thing was shabby. All the same, the situation was humorous, and he saw, with an ironical smile, the advantages of Mrs. Cartwright's plan.

"I'm not a business woman, but I have noted you're sometimes moody, as if you were anxious, and I want to help," she resumed.

"You do help. The storms I've weathered have left a mark, and now I'm old and strained it's much to make a quiet port at night. You take all bothers from me, and send me out in the morning, braced for another watch in the pilot-house."

"Some time you must give another the helm," said Mrs. Cartwright quietly. "I wish I could persuade you to do so soon."

Cartwright sighed, for the strain was heavy and he wanted to rest. The trouble was the put-off reckoning for past extravagance was at hand and he shrank from asking his wife to pay. He had not been very scrupulous, but he had his code. Then Hyslop came through the arch, and stopping, noted Cartwright's awkwardly stretched-out leg.

"Gout bothering you again, sir?" he said. "You ought to lie up for a few days, but I expect you're needed at the office. I heard the E.P. line had a stormy meeting and the dissatisfied shareholders came near turning out the directors. Johnson declared they only saved the situation by a few votes."

"They ought to be turned out! A blundering lot! They've let a good fleet down."

Hyslop smiled. He had pale and watery blue eyes that generally annoyed Cartwright. "An awkward doctrine, sir! If all the steamship directors who might have used the shareholders' money to better advantage were called to account, I imagine a number of respectable gentlemen would find their occupation gone. Besides, when people start deposing rulers they don't know where to stop. The thing's, so to speak, contagious, and panicky investors are not logical."

He went off and Cartwright braced himself. Mortimer meant to be nasty, but his languid malice bit deeper than he knew. Cartwright had hesitated, weighing the value of his wife's help against his scruples, until his step-son's hints had tipped the beam. After all, if he used Clara's money and saved his skin at her cost, the pup would have some grounds to sneer.

"I must keep control for some time yet," he said. "Times are bad, and if I let go the helm I doubt if my successor could steer a safe course. When the need is gone I'll willingly give up, but I must bring the old ship into port first. In the meantime, you had better let Stormont's buy you sound Corporation stock."

Mrs. Cartwright acquiesced and Cartwright watched the young people beyond the arch. With the stiff curtains for wing-scenes and the lights concealed, the end of the room made a proscenium: it was like looking at a drawing-room comedy on the stage. Two of the girls were pretty and he approved their fashionable clothes. When she was quiet, Grace was almost beautiful, but somehow none had Barbara's charm. Yet Cartwright thought the girl was getting thin and her color was too bright. A friend of Mortimer's occupied the music stool and Cartwright admitted that the fellow played well, although he was something like a character from a Gilbert opera.

Lister sat near the piano, and talked to Barbara, He smiled, but his smile had a touch of gravity. Cartwright thought him a good Canadian. A bit rugged perhaps, but staunch, and his quiet sincerity was after all better style than the cleverness of Mortimer's friends. Cartwright imagined Barbara studied Lister, who did not know. In fact, it looked as if he were puzzled, and Cartwright smiled. Lister had not his talents; when Cartwright was young he knew how to amuse a pretty girl.

The man at the piano signed to Barbara, who got up and began to sing. The song was modern and the melody not marked. Cartwright liked the Victorian ballads with tunes that haunted one and obvious sentiment, but because Barbara sang he gave the words and music his languid interest. After all, the thing was clever. There was, so to speak, not much on the surface, but one heard an elusive note of effort, as if one struggled after something one could not grasp. On the whole, Cartwright did not approve that kind of sentiment; his objects were generally plain. Then he thought the hint of strain was too well done for a young girl, and when Barbara stopped he turned to his wife.

"Are you satisfied about Barbara?" he asked.

"Why should I not be satisfied?"

"I have felt she's not quite up to her proper form. Looks thin and sometimes she's quiet. Then why has young Vernon gone off? I haven't seen him recently."

"Harry's in town; he goes home in a few days," Mrs. Cartwright replied. She hesitated and resumed, "I imagined he wanted to marry Barbara, although she told me nothing about this. Barbara does not tell one much."

"Do you think she likes him?"

"I don't know, but I rather think if she had liked him she would have refused."

"Ah!" said Cartwright thoughtfully. "Well, Vernon's a good sort, but I see some light; the girl is sensitive and very proud! No doubt, she feels her Canadian adventure—ridiculous, of course! But Barbara's hard to move. All the same, if Vernon's the proper man and is resolute—"

"I doubt if he is the proper man," Mrs. Cartwright replied.

Cartwright pondered. Sometimes Clara did not say all she thought, and his glance wandered back to the group at the other end of the room. Barbara was again talking to Lister. He looked thoughtful and her face was serious. They were obviously not engaged in philandering; Cartwright felt their quiet absorption was significant. After a minute or two, however, the party about the piano broke up and went off. Barbara stopped to put away some music and then came through the arch.

"Mr. Lister wants to go a voyage," she said to Cartwright. "I suggested you might help him to get a post on board a ship."

"I imagine he did not suggest you should persuade me?"

"Certainly not! He refused to bother you," Barbara replied and, with some hesitation, added: "However, perhaps in a sense we ought to help."

"That is so," Cartwright agreed. "Why did Mr. Lister come to Liverpool?"

"He wanted to go round the shipping offices. Mother told him our house was always open—"

Cartwright nodded, "Of course! Well, I'll think about it and may see a plan."

Barbara went off and Cartwright looked at his wife. "I don't know if this is a fresh complication; but if she refused Harry, she'd no doubt refuse the other. Perhaps it's important that she's willing he should go to sea."

"One is forced to like Mr. Lister and we owe him much," Mrs. Cartwright remarked.

"Certainly," Cartwright agreed. "However, it looks as if some engineering talent is all he has got, and I think a long voyage is indicated—" He stopped, and resumed with a twinkle: "For all that, the fellow is not an adventurer, and I married a rich woman."

Mrs. Cartwright gave him a gentle smile. "I have been happy and Barbara is not; but, in one sense, I don't imagine we need be disturbed. Barbara has not recovered from the jar."

She got up, and Cartwright dozed until he heard a step and Lister crossed the floor.

"Hallo!" he said. "Are you going? There is no train just now."

Lister said he meant to walk to the tramline, but Cartwright asked him to stop for a few minutes.

"Barbara tells me you are trying for a post in an engine-room," he remarked.

"That is so," said Lister with a touch of embarrassment. "Still, I didn't mean Miss Hyslop to bother you."

"Barbara likes to meddle and I'm a ship-owner. To begin with, why d'you want to go to sea?"

"I must go to sea or back to Canada," Lister said, smiling. "I've had a pretty good holiday, but my wad's nearly gone."

"Then, wouldn't it be prudent to return to your occupation?"

"I haven't an occupation; I turned mine down. It's possible I'll find another, but I'm not ready yet. In Canada, we're a restless, wandering lot, and I want to look about the world before I go back. You see, when you only know the woods and our Western towns—"

Cartwright saw and sympathized. He remembered how adventure called when he was young. Well, he had got adventure, but perhaps not the kind Lister seemed to enjoy. Anyhow, he had not started off with an empty wallet to look about the world.

"How much does your roll amount to?" he asked with a bluntness he sometimes used.

When Lister told him he laughed. The young fellow was good stuff; Cartwright liked his rashness.

"Well," he said, "you have pluck, and if you're obstinate, pluck takes you far. Have you got a promise from any of our shipping offices?"

Lister said he had not. There were some difficulties about certificates. He had sailed on lake boats and made coasting voyages, but the English Board of Trade rules were strict. Then he looked at the clock and Cartwright gave him his hand.

"Come and see me at the office. We'll talk about this again."

Lister thanked him, and when he had gone Cartwright mused. The young fellow was not an adventurer; anyhow not in the sense Shillito was an adventurer. His honesty was obvious, it was plain he did not want Barbara's money, and Cartwright thought he did not know she was rich. In fact, he was Barbara's sort. There was the trouble. Cartwright weighed this for a time and then went to sleep.

CHAPTER VI

A NASTY KNOCK

Frost sparkled on the office windows and Cartwright, with his feet on the hearthrug studied an Atlantic weather chart. The temperature reported by the liners' captains was low, and winter had begun unusually soon. Since Cartwright had hoped for a mild November, this was unlucky. As a rule, cargo is plentiful at Montreal shortly before the St. Lawrence freezes and the last steamers to go down the river do so with heavy loads. Cartwright's plan was to run a boat across at the last moment and pick up goods the liners would not engage to carry, and he had sent *Oreana* because she was fast. When the drift ice began to gather, speed was useful.

A cablegram two or three days since stated that she had sailed, and Cartwright, who knew the St. Lawrence, calculated the progress she ought to have made. Perhaps he had cut things rather fine, but Captain Davies was a good navigator and would push on. Although the narrow waters below Montreal, where the stream runs fast between the islands, would be open, Lake St. Peter was freezing, and the liner *Parthian* had some trouble to get through. Still the channels were not yet blocked, and when Davies had passed the Narrows he would get open water down the gorge to Quebec. Allowing for cautious navigation, Davies ought to be near Rimouski at the mouth of the river, and his passing would, no doubt, soon be telegraphed from the signal station. Cartwright admitted that to get the message would be some relief.

By and by his bookkeeper came in.

"Direct cablegram from Davies, sir."

Cartwright took the form and frowned. The message was not from Rimouski and ran: "Delayed Peter; passing Quebec."

"Awkward, sir," Gavin remarked sympathetically.

"Very awkward," said Cartwright. "Davies needed all the time he's lost. It will be a near thing if he gets out."

He picked up the weather chart and got no comfort. "Cable Malcolm at St. Johns. You'll find questions in the code-book about ice and wind."

Gavin withdrew and Cartwright grappled with disturbing thoughts. He had counted on *Oreana's* earning a good sum, and had engaged a paying cargo for her when she got back. In fact, the two good runs ought to have made the disappointing balance sheet he must shortly submit to the shareholders look a little better. All the same, there was no use in meeting trouble. Davies had passed Quebec, and if he made good progress in the next twenty-four hours, one might begin to hope.

Below Quebec there were awkward spots where steamers used buoyed channels, and if these were blocked by ice Davies must risk crossing the shoals. If he got across, the water was deep and he need only bother about the floes until he came to the Gulf. Since Belle Isle Strait was frozen, Davies would go South of Anticosti and out by the Cabot passage, but the Gulf was often dark with snow and fog, and one met the old Greenland ice. Well, much depended on the weather, and Cartwright went to get his lunch.

The restaurant under a big building was warm, and for a time Cartwright occupied his favorite corner of the smoking-room. His tips were generous, and so long as he was punctual the waitress allowed nobody to use his chair. The noise of the traffic in the street was softened to a faint rumble, the electric light was cleverly shaded, and his big chair was easy. He got drowsy, but frowned when he began to nod. The trouble was, he was often dull when he ought to be keen. His doctor talked about the advantages of moderation, but when one got old one's pleasures were few and Cartwright liked a good meal. At the luncheon room they did one well, and he was not going to use self-denial yet.

By and by a merchant he knew pulled up a chair opposite. "Very cold and slippery outside," he remarked. "I nearly came down on the floating bridge, and looked in for a drink. A jar shakes a man who carries weight."

"What were you doing on the floating bridge?" Cartwright asked.

"I went to the stage to meet some Canadian friends on board the *Nepigon.* They'd a bad voyage; thick mist down the St. Lawrence, and they lost a day cruising about among the floes in the Gulf. What about your little boat?"

"I understand she's coming down river."

"Hasn't she started rather late?"

"If I'd sent her sooner, the *Conference* would have knocked me out," Cartwright rejoined. "I'd have got nothing but low-rated stuff the liners didn't want. One must run some risks."

The other nodded. "That is so, when shareholders must be satisfied. Well, I expect I'm lucky because my partner's a good sort. When you needn't bother about other folk's greediness, you can take a cautious line. Now I come to think of it, I heard some of your people grumbling. I hope your boat will get across all right."

He got up and Cartwright pondered. If outsiders knew his shareholders were dissatisfied, things were worse than he had thought and he might expect trouble at the next meeting. Then he looked at his watch, but his chair was deep and when he tried to get up his leg hurt. He sank back again. Gavin knew where to find him if a reply from St. Johns arrived.

By and by his office boy, carrying a cable company's envelope, came in, and Cartwright's hand shook when he opened the message. It stated that an easterly gale and snowstorm raged about the Newfoundland coast and the thermometer was very low. The gale would drive the drift ice up the Gulf and pack the floes. Things looked bad. Cartwright felt he ought to get about and make some plans to meet the threatened blow, but he did not see what he could do.

He sat still. The other customers had gone, and all was quiet but for the faint rumble of traffic and soothing throb of an electric fan. Cartwright mused about *Oreana* and pictured Davies sheltering behind the wind-screens on his bridge and trying to pierce the snow, and the look-out man half frozen in the spray that leaped about the forecastle. *Oreana* was a wet boat when she was loaded deep. Now and then, perhaps, a buoy loomed in the tossing flakes. One tried to read the number and see the color. Then the steering-engine rattled as the rudder was pulled across and *Oreana* headed for another mark.

The work was nervous, because dangerous shoals bordered the channels and Davies must let the steamer go. He knew when a risk must be run and the engineer was staunch. The trouble was, *Oreana's* boilers were bad; the money Cartwright durst not spend on repairs would have been a good investment now. Still, the old boat was fast, and Davies would drive her full-speed.

The captain's job would not be easier when he left the shoals. The easterly gale would send the floes up stream. Cartwright knew the strange chill one felt when ice was about and the faint elusive *blink* that marked its edge in the dark. Sometimes one did not see the blink until the floe was almost at the bows, and when the look-out's startled cry reached the bridge one must trust to luck and pull the helm over quick. Then to dodge the floe might mean one crashed upon the next. It was steering blind, but, as a rule, the sailor's instinct guided him right. Farther on, the river got wide and in thick weather one saw no lights: Davies must keep mid-channel and trust his reckoning while he rushed her along. For a thousand miles the old boat's track was haunted by dangers against which one could not guard, and Cartwright thought she carried his last chance to mend his broken fortunes.

If she were wrecked, the reckoning he had long put off must be fronted, for when his embarrassments were known his antagonists would combine and try to pull him down. One must pay for one's extravagance, but to pay would break him, and if he were broken, Mortimer would sneer and Grace treat him with humiliating pity. He would be their mother's pensioner, and to lose his independence was hard. He had long ruled, and bullied, others.

By and by a waitress moved some glasses and Cartwright looked up with a start. The afternoon was nearly over; he must have gone to sleep. Returning to the office, he gave his bookkeeper some orders and then went to the station. The pavements were slippery with frost, and tall buildings with yellow lights loomed in the fog. Cartwright shivered, but reflected that Davies, fighting the snow and gale, was no doubt colder. For a day or two he must bear the suspense, and then, if no cablegram arrived, he could take it for granted that *Oreana* had reached the Atlantic. After dinner he sat by the fire and smoked while Mrs. Cartwright knitted.

"In the afternoon I went to Mrs. Oliver's and met Mrs. Seaton," she said presently. "She talked to me for some time. At the beginning, I thought it strange!"

"It's pretty obvious that you don't like her," Cartwright remarked.

"Ellen Seaton is not my sort, but I understand she was a friend of yours."

"She was my friend," said Cartwright carelessly. "It's long since, and I rather doubt if she is my friend now."

"Then why did she buy her shares in the line?"

"Ellen did not buy the shares. Seaton bought them when shipping was good."

Mrs. Cartwright looked relieved and Cartwright resumed: "All the same, I don't see her object for telling you she was a shareholder."

"She wanted to sell her shares to me; I knew she had some plan when she crossed the floor. I was talking to Janet, but Ellen got Janet away and persuaded a young man on the other side to move. It was clever. I don't think Mrs. Oliver or anybody else remarked what she was doing. But you know Ellen!"

"I know Ellen rather well," said Cartwright dryly. "However, when you saw she wanted to get you alone, why did you indulge her?"

"For one thing, I was curious; then it wasn't worth while to spoil her plan. I didn't think Ellen would persuade me, if I did not approve."

Cartwright smiled. Clara did not argue much and generally agreed with him, but sometimes she was as immovable as a rock. He pictured with amusement the little comedy at Mrs. Oliver's, but all the same he was annoyed.

"Well, Ellen wanted you to buy her shares? Did she give you any grounds?"

"She declared she wanted money. Then she said it would help you if I took the lot. There might be a dispute at the meeting; the directors' report would not be satisfactory. People would ask awkward questions, and she expected some organized opposition. It would be useful for you to command a large number of votes."

Cartwright's face got red. Ellen was well informed; in fact, it was ominous that she knew so much. Had she not been greedy, he thought she would have kept the shares in order to vote against him, but she obviously meant to sell them before the crash she expected came. If a number of others agreed with her, his retirement would be forced.

"What price were you to pay?" he asked.

Mrs. Cartwright told him, and he laughed. "If Ellen found a buyer at a number of shillings less, she would be lucky! Well, I understand you didn't take her offer?"

"I did not," said Mrs. Cartwright tranquilly. "When I wanted to buy some shares not long since, you did not approve. Since you refused to let me help, I didn't mean to be persuaded by Ellen Seaton!"

"You're staunch," said Cartwright and Mrs. Cartwright resumed her knitting. In the morning he went to the office sooner than usual, but there was no news and the dark, cold day passed drearily. When he started for home Gavin promised to wait until the cable offices closed, and Cartwright had gone to dinner when he was called to the telephone. When he took down the instrument his hand shook.

"Hallo!" he said hoarsely. "Is that you, Gavin?"

"Yes, sir," said a voice he knew. "Cablegram from Davies just arrived, part in code. I'll give it you slow—"

"Go on," said Cartwright.

"*Oreana* ashore east Cape Chat, surrounded ice, water in fore hold. Think some plates broken; have abandoned ship. Salvage impossible until ice breaks."

There was a pause, and Gavin added: "That's all. Have you got it, sir?"

"I've got enough," Cartwright replied.

He hung up the instrument, and going back to the dining-room, drained his glass. Then he turned to Mrs. Cartwright, who had remarked his grim look.

"I've got a nasty knock. *Oreana's* in the ice and may be wrecked. Anyhow, we can't get her off until spring, and she's the best of the fleet."

Mrs. Cartwright gave him a sympathetic glance and signed a servant to bring another plate. As a rule she did not say much. She studied her husband quietly and was not much comforted when he resumed his dinner. This was characteristic, but it was plain he had got a nasty knock.

CHAPTER VII

THE SHAREHOLDERS' MEETING

The afternoon was dark and electric lights burned along the cornice of the room engaged for the shareholders' meeting. The room was big and cold, and as Gavin moved about the table on the platform his steps echoed hollowly. He was the company's secretary and was putting down papers by the blotting pads. A group of gentlemen, engaged in thoughtful talk, stood by the fire. They were directors of the line and did not look happy. Nominally, by the company's constitution, the shareholders elected the Board; in practice, Cartwright had, so far, appointed the directors, and meant, if possible, to do so again. The gentlemen by the fire were eligible for reëlection, and Cartwright was satisfied, although he had not chosen them for their business talent. Their names were good in Liverpool and their honesty was known. Cartwright did not want clever men. He was head of the house and knew it would totter to a disastrous fall unless he kept his firm control.

Now and then Gavin gave his employer a keen glance. Cartwright's lips were rather blue and the lines round his eyes were sharply drawn. His white mustache stuck out, and one got a hint of stubbornness, but except for this his face was inscrutable. Although Gavin thought Cartwright would score again, he was anxious. Nobody but Cartwright could persuade the dissatisfied shareholders to accept *that* balance sheet.

Cartwright himself felt in rather good form. He had curtailed his lunch and been satisfied with a single glass of liquor that generally braced him up. He imagined he would need all his skill and coolness before the meeting was over. The trouble was, he might not get much support. The directors did not know all he knew, but they knew something, and he saw one or two hesitated. Then Mrs. Cartwright was ill, and although she had given her husband her proxy votes, had sent Mortimer. Mortimer was entitled to come because he had some shares, but Cartwright did not know the line he meant to take. The pup did not like him and was cunning. Presently Cartwright looked at his watch.

"They won't be long. I imagine we are going to have some opposition."

"It's very possible," one of the others agreed. "A two-per-cent dividend is disappointing and we are paying this by cutting down the reserve fund. Then people know we have lost the use of our best boat for six months and may lose her for good. When we reduced our insurance, I urged that we were rash."

"We saved a good sum and economy was needful," Cartwright rejoined. "Insurance is expensive for our type of boats."

"The balance sheet looks bad. I'll admit I'd sooner not be accountable for a state of things like this," another remarked.

Cartwright smiled. The balance sheet looked better than it was, but Jordan had given him a useful lead. He knew his colleagues' weaknesses and how they might be worked upon.

"We are all accountable. I have consulted you frankly and you approved my plans."

Jordan gave him a rather doubtful look. "Anyhow, we must front an awkward situation. Suppose the shareholders ask for an investigation committee?"

"We must refuse," said Cartwright, with quiet firmness. "A frightened committee would probably urge a drastic re-construction scheme, the writing off much of our capital, and perhaps winding up the line. When rates are bad and cargo's scarce, one must take a low price for ships; our liabilities are large, and I imagine selling off would leave us much in debt—"

Cartwright paused. He saw his remarks carried weight and knew his co-directors. He would give them a few moments for thought before he finished his argument.

"Very well," he resumed. "Jordan declares he does not like to be accountable for an unsatisfactory balance sheet. I take it he would much less like to be made accountable for a bad bankruptcy! No doubt you sympathize with him?"

It was obvious that they did so and one said, "If I thought my occupying a seat on the Board would lead to this, I would sooner have given my shares away!"

"I have not talked about my feelings," Cartwright went on. "All the same, I am head of the old house; you can imagine I do not want to see it fall. But rates are not always low, and if I'm not embarrassed by rash meddlers, my persuasion is, I can keep the fleet running until better times arrive."

He saw he had won them. The number of shares they owned was not very large: for the most part, the men were rich and not disturbed about their money. They valued a high place in business and social circles and their good name. To be entangled by a bankruptcy was unthinkable.

"Then, I feel we ought to support you," Jordan replied. "For all that, our power's not very great. We are going to meet some opposition and if the dissatisfied people are resolute they can turn us out."

"So long as I know the Board will back me, I'm not afraid of the shareholders," Cartwright declared.

"You imagine you can save the situation?" a red-faced gentleman remarked.

"It's possible," said Cartwright dryly.

"Very well," said the other. "We must try to see you out."

They went to the table soon afterwards and the shareholders began to arrive. They were not numerous, and the scattered groups emphasized the bareness of the big echoing room. Cartwright studied the people as they came in. Some looked gloomy and some stubborn; a few looked frankly bored. There were five or six women and two whispered, while the others glanced about with jerky movements. Cartwright's face hardened when he saw Mrs. Seaton, and then he noted Hyslop in a back row. He thought Hyslop looked languidly amused.

When all was quiet, he took the notes Gavin handed him, glanced at the paper, and put it down. Then, speaking in a steady voice, he gave the report of the year's work and talked about the balance sheet. He was frank but not apologetic, and claimed, in view of the difficulties, that the directors had well guarded the company's interests. When he stopped there were murmurs of approval, as if some of the despondent had begun to hope; the cautious admitted that Cartwright had made a bad situation look better.

One or two asked questions, which he answered candidly, and then there was a pause and somebody moved the adoption of the chairman's report and balance sheet. His seconder made a short nervous speech, and Mrs. Seaton got up at the end of the room. She pushed back her veil, took out her handkerchief, put her hand on a chair in front, and gave the directors an apologetic smile.

"I don't know if it is usual for a woman to speak at a business meeting, but I have a number of shares in the line and it's long since I got a good dividend," she said. "Two per cent is ridiculous and my lawyer tells me I could get four per cent, where the security is really good." She paused and added naïvely: "To have twice as much to spend would be very nice."

Somebody laughed and Cartwright braced himself. Ellen Seaton was cleverer than she looked, and he thought her dangerous, but in the meantime he durst not stop her.

"One feels that security's important and it's plain ours is not first-class," she resumed. "Well, I suppose if we accept the report, it means we are satisfied to let the company's business be managed on the old plan?"

"It does mean something like that," a man agreed.

"Then I'm *not* satisfied. For one thing, I want a proper dividend."

"We all want a proper dividend," somebody remarked.

Mrs. Seaton smiled, as if she were encouraged. "To go without is disappointing, but perhaps the dividend is not most important. I'd like to feel my shares were worth the money they cost, and find out they are not. We have drawn on the reserves and I expect this implies we are losing money. You can't go on losing money very long, and we ought to stop while we have some capital left."

A number of the others applauded and she continued: "Our directors have worked very hard. To manage ships that don't pay must be tiring and perhaps we oughtn't to ask them to bear the heavy strain. Could we not choose somebody with fresh ideas to help?"

"That's what we want!" said one. "The Board needs new blood!"

Then the storm broke and for a time Cartwright lost control of the meeting. Mrs. Seaton had loosed passions he might have restrained and the shareholders were frankly moved by fear, distrust, and greed. Men got up, asking angry questions and shouting implications, but for a few minutes Cartwright sat like a rock and let them rage. When they stopped and there was an awkward pause, Mortimer Hyslop got up. He looked languid and his voice was soft, but Cartwright admitted his speech was clever.

He and Mrs. Cartwright, whom he represented, owned shares in the line, and he had not risen before because the chairman was his relation. Now, when attacks, perhaps not altogether justified, had been made on the Board, he was forced to state his conviction that nobody else could have steered the company past the dangers that threatened. One must admit the situation was bad; and for a minute or two Mortimer cleverly indicated its drawbacks. For all that, he argued, it was rash to change pilot and officers in the middle of a storm. The officers they knew and had trusted must be left control until the gale blew over.

Mortimer sat down and Cartwright knitted his brows. On the surface, his step-son had taken the proper line. Mortimer meant to support the Board, but he had indicated that he did so because it was his duty. His remarks about the dangers by which the company was surrounded had made things look worse. All the same, he had calmed the meeting, but Cartwright did not know if this was an advantage. Criticism was harder to meet when the critics were cool.

Another man got up and began to talk in a quiet voice.

"Mr. Hyslop has an object for trusting the chairman that we have not got. We won't grumble about his staunchness, but we are entitled to weigh his arguments, which are not altogether sound. He owns the situation is awkward and the outlook dark, but he urges us to trust the officers who got the ship in danger. One feels this is not remarkably logical. Then he declares nobody else could have kept the fleet running. I think the claim is rash. In this city we are conservative and names long known in business circles carry an exaggerated weight; we expect a man to work wonders because his father started a prosperous line, and another because he long since made a lucky plunge. Men like these are often satisfied with former triumphs while times and methods change. We want fresh thought and modern methods. It's obvious the old have brought us near the rocks!"

Cartwright saw the shareholders were moved and the time for him to speak had come. He got up and fronted a doubting and antagonistic audience. His face was inscrutable, but he looked dignified.

"We have heard angry criticism and hints about slackness," he began. "Some of you have suggested rejecting the report, a committee of inquiry, and new members for the Board, but no substantive motion has been put. Well, before this is done, I claim your patience for a few minutes. If you are not satisfied, I and your directors are jointly accountable. We stand together; if you get rid of one, you get rid of all. This is a drastic but risky cure—"

He paused and one or two of the gentlemen at the table looked surprised. It was plain they felt the chairman had gone farther than he ought. The red-faced man, however, smiled as if he approved and Cartwright resumed:

"Times are bad, the markets are flat, and goods are not moved about the world. I venture to state no steamship company is free from embarrassments. You can, no doubt, find men with business talent equal to ours and give them control; but you cannot give them the knowledge, gained by long experience, one needs to grapple with the particular difficulties the Cartwright line must meet. The personal touch is needed; your manager must be known by the company's friends, and its antagonists, who would not hesitate to snatch our trade from a stranger. They know me and the others, and are cautious about attacking us. In all that's important, until times get better, *I am the company*—"

Cartwright stopped and drank some water. He saw he had struck the right note and began again:

"I will not labor the argument; the thing is obvious! If I go, the line will stop running before the new men learn their job. Well, I'm old and tired, but it would hurt to see the house-flag hauled down; it was carried by famous oak clippers in my grandfather's time. You hesitate to risk your money? I risk mine and much that money cannot buy; the honor of a house whose ships have sailed from Liverpool for a hundred years!"

The shareholders were moved and one heard murmurs of sympathy. Boldness paid, and Cartwright saw he was recovering his shaken power, but it was not all good acting. To some extent, he was sincere. He got his breath and resumed:

"I don't urge you with a selfish object to let me keep my post; I'd be relieved to let it go. Counted in money, the reward for my labor is not large. I want to save the Cartwright line, to pilot it into port, and, if there is no rash meddling, I believe I can. But I warn you the thing is in no other's power. Well, I have finished. You must choose whether your directors go or not."

There was an awkward silence, and then somebody asked: "Will the chairman state if he has a plan for meeting a situation he admits is difficult?"

Cartwright smiled rather grimly. "I will not make a public statement that might be useful to our antagonists! So long as I am chairman, you must trust me. My proposition is, give us six months, and then, if things are no better, we will welcome a committee of inquiry. In the meantime, a motion is before the meeting—"

"It is proposed and seconded that the directors' report and balance sheet be accepted," Gavin remarked.

The resolution was carried, the directors were reelected, and the meeting broke up. Cartwright sat down rather limply and wiped his face.

"I pulled it off, but they pushed me hard," he said. "At one time, it looked as if our defenses would go down."

"You have put off the reckoning; I think that's all," one of the directors remarked.

"We have six months," said Cartwright. "This is something. If they call a meeting then, I imagine I can meet them."

He signed to Gavin, who helped him with his big coat, and went off to the underground restaurant, where he presently fell asleep in a chair by the fire.

CHAPTER VIII

A STOLEN EXCURSION

Barbara stopped at the top of James Street and looked down hill to the river. The afternoon was dark and the pavement wet. Thin fog drifted about the tall offices, lights shone in the windows, and she heard steamers' whistles. Down the street, a white plume of steam, streaking the dark-colored fog, marked the tunnel station, and Barbara glanced at a neighboring clock.

She could get a train in a few minutes, but she would be forced to wait at a station on the Cheshire side, and there was not another train for some time. She had bought the things she needed and did not know what to do. One could pass half an hour at a café; but Mrs. Cartwright did not like her to go to a café; alone and Barbara frowned impatiently. Her mother was horribly conventional and Barbara missed the freedom she had enjoyed in Canada. In fact, it was very dull at home; Grace's correct serenity and cold disapproval made one savage; Mortimer's very proper friends were tiresome.

Barbara was restless and dissatisfied. She wanted to play an active part and feel she was alive. Moreover, since she came home she had felt she was being watched, and, so to speak, protected from herself. Her relations had forgiven her Canadian escapade, but they meant to guard against her doing something of the kind again. Perhaps from their point of view, they were justified, but Barbara was not tempted to make a fresh experiment. She had not yet got over the shock; she saw how near her romantic trustfulness had brought her to disaster and thought her faith in men and women had gone. This was perhaps the worst, because she was generous and had frankly trusted people she liked.

Now she imagined the gloomy day had re-acted on her spirits. She was moody and longed for something that would banish the dreariness. Starting down hill for the station, she stopped abruptly a few moments afterwards. Lister was crossing the street, and if she went on they would meet. It was some time since she had seen him and she noted with surprise that he wore a rather soiled blue uniform. His cap, which had a badge in front, was greasy, and he carried an oilskin coat.

He walked quickly, looking straight in front, with his head well up, and Barbara got a hint of purposeful activity. Barbara liked him much, but she had, as a rule, quietly baffled his efforts to know her better. She waited, rather hoping he would pass, until he looked round and advanced to meet her.

"I'm lucky!" he remarked, and his satisfaction was comforting. "It's long since I have seen you."

"You know our house," Barbara rejoined.

"Oh, well," he said with a twinkle, "when I last came, you talked to me for about two minutes and then left me to play billiards with your brother. He was polite, but in Canada we play pool and my game's not very good. I imagined he was bored."

"Mortimer is like that," said Barbara. "But why are you wearing the steamship badge and sailor's clothes?"

Lister laughed. "They're engineer's clothes. I go to sea; that's another reason I didn't come over."

"Ah," said Barbara. "Did my step-father get you a post on board ship?"

"He did not. He told me to look him up at the office, but I didn't go. One would sooner not bother one's friends."

"Canadians are an independent lot," Barbara remarked. "In this country, we use our friends for all they are worth, and we're justified so long as they want to help. If Cartwright said he would help, he meant to do so. But what ship are you on board?"

"*Ardrigh*, cross-channel cattle boat. She's unloading Irish steers, sheep and pigs not far off. Will you come and see her? I don't suppose you've been on board a Noah's ark before."

Barbara did not hesitate. She doubted if Mrs. Cartwright would approve and knew Grace would not, but this was not important. Grace disapproved all she did and the stolen excursion would break the monotony. Then Lister's twinkling smile appealed, and somehow her reserve vanished when she was out of doors with him.

"I'd like to go," she said.

"Then, come along," he urged, and they started for the elevated railway at the bottom of the street.

While the electric cars rolled along the docks Barbara's moodiness went. She could not see much in the fog. Wet warehouse roofs, masts and funnels, and half-seen hulls floating on dull water, loomed up and vanished. Inside the car, lights glimmered on polished wood; the rattling and shaking were somehow cheerful. Barbara felt braced and alert. Lister talked and she laughed. She could not hear all he said, because of the noise, and thought he did not hear her, but she did not mind. She liked his cheerfulness and frank satisfaction. The gloom outside and the blurred lights in the fog gave the excursion a touch of romantic adventure.

They got down at a station by a muddy dock-road. Ponderous lorries with giant horses rolled out of the gloom between stacks of goods; wet cattle were entangled in the press of traffic, and Barbara was relieved when Lister pushed back a sliding door. Then she stopped for a moment, half daunted by the noise and bustle, and looked about.

Big lights hung from the room of the long shed, but did not pierce the gloom that lurked between the piles of cargo. A flock of sheep, moving in a dense woolly mass, came down a gangway; squealing pigs occupied a bay across the piles of goods. The front of the shed was open and in places one saw a faint reflection that looked like water. Opposite Barbara, the gap between the low roof and dock-sill was filled by a deckhouse and a steamer's funnel. Steam blew across the opening farther on, and in the vapor bales and boxes shot up and rattling chains plunged down. Through the roar of the winches she heard coarse shouts and the bellowing of cattle.

Lister took her to a slanting plank that spanned a dark gulf and she saw dim water and then the hollow of a steamer's hold. Men who looked like ghosts moved in the gloom and indistinct cattle came up a railed plank. Barbara could not see where they came from; they plunged out of the dark, their horns glimmering in the beam of the lamps.

After a few moments Lister helped her down on the steamer's bridge-deck. The boat listed away from the wall. Her tall red funnel was inclined sharply, much of her side was above water, and muddy streams poured from the scuppers on the after deck, where men with long boots pulled a hose-pipe about. The boat was horribly dirty, but her lean bows and the length of the iron engine-room casing indicated speed.

A man came along the bridge-deck, and Barbara thought the gold bands on his cap indicated the captain. He stopped and when he glanced at Lister she blushed, for there was a hint of sympathetic understanding in her smile.

"We won't want you until high-water," he said and went off.

Barbara hoped Lister had not seen her blush and thought he had not. He took her down some iron steps and to a door in a dark passage.

"Our mess-room," he said. "I expect it's the quietest spot on board the ship."

He pushed the door open and stopped. The small room was bright with electric light and a young man and woman sat opposite each other at the table. The man's uniform was stained by oil; the girl was pretty and fashionably dressed, but Barbara knew her clothes were cheap. She stood at the door, hesitating, and the man gave Lister a smile like the captain's.

"I didn't expect you yet, but come in," he said. "The tea's not cold, and Mike has made some doughnuts."

"Mr. Robertson, my chief," Lister said to Barbara, and the man presented Lister to his companion, and put a machine in a box on the floor. "Now there's room; I was pulling out the indicator diagrams," he added. "Won't you take off your coat, Miss Hyslop, and try Mike's doughnuts?"

The little room was hot, and when Barbara hung up her furs she noted the other girl's appraising glance. Miss Grant poured some black tea from a big cracked pot and pushed across a tin of condensed milk and a plate of greasy buns. When Barbara picked one up and looked at it doubtfully Robertson opened a drawer.

"We pull ours in two, but I expect you'd like a knife," he said.

He found a knife, which he rubbed on the table-cloth. "I used the thing on the indicator, the contraption in the box, but I think it's clean enough."

Barbara ate her doughnut and drank the bitter tea. Miss Grant looked friendly and she liked the engineer. They were frank, human people, and she thought them kind. Robertson began to talk about carpets, gas-stoves and pans, and Miss Grant told Barbara what the articles cost. They had been buying furniture and Robertson stated they were to be married soon.

"I reckon you haven't got so far yet," he said to Lister, and when Barbara saw Miss Grant touch him she blushed. It was ridiculous, but the blood came to her skin, and then, noting Lister's embarrassment, she began to laugh.

"Jim *will* talk like that!" Miss Grant remarked.

"Oh, well," said Robertson, "I expect it's rather soon. Mr. Lister hasn't joined us long, and you don't begin at the top." He turned to Barbara with an encouraging smile. "All the same, he knows his job and has got one move up. Perhaps if he sticks to it, for a year or two—"

Miss Grant stopped him and asked Barbara's views about curtains. She had some patterns, and while they contrasted the material and the prices the door opened and a greasy, red-haired fellow gave the group a benevolent grin.

"Was thim doughnuts all right?" he inquired.

"I've had better, but you've made some worse, Mike," Robertson replied.

"Yez said *tea for two.* If ye'd told me it was a party, I'd have been afther stealing the captain's Cork butter. A cook cannot do his best whin the shore-steward sends him engine-grease. Annyhow, whin ye're young an' romantic, what's it mather what ye ate?"

He went off and Robertson began to talk about *Ardrigh.* He was naïvely proud of the boat and his engines, and narrated hard runs in bad weather to land the livestock in time for important markets. Sometimes the hollow channel-seas that buried the plunging forecastle filled the decks and icy cataracts came down the stokehold gratings. Sometimes the cattle pens broke and mangled bullocks rolled about in the water and wreckage.

Robertson had a talent for narrative and Barbara felt something of the terror and lure of the sea. She liked the *Ardrigh's* rather grimy crew, their cheerfulness and rude good-humor. They did useful things, big things now and then; they were strong, warm-blooded fellows, not polished loafers like Mortimer's friends. Then she approved Miss Grant's frank pride in her lover. There was something primitive about these people. They were, so to speak, human, and not ashamed of their humanity. Lister was somehow like them; she wondered whether this had attracted her. Perhaps she was attracted, but the attraction must not be indulged.

By and by Miss Grant resumed her talk about curtains, and when they had agreed about the material that ought to wear best Barbara looked at her watch. Miss Grant gave her her hand and Robertson declared she must come back when the boat was in port again. Lister took her down the gangway and was quiet until they reached the station. Then he smiled apologetically.

"You played up well. I didn't know Robertson was on board, but he's a very good sort. So's the girl, I think."

Barbara laughed. "I didn't play up; I liked the people. The excursion was delightful; I've enjoyed it all."

Lister saw she was sincere and thrilled. He had begun to think he ought not to have suggested the adventure, but he was not sorry now; Barbara was not bothered by ridiculous conventions. She talked gayly while the cars rolled along beside the warehouse walls, but when they got down at the station she stopped in the middle of a sentence. Cartwright had alighted from the next car and was a yard or two in front. Lister knew his fur coat and rather dragging walk. If he and Barbara went on, they would confront Cartwright when he turned to go down the steps.

Barbara gave him a twinkling glance and remarked that he knitted his brows but did not hesitate. In the few moments since her step-father left the train she had seen three or four plans for avoiding him. Lister obviously had not, and on the whole she approved his honesty. He advanced and touched Cartwright.

"I didn't know you were on board our train, sir."

Cartwright looked at him rather hard and Barbara waited. Although she had been caught enjoying a stolen excursion, she was not afraid of her step-father, but she was curious.

"I was in front," said Cartwright dryly. "Barbara has picked a rather dreary day for a run to the north docks. I understood she was going to the shops."

"Miss Hyslop met me near the station and I persuaded her to come and see my ship."

"Then you have got a ship?" said Cartwright. "If you are not on duty, come to the office in the morning and tell me about the boat. In the meantime, I'll put Barbara on the tunnel train."

He went off with the girl, but Barbara turned her head and Lister saw her smile.

CHAPTER IX

CARTWRIGHT SEES A PLAN

In the morning Lister went to Cartwright's office. To some extent, he was embarrassed, because he had begun to see that Barbara's relations might not approve her going on board his ship and he imagined Cartwright meant to talk about this. When he came in Cartwright gave him a nod and indicated a chair.

"I understand you did not arrange for Barbara to meet you and go to the dock?" he said.

"No, sir. I didn't expect to meet Miss Hyslop. I was talking about the boat and thought Miss Hyslop might like to see her."

Cartwright turned and the electric light touched his face. He looked thoughtful, but somehow Lister imagined he was not thinking about his step-daughter.

"Oh, well!" he said, as if the matter were not important, and went on: "I might have got you a post had you looked me up. What boat are you on board?"

"*Ardrigh.* Perhaps you know her?"

"Yes. Belfast model; long bow and fine lines aft. Don't know if I approve the type. Give you speed, at the cost of carrying power, but makes a wet ship in a head sea."

"She is wet," Lister agreed with a smile. "Last run we couldn't keep the water out of the stokehold. Had to cover and batten gratings, and then a boat fetched adrift and smashed the engine skylights."

"What's your rating?" Cartwright asked.

Lister told him and he remarked: "You have made some progress!"

"I was lucky. She burst some boiler tubes in my watch. We were steaming hard, head to an ugly sea, with a lot of cattle on board, and were forced to keep her going. Two firemen were scalded, but I was able to put the patent-stoppers in the tubes. I used a trick I'd learned on a Canadian lake boat; rather risky, but it worked. Afterwards the company moved me up."

Cartwright was not surprised. He knew men and saw the young fellow was all he had thought. All the same, it might be worth while to get some particulars about the accident from the *Ardrigh's* owners.

"You won't go far in the cross-channel trade. Why did you not try for a berth with an Atlantic line!"

"There was some trouble about your Board of Trade rules and I might have been required to prove my qualifications for an English certificate. While I was inquiring I heard an engineer was wanted on board *Ardrigh*. The regulations don't apply to coasting voyages."

"You might have got your certificate. Would it not have been worth while?"

Lister hesitated. His main object for joining the *Ardrigh* was that she sailed from Liverpool and he wanted to see Barbara now and then. As a rule, he was frank, but he did not think it prudent to enlighten Cartwright.

"I don't know," he said. "You see, I may go back to the railroad soon."

He wondered whether Cartwright did see and thought he had remarked his hesitation; the old fellow was very keen. Cartwright's look, however, was inscrutable and for a few moments he said nothing. Then he picked up some papers on his desk.

"Look me up now and then when you're in port. I might have a job for you, but I don't know yet," he said, and added in a meaning voice: "If you want to see my family, Mrs. Cartwright will receive you at her house."

Lister colored and got up. "I'll remember, sir! Perhaps I oughtn't to have persuaded Miss Hyslop—I didn't stop to think—"

When he went off Cartwright smiled, but soon afterwards he put his cigar-case in his pocket and told Gavin he was going out. He thought he knew where to find the cattle boat's shore-engineer, and when he did so the waitress gave them a table at which they would not be disturbed. In half an hour Cartwright had found out all he wanted to know, and returning to his office, he smoked and mused.

Lister had not exaggerated; his pluck and coolness had kept *Ardrigh's* engines going when to stop might have meant the loss of the livestock on board. Well, Cartwright had known the fellow was good stuff and he might soon want a man like that. Somebody staunch and resolute who knew his job! He had beaten his antagonists at the shareholders' meeting, but doubted if he could do so again. In fact, he had only put off the reckoning for six months, in which he must make good, and he knitted his brows while he studied *Titania's* picture. He thought about her sister ship, wrecked and abandoned on the African coast.

Arcturus was a useful boat and cheap to run. Although times were bad, Cartwright could run her and earn some profit. He had known the company that bought her was getting near the rocks, but they had insured her heavily and there was something strange about the wreck. Cartwright understood the underwriters had hesitated before they paid. He, himself, would not have paid; he had a notion—.

An effort had been made to float *Arcturus*, but the salvors did not know all Cartwright thought he knew. If his supposition were correct, the wreck might be worth buying and one could, no doubt, buy her very cheap. The boat had for some time lain half-buried in shifting sands at the mouth of an African river.

The underwriters would be lucky if they sold her for old iron.

Cartwright weighed the cost of floating. If he employed a regular salvage company, this would be high, because they would bargain for a large part of the value recovered; his plan was to do the job himself, with cheaper appliances than theirs. The trouble was, he could not go out and superintend. He was too old, and one ought to be an engineer; Cartwright had grounds for imagining the job was rather an engineer's than a sailor's. Well, he knew a young fellow who would not be daunted and would work for him honestly, but to get the proper man was not all.

He pondered about the money. Somehow he might get the necessary sum, but if the venture failed, it would be the last. Nobody would trust him again; he would be forced into retirement and dependence on his wife. It was a risk he hesitated to run and he resolved to wait.

In the evening after dinner Barbara joined him in the drawing-room, and Cartwright waited with some amusement, for he thought he knew what she wanted.

"Did Mr. Lister come to the office?" she asked presently.

"He did come. Did you think he would not?"

"Oh, no!" said Barbara, smiling, "I knew he would come. Mr. Lister is like that!"

"I suppose you mean he's honest?"

"I think I mean he's scrupulous. When you crossed the station platform in front of us he got a jolt."

"Then, you did not get a jolt?"

"Not at all," said Barbara. "To keep behind and meet you after I'd sent Lister off would not have bothered me. However, I was curious, although I think I knew the line he'd take. You see, for an unsophisticated young man, the situation was awkward."

"If he felt it awkward, it indicated he knew he ought not to have taken you on board his boat."

"You're horribly logical," Barbara rejoined with a twinkle. "When we started he didn't know I ought not to have gone. Mr. Lister is not like you; he's very obvious. Of course, I did know, but I went!"

"I wonder why!" said Cartwright dryly.

"Sometimes you're keen, but you didn't remark, I meant to give you a lead. Well, I didn't go altogether because I wanted to enjoy Mr. Lister's society. To see a cattle boat was something fresh and I was dull."

"Then, when did Lister see a light? Since he stopped me, it's plain he'd got some illumination."

"I think it was when the engineer and the girl Robertson is going to marry began to talk about house furnishings in the *Ardrigh's* mess-room. They took it for granted Lister was my lover and he was horribly embarrassed. The thing really was humorous."

"Folks have hinted I'm getting a back-number," Cartwright remarked. "To talk to a modern girl makes me feel I am out-of-date."

"Grace is not modern and to talk to her makes you tired," Barbara rejoined. "But I'll tell you about the tea-party in the mess-room if you like."

"Then you got tea in the cattle boat's mess-room?"

"Of course," said Barbara. "Black tea and condensed milk, and a ruffian with red hair whom they called Mike had made some doughnuts with lard like engine-grease. For all that, they were very nice people, and if you don't interrupt, I'll tell you—"

She told him about the party and Cartwright chuckled. He pictured her in the dirty mess-room, looking exotic in her fashionable clothes and expensive furs, but no doubt quite serene. She said the other girl was pretty, but Cartwright admitted that Barbara was beautiful. He rather sympathized with Lister's embarrassment, and wondered whether Barbara meant to throw some light on the young man's character.

When she stopped, he asked: "Did they talk about some burst boiler tubes?"

"No," said Barbara. "We talked about gas-stoves and kitchen pans." Then she gave Cartwright a keen glance. "But what are boiler tubes? Do they sometimes burst?"

"They carry the flame from the furnace through the water. If you're much interested, Gavin will show you a plan of a ship's boiler when you come to the office. In the meantime, have you found out all you want to know?"

"You really are keen!" Barbara rejoined.

"I was a little curious about what you said to Mr. Lister."

"Ah," said Cartwright, "I imagined something like this. I told him if he wanted to see my family, he must come to the house."

Barbara looked thoughtful. "This was all? Was it worth while to tell him to come to the office? To order him, in fact?"

"It was all that's important. I think it was important and expect you to agree."

"Well, you have carried out your duty and ought to be satisfied," said Barbara, who got up and gave Cartwright a smiling glance. "All the same, if you want a man for an awkward job, I think you can trust Mr. Lister!"

She went off and Cartwright laughed. Barbara was clever. The strange thing was, she had been cheated by a theatrical rogue, but clever girls were sometimes like that. He imagined she liked Lister, but this was perhaps all, since she had been frank. In one sense, Lister was the man for Barbara; he was honest, sober, and resolute, and she needed firm control. The girl was as wild as a hawk, and although she was marked by a fine fastidiousness, would revolt from a narrow-minded prig. Lister was not a prig; his blood was red.

In another sense, perhaps, the thing was ridiculous. Barbara was rich and ought to make a good marriage, but good marriages sometimes brought unhappiness.

Human nature was stubborn; one paid for forcing it to obey the rules of worldly prudence. Then Barbara had a romantic vein. She would risk all for her lover and not grumble if she were forced to pay for her staunchness. Besides, she and Lister had qualities he had not. They were marked by something ascetic, or perhaps he meant Spartan, and if it were worth while, could go without much that he required.

Cartwright admitted that indulgence had cost him dear. He had paid with grim philosophy, but he did not want Barbara to pay. Although she was not his daughter, he loved the girl, and her recent moodiness bothered him. If she did not love Lister, why was she disturbed? Sometimes Cartwright thought he saw a gleam of light. Suppose she did love the fellow and was trying to keep him off because of her Canadian adventure? Lister knew about that and Barbara was proud.

Cartwright's eyes got bloodshot and he clenched his fist. He would very much like to meet Shillito. His muscles were getting slack, but he had not lost all his power; anyhow, he could talk. Well, the thing was humiliating, but he must not get savage. When he let himself go he suffered for it afterwards. Getting up, he threw away his cigar, and went off to talk to his wife.

CHAPTER X

A BOLD SPECULATION

After weighing for some weeks all he could learn about the wreck on the African coast, Cartwright went to London and was carried up one morning to the second floor of an imposing office block. Black marble columns supported the molded roof of the long passage, the wide stairs were guarded by polished mahogany and shining brass, and a screen of artistic iron work enclosed the elevator shaft. Cartwright's fur coat and gloves and varnished boots harmonized with the surroundings; he looked rich and important, but as he went along the corridor his face was stern. He was going to make a plunge that would mend or break his fortune. Unless he got straight in the next six months, he must retire from the Board and make the best bargain possible with his creditors.

He opened a door, and giving a clerk his card, was shown into a handsome private office. Mr. Morse at a writing-table indicated a chair, and when Cartwright sat down, rested his chin in his hand.

"We have considered your letters, and my partner, Mr. Bull, agrees that, if we can come to terms, your suggestion has some advantages," he said.

"The advantages for your clients are obvious," Cartwright remarked.

The other smiled. "They paid out a good sum when *Arcturus* was wrecked, and would frankly like to get something back. Well, we understand you are willing to buy her, *as she lies*."

"At my price! I'll give you a check when the agreement's signed."

"Then, I expect you have made some calculations and know all about the efforts to float the wreck. If we sell her to you, the job is yours, but I admit some curiosity. Why do you expect to float her when the salvage company failed?"

"For one thing, they started the job on extravagant lines," Cartwright replied. "They sent out two first-class tugs and a number of highly-paid men; they ought to have hired negro laborers at the spot. The surf is often bad, they could only work when it was calm, and while they were doing nothing, wages mounted up. So did their bills for the coal they must bring from Sierra Leone, where coal is expensive. Then they were bothered by fever and were forced to send men home. They saw the contract would not pay and let it go. The job was not impossible; it was costing too much."

Mr. Morse agreed that Cartwright's statement was plausible and probably accurate, but thought he rather labored his argument.

"You mean to use another plan?" he said.

"My outfit will be small and cheap. This has the advantage that when my men can't work, I won't pay much for wasted time. All the same, my risk is obvious. The thing's a rash speculation, on which I can't embark unless you are satisfied to take a very small price."

For a few moments the ship broker pondered. Cartwright's line was the line a man who wanted to buy something cheap would take. All the same, Mr. Morse did not altogether see why he wanted to buy the wreck.

"What about the cargo?" he suggested. "Of course, you understand that I have no authority to sell this; you noticed the wording of our original advertisement? 'And for the salving of the cargo,' Precisely it is on that basis alone that the cargo underwriters will deal. Together with your offer for the steamer as she lies, you must accept a percentage of the value of the cargo you save."

"What is the cargo?"

"She carried palm-kernels in the forehold; I expect they have fermented and rotted. Perhaps the palm oil aft isn't spoiled."

"The barrels will have gone to bits."

"Oak barrel staves stand salt water long."

"The iron hoops do not," Cartwright rejoined. "Anyhow, I don't reckon on the cargo; I expect to make my profit on buying the hull."

"Yet the cargo is worth something. I imagine you know she carried some valuable gums, ivory and a quantity of gold?"

Cartwright smiled. "I do know the goods were on the ship's manifest. How much gold did the salvage company get?"

"Six boxes; but this was not all that was shipped."

"I imagine it's all that will be recovered!" Cartwright remarked.

The other looked hard at him, but his face was inscrutable and he went on: "Well, I don't want the cargo, and may be forced to heave much of it overboard in order to lighten the hull. However, if we find stuff worth saving, we'll put it on the beach and I'll take a third-part of the value, and you can send out an agent to tally the goods."

"Very well," said the other, who approved the latter plan, although he imagined Cartwright knew something he did not. "Let's be frank," he resumed. "Personally, I felt from the beginning there was a mystery about the wreck."

"Oh, well," said Cartwright, "the owners of the boat went broke, and the merchant who put the goods on board died. His son sold the business to a small company, in which he took shares. The new house is prosperous and respectable; it would be necessary to know your ground well before you bothered them. Then I have nothing to go upon but a vague supposition. In fact, the thing's a risky plunge, and if you refuse my offer, I won't grumble. All the same, I doubt if anybody else would give you, for example, five hundred pounds for *Arcturus*."

"Five hundred pounds is, of course, ridiculous," the other rejoined, and they began to bargain.

When Cartwright left the office he was, on the whole, satisfied. He could finance the undertaking, but this was all. There would be no margin to cover unforeseen difficulties. It was his last gamble, and, besides his money, he staked his post and reputation. If he lost, he was done for, and the house must fall. Soon after his return he sent for Lister and told him about the wreck and his salvage plans.

"I had some bother to get a captain," he said. "The job has not much attraction for a sober man, but Brown is not sober; he's frankly reckless and irresponsible. The strange thing is, I've known him make good where cautious men have failed. Then much depends on the engineer. I brought you across to ask if you would go."

Lister's eyes sparkled. "Yes, sir. I've been looking for a chance like this."

Cartwright studied him quietly. Lister's keenness was obvious; the young fellow liked adventure, but Cartwright imagined this did not account for all.

"From one point of view, I think the chance is pretty good," he said. "If you can float the wreck and bring her home, I expect some of the big salvage companies will offer you a post. Anyhow, you'll get your pay, and if we are lucky, a bonus that will depend on the cost of the undertaking and the value of all we salve."

"I'm going," Lister declared, and Cartwright noted that he did not inquire about the pay. Then he hesitated and resumed: "But I haven't got an English chief-engineer's certificate."

"I don't know if it's important. I expect you'll find the adventure is marked by a number of small irregularities. However, to satisfy the Board of Trade is my business."

"Then you can reckon on me; but there's another thing. Why do you hope to lift the wreck when the salvage men could not?"

Cartwright smiled. "I have been asked this before, but saw no grounds for satisfying the inquirer's curiosity. All the same, I'll enlighten you."

He did so, and Lister looked up sharply. He had known Cartwright was clever, but the old fellow was cleverer than he thought. It was possible he had solved a puzzle that had baffled the salvage engineers. After all, perhaps, it was not strange they were baffled. They had reckoned on mechanical obstacles; Cartwright had reckoned on the intricacies of human nature.

"I expect you have got it, sir," Lister agreed. "If her bilge was in the sand and the divers couldn't break into the engine-room—" He paused and laughed. "A powerful centrifugal pump lifts some water, but you can't pump out the Atlantic!"

"It looks as if the salvage company tried," said Cartwright, dryly. "However—"

He talked about the undertaking, giving Lister particulars he thought he ought to know, and when the young man went off, all important plans had been agreed upon. Soon afterwards Cartwright went home and found Mrs. Cartwright had gone to bed. He was getting disturbed about her, but since the doctor had said she must rest, he talked to Barbara in the evening. He told her about the wreck, and smiled when he stated that Lister would have control.

"I think you declared he was the man for an awkward job," he said.

Barbara looked at him rather hard. "Perhaps I did say so. You don't imply you are sending Mr. Lister because you thought I'd like it?"

"Not at all," said Cartwright. "The thing's a business venture. Still your statement carried weight. I admit your judgment sometimes is sound."

She turned her head and when she looked up and replied, her voice was rather hard.

"You must not trust my judgment. I have been cheated."

"My dear!" said Cartwright. "Perhaps my remark was unlucky, but the cleverest of us is sometimes cheated, and you were not cheated long. We'll let it go. I'm bothered about your mother. She feels the damp and cold and is not picking up. Perhaps we ought to send her South. I must talk to the doctor."

In the morning he saw the doctor, who said they had better wait for a time, and Cartwright occupied himself by outfitting the salvage expedition. Finding it necessary to go to London, he called on the gentleman from whom he had bought the wreck a short time ago.

"When we made the agreement, you asked if I knew anybody who would give me five hundred pounds for the boat," remarked Mr. Morse. "Just then I did not know, but not long since I was offered a better price than yours."

"Ah," said Cartwright, thoughtfully. "She lay in the sand for some time and nobody bothered about her. Who was willing to buy?"

The other smiled. "A shipbroker stated a sum at which he would take her off our hands. It was plain he was an agent, but he wouldn't give his customer's name. I don't imagine you will find out from him. I tried!"

Cartwright said it was strange, and went off soon afterwards. When he went down in the lift he smiled, for he thought he saw a light; after all, his speculation was not as rash as it looked.

When he got home Mrs. Cartwright had come downstairs and she joined the others at dinner. The doctor said she was stronger and might soon undertake a journey South; he suggested the Canaries, and Cartwright approved.

"If you sail by a Cape liner, it's a short run, and after you leave the Spanish coast the sea is generally smooth," he said. "Since I must stay at the office, we must decide who is going with you."

Hyslop said he would like to go, and would do so if it were necessary, but to get away just then was awkward. Grace declared somebody must stop to look after Cartwright and the house, and she imagined this was her post. For all that, since she was older than Barbara, it was hard to see her duty. Mrs. Cartwright did not indicate whom she wanted, although she glanced at Barbara. Since she was ill she had got very languid, and Cartwright did not meddle. He knew his stepchildren, and it was characteristic that Grace talked about her duty; taking care of an invalid at a foreign hotel had not much charm for Grace.

"Very well," said Barbara, "I gave you and Mortimer first chance, because I'm not important, but since you have good grounds for staying, we won't argue." She turned to Mrs. Cartwright: "I'm going, because I want to go."

Mrs. Cartwright gave her a gentle smile and it was plain that she was satisfied, but when she had gone to bed and Cartwright was alone, he pondered. Barbara loved her mother and would have gone had she not wanted to go, but he thought she did want and had an object. He had told her something about his plans, and had stated that he would use Grand Canary as a supply depot for the expedition; then he had found the girl studying an Atlantic chart in the library. Barbara had no doubt noted the island lay conveniently near the African coast, and knew it was an important coaling station, at which steamers bound South from Liverpool called. Cartwright wondered whether she had argued she might see Lister at Grand Canary.

CHAPTER XI

THE START

Rain was falling and the light had hardly reached the opening between the tall warehouses. In the dock the water was smooth and shone with dull reflections, but the gates were open and the muddy swell the flood tide brought up the river splashed about the entrance. Ponderous lorries rumbled across a bridge, indistinct figures moved and shouted on the pierhead, and men in wet oilskins splashed about *Terrier's* deck.

She was a battered propeller tug and lay against the wall, with large cases of machinery lashed to her bulwarks, and a stack of coal built up beside the engine-skylights. Her bunkers were full, but the fuel she carried would not last very long, and coal is dear at foreign ports. Coils of thick wire rope and diving gear occupied her shallow hold, and Cartwright was annoyed because she could not take the massive centrifugal pump which he had sent by an African liner. Some extra coal and supplies were loaded on a clumsy wooden hulk, but he durst not risk her carrying expensive machinery.

When he talked to the captain in the pilot-house, he was, on the whole, satisfied. Brown's face was flushed and his voice was hoarse, but he would pull himself together after he got to sea. Cartwright knew Brown's habits when he gave him the job, although, in an important sense, the job was Lister's. To trust the young fellow was a bold experiment, but Cartwright did so. If Lister were not the man he thought, Cartwright imagined his control of the line would presently come to an inglorious end. To some extent this accounted for his bringing Barbara to see the salvage expedition start. He knew the power of love.

Barbara had not gone up the greasy ladder to the bridge and waited on deck. She had left home without much breakfast, in the dark, and was cold and rather depressed. All was gloomy and strangely flat. The tug looked small and was horribly dirty. Coal-dust covered rails and ropes; grimy drops from the rigging splashed on the trampled black mud on deck. The crew were not sober and their faces were black. Two or three draggled women called to them from the pierhead, their voices sounding melancholy and harsh.

Barbara had not seen Lister and wondered where he was, until a man plunged out from the neighboring door of the engine-room. The abruptness of his exit indicated that he had been rudely propelled by somebody behind, and as he lurched across the deck, Lister appeared at the door. His cap was dark with grease, his overalls were stained, and a black smear ran from his eye to chin.

"Hustle and get that oil drum on the wharf, you drunken hog!" he shouted. "If I hadn't watched out you'd have left half the truck."

He stopped when he saw Barbara. "This is very kind," he said to her. "I knew Cartwright was on board, but hadn't hoped you would come to give us a good send-off."

Barbara noted his satisfaction and was moved by something in his voice. He looked thin and fine-drawn in his stained engineer's clothes, and his hands were greasy. The surroundings were not romantic, but somehow they got brighter and her gloom vanished. Lister's eyes sparkled; he wore the stamp of strength and confidence.

"I doubted if my step-father would bring me, but I really meant to come," she said. "For one thing, I wanted to ask you—"

She hesitated, for it was hard to strike the right note. She had begun to see there was something exciting and perhaps heroic about the adventure. The handful of men had undertaken a big thing; there was much against them, and daunting risks must be run. Moreover, she had studied Cartwright and remarked the anxiety he thought he had hid. Cartwright was rather inscrutable, but sympathy had given her power to understand. She thought he was engaged in a reckless gamble and could not afford to lose.

"Whatever you want—" Lister declared, but she stopped him.

"I want you to do your best."

"You can reckon on that, anyhow! Cartwright has hired me; I'm his man."

Barbara smiled. "Yes; I know! You're honest and will do all you engaged; but in a sense, this is not enough. I want you to make an extra effort, because—"

She paused and the blood came to her skin when she went on: "You see, it's important you should float the wreck and bring her home. It means much to my step-father; very much, I think. He's kind and I love him. I feel I ought to help."

Lister saw her statement was significant, and her embarrassment indicated that she knew it was so. In fact, she had admitted that she knew he would, for her sake, use all his powers. He was moved, but he was not a fool. The girl, wearing her costly furs, looked rich and dignified; he was a working engineer and conscious of his greasy clothes. He loved her, but for a time he must be cautious. To begin with, he would not have her think he made a claim.

"You're not very logical," he replied carelessly. "When I took the job I undertook to earn my pay. Cartwright sends me off to float the wreck, and if it's possible, I must make good."

"I am logical," Barbara declared, while her color came and went. "One thinks one does one's best, but sometimes when the strain comes, one can do better. It really isn't ridiculous! Emotion, sentiment, give one extra force—" She stopped and resumed in a strangely gentle voice: "You are young, and if you don't make good it won't hurt very much. Mr. Cartwright's old; he can't try again. Then he's not my step-father only. He's my friend, and I know he trusts you. For his sake, I must be frank—I trust you!"

Lister smiled, but his voice betrayed him, although he thought he used control.

"Very well! If it's possible for flesh and blood, we'll bring *Arcturus* home. That's all. The thing's done with."

She gave him her hand, and kept the glove with the dark grease stain. Then, seeing there was no more to be said, she looked about. Ragged clouds rolled up from the Southwest, and the disturbed swell that splashed about the dock gates indicated wind down channel. A shower beat upon the engine skylights and Barbara moved beneath the bridge. A great rope rose out of the water as the men at the winch hauled up the clumsy hulk. Two or three others, dragging a thin, stiff wire rope, floundered unsteadily across the deck.

"They look rough, and they're not very sober," Barbara remarked.

Lister laughed. "They're frankly drunk! A pretty hard crowd, but Brown and I have handled a hard crowd before. In fact, I reckon Cartwright has got the proper men for the job."

"Captain Brown is like them," said Barbara, thoughtfully. "You are not."

"You haven't seen me hustling round when things go wrong."

"I saw you throw a man out of the engine-room not long since!"

"With a gang like ours, one must prove one's claim to be boss at the start. Anyhow, there are different kinds of wastrels, and the fellow who gets on a jag at intervals is often a pretty good sort. The wastrel one has no use for is the fellow who keeps it up. But I see Mr. Cartwright coming and mustn't philosophize."

A gateman on the pierhead began to shout to the captain, and Cartwright gave Lister his hand.

"They are waiting for you and we must get ashore," he said. "Well, I've given you and Brown a big job, but I expect you'll see me out."

"We'll put in all we've got, sir," said Lister quietly.

Cartwright nodded, as if he were satisfied, and touched Barbara, who turned and gave Lister a smile.

"Good luck!" she said, and following Cartwright, went up the steps in the wall.

She thought it significant Cartwright had left her for some time and had given Lister a quick, searching glance. Lister had said nothing about their talk and his promise; she had known he would not do so. Yet this was not because he was clever. He had a sort of instinctive fastidiousness. She liked his reply to Cartwright; he *would* put in all he had got, and a man like that had much. Fine courage, resolution and staunch loyalty.

When Barbara reached the pierhead, *Terrier's* engines began to throb. The propeller churned the green water, and the tug bumped against the wall. Gatemen shouted, the big tow-rope splashed and tightened with a jerk, and the hulk began to move. Then the tug's bow crept round the corner and swung off from the gates. The engine throbbed faster, and a blast of the whistle echoed about the warehouses. Brown waved his cap and signed to a man in the pilot-house. The hulk swung round in a wide sweep, and the adventurous voyage had begun.

Terrier, steaming across the strong current, looked small and dingy; when she rolled as the helm went over, the swell washed her low bulwarks. She got smaller, until a rain squall blew across from the Cheshire side and she melted into the background of dark water and smoke. Barbara felt strangely forlorn, and it was some relief when Cartwright touched her arm and they set off along the wall.

After the rain the wind freshened, and when Brown steamed out from the river, a confused sea rolled across the shoals. The light was not good, but a double row of buoys led out to sea, the ebb-tide was running, and *Terrier* made good progress. She shipped no water yet, and the hulk lurched along without much strain on the rope. The rope was fastened to a massive iron hook and ran across a curved wooden horse at the tug's stern. Sometimes it slipped along the horse and tightened with a bang, for the clumsy hulk sheered about. When her stern went up one saw an indistinct figure holding the wheel.

When they passed the Bar Lightship, Lister climbed to the bridge and for a few minutes looked about. The plunging red hull to starboard was the last of the Mersey marks, for the North-West ship was hidden by low clouds.

Ahead the angry gray water was broken by streaks of foam. *Terrier* rolled and quivered when her bows smashed a sea, and showers of spray beat like hail against the screens on the bridge.

"She's loggish," Brown remarked. "If you don't burn up that coal soon, she'll wash it off. Looks like a dirty night, and I'm pushing across for Lynas Point. With the wind at south-west, I want to get under the Anglesey coast. There'll be some sea in the channel when we open up Holyhead."

"The boat's good," said Lister. "Engines a bit neglected, but they're running smooth and cool, and she has power to shove her along. Cartwright has an eye for a useful craft."

Brown nodded. "The old fellow has an eye for all that's useful; I reckon he sees farther than any man I know. There's something encouraging about this, because the job he's given us looks tough—"

He stopped, for the tow-rope slipped noisily across the horse. There was a clang of iron as the hook took the strain, and the captain frowned. "That hulk is going to bother us before very long."

Lister seized the slanted rails. The lightship had vanished, but a bright beam pierced the haze astern. Ahead the sea was empty; gray water rolled beneath low and ragged clouds. Spray flew about the plunging bows, and the tug rolled uneasily. Lister turned and left the bridge, but stopped for a few moments at the engine-room door. Barbara had stood just opposite, where the iron funnel-stay ran down. Her rich furs gave her girlish figure a touch of dignity, the color was in her face, and her eyes shone.

Lister knew the picture would haunt him, and he would come to the engine door to recapture it when he needed bracing. He would need bracing, for there were obstacles ahead, but he had promised Barbara to help Cartwright out. Stepping across the ledge to a slippery platform, he went below.

PART III
THE BREAKING STRAIN

CHAPTER I

THE FIRST STRUGGLE

The engine-room floor-plates slanted, and light and shadow played about the throbbing machinery. It looked as if the lamps swung in a semicircle, but they did not. All else slanted at an ever-changing angle; the swiveled lamps were still. Overhead the dark and bulky cylinders cut against the reflected glimmer on the skylights; below, valve-gear and connecting-rod flashed across the gloom, and the twinkling cranks spun in their shallow pit. One saw the big columns shake and strain as the crosshead shot up and down; the thrust-blocks groaned with the back push of the propeller.

A door in the bulkhead was open, and now and then a blaze from the stokehold lighted the engine-room. Shovels clanged and the thud of a hammer jarred upon the throb of machinery. Men moved about like ghosts. Their feet made no noise; for a moment one saw their sweat-streaked faces and then they vanished. Lister sat on a tool-box, an old pipe in his mouth, and was happier than he had been for long. For one thing, his men were getting sober and he saw they knew their job; then he was satisfied with his engines and relished the sense of control. He was *chief*, and until the tug came back from Africa the engines were his.

In the meantime he need not move about. It was like listening to an orchestra of which he knew all the instruments, and he heard no jarring notes. The harmony was good and the rhythm well marked. The clash and clang rose and fell with a measured beat; but the smooth running of his engines did not account for all Lister's satisfaction. In a sense, Barbara had given him his job, he was her servant, doing her work, and this was much, although he scarcely durst hope for another reward.

Cartwright had not without careful thought sent Lister on board. He knew the young fellow's staunchness as he knew Barbara's, and, because his need was great, had not hesitated to use him and the girl. He was old and must be resigned to sit at his desk and plan, but, as a rule, his plans worked, and he had a talent for choosing his tools. When it was possible, he used his tools carefully; he hated to overstrain fine material.

Terrier's regular lurch and roll indicated that she was steaming along the coast, in some shelter from the wind that blew obliquely off the land. By and by, however, the lurches got violent, and when Lister heard the thud of water on deck he went up, and opening the door on the lee side, looked out. Water splashed against the ledge that protected the engine-room; the stack of coal worked and he heard big lumps fall. Spray blew across the bulwarks and fell in heavy showers from a boat on the skids. For a few moments this was all he could distinguish, and then he saw slopes of water slanting away from the tug's low side. A half-moon shone for a few moments between ragged clouds and was hidden.

Lister stepped across the ledge and went aft. *Terrier* felt the drag of the hulk astern, and he wanted to see how she was towing. He heard the iron ring clang on the hook, and when he stopped by the horse, the big tow-rope surged to and fro across the arch. The hulk steered wildly, and if the sea got worse, he doubted if they could hold her. He knew where he was, because he had steamed along the coast on board the cattle boat. The Anglesey shore was fringed by reefs, the tide-races ran in white turmoil across the ledges. The tide had now nearly run out, but when they turned the corner at Carmel Point they would meet the flood stream and the big combers the gale drove up channel. Going to the pilot-house, Lister lighted his pipe.

"A fierce night!" he remarked to Brown, who peered through the spray-swept glass. "I reckon you'll want to slow down when we make Carmel."

The house was dark, but Lister saw the captain turn. "I'm bothered," Brown admitted. "We ought to push on, but while we might tow the hulk under, we can't tow her down channel. We can't turn and run; it's blowing down the Menai Strait like a bellows spout, and there's all the Mersey sands to leeward. We have got to face the sea and try to make Holyhead. Will your engines shove her through?"

"They'll give you six or seven knots, head to wind. Will your tow rope hold?"

"I doubt. We have a steel hawser ready, but if she breaks the hemp rope she'll probably break the wire."

Lister agreed. The thick hemp rope stretched and absorbed the strain; the wire was less elastic. They were approaching Carmel Point, and Holyhead was not far, but they must front the gale when they got round the corner. In the meantime, the engines were running smoothly, and Lister smoked and waited while the sea got worse. Flashing lights ahead and the violent lurching indicated that they crept round the point. Then *Terrier* plunged into a white sea and deck and bulwarks vanished. Her bows swung out of the foam and Lister ran to the door. He felt the tug leap forward and knew the rope had gone.

He got out in front of Brown and plunged down the ladder. Since *Terrier* must be stopped and turned, he was needed. Water ran from his clothes when he reached a slanted platform and seized a greasy wheel. The telegraph gong was clanging and the beat of engines slackened as he followed the orders. Then the spinning cranks stopped altogether and for a minute or two there was a strange quietness. One heard the wind, and water splashed in the bilges.

Lister got the signal *Ahead slow*, and when he restarted his engines ran up the ladder. He could trust the man he left, and wanted to see what was happening. It was a moment or two before he could satisfy his curiosity, and then a bright beam illuminated the tug and angry water. Brown was burning a blue-light while *Terrier* crept up to the hulk. He meant to pass the fresh hawser, but could not launch a boat, and Lister doubted if the men on the hulk could heave the heavy wire rope on board. Although one must get near to throw a line, it looked as if Brown were going alongside.

Two dark figures, crouched on *Terrier's* rail like animals ready to spring, cut against the blaze. Brown was going alongside; anyhow, he was going near enough for the men to jump, but the thing was horribly risky. If the rolling hulk struck the tug planks and iron plates would be beaten in; moreover the men must jump from the slanted rail, and if they jumped short, their long boots and oilskins would drag them down.

It looked as if Cartwright knew how to choose men for an awkward job, for as the tug got nearer Lister saw the men meant to go. She swung up on the top of a white sea; the hulk, swept by spray, rolled down, with her deck close below the steamer's rail. One felt they must shock, but they did not. The dark figures leaped, there was a faint shout, a line whirled out from *Terrier's* bridge and the hulk drove astern. Then the blue light vanished and Lister plunged into the engine-room. Somehow the thing was done.

The gong signaled *Half-speed*, the rhythmic clash of engines began, and Lister felt *Terrier* tremble as she tightened the rope. Brown had played his part and Lister's had begun. He wondered whether they could keep the water out of the engine-room. They had drifted off-shore, and now they had opened up the channel the combers leaped on board. The seas were not regular; they ran in short, steep ridges, and gave the tug no time to lift. While she swung her bows from the foaming turmoil the next swept her deck. But to watch the seas and keep the hulk in line was the captain's business, and Lister was occupied by his.

Standing on a slanted platform with his hand on the throttle, he waited for the lurch that lifted the spinning screw. When the blades left the water, the engines raced with a horrible din and he must cut off steam. If he let the engines go, something might break when the propeller got hold again. The work demanded a firm but delicate touch, since the pressure must change with the swiftly-changing load. One could not argue when the bows would plunge and the stern swing clear; one must know instinctively. The muscular effort was not hard, but Lister's face was wet with sweat, and when he was slow and the engine-room rang with the clash of machinery his heart beat. The big columns that held the cylinders rocked; crank and connecting-rod spun too fast for him to see. There was a confusing flash of steel and a daunting uproar.

For the most part, he was able to get control before the stern came down. Moreover, he was not using full steam; to let her go would swamp the boat and wash the men off the laboring hulk. Lister knew the rope held because he felt the heavy drag. Although she rolled and plunged, there was no life in *Terrier's* movements. She was sluggish, embarrassed by the load she hauled.

Lister thought about the men on board the hulk. Two, buffeted by wind and spray, must hold the wheel on the short quarter-deck that lifted them above the shelter of the bulwarks. Forward of this, the water rolled about, washing on board and pouring out. The men could not for a moment slack their watchfulness. Sweating and straining at the spokes, they must hold her straight. To let her sheer when she crossed a comber's top would break the rope.

The strain on the laboring engines indicated that the men held out and Lister fixed his thoughts on his machinery. One could not see much, but while he turned the valve-wheel he listened. If a bearing got hot or a brass shook loose, he would hear the jar. An engine running as it ought to run was like a well-tuned instrument.

He heard no discord. The heavy thud of the cross-heads, flashing between their guides, beat time to the clang of the valve-gear, a pump throbbed like a kettledrum, and something tinkled like a high-pitched triangle. All went well, the engines were good and *Terrier* stubbornly forged ahead.

By and by the strain was less marked. The load was getting lighter and after a time Lister let go the wheel and wiped his wet face. He could stand on the platform without support, the plunges were easy and regular. Calling a man to relieve him, he went to the door.

The sea was white, but it no longer ran in crested ridges and a vague dark line crossed the foam ahead. Sometimes part of the line vanished and reappeared like a row of dots with broad gaps between. Lister knew it was breakwater. On the other side anchor-lights tossed, and in the background a dull, reflected illumination indicated a town. Then the gong rang and Lister went back to the platform. In a few minutes he would get the signal to stop his engines. The first struggle was over; Brown had made Holyhead.

CHAPTER II

THE WRECK

The night was calm, but now and then a faint, hot wind blew from the shadowy coast, and rippling the water, brought a strange, sour smell. Lister did not know the smell; Brown knew and frowned, for he had been broken by the malaria that haunts West African river mouths. Heavy dew dripped from the awnings on *Terrier's* bridge and in places trickled through the material, since canvas burns in the African sun. Brown searched the dark coast with his glasses, trying to find the marks he had noted on the chart. Lister leaned against the rails and mused about the voyage.

They had ridden out a winter's gale in the Bay of Biscay and for a night had lost the hulk and the men on board. Then they went into Vigo, where Lister's firemen wrecked a wine shop and it cost him much in bribes to save them from jail. He had another taste of their quality at Las Palmas, where they made trouble with the port guards and Brown brawled in the cheap wine shops behind the cathedral. In fact, it was some relief when the captain fell off the steam tram that runs between town and port, and a cut on his head stopped his adventures.

Then they steamed for fourteen-hundred miles before the Northeast Trades, with a misty blue sky overhead and long, white-topped seas rolling up astern. The Trade breeze was cool and bracing, but they lost it near the coast, and now the air was hot and strangely heavy. One felt languid and cheerfulness cost an effort. The men had begun to grumble and Lister was glad the voyage was nearly over and it was time to get to work.

Lightning flickered on the sea, touching the back of the smooth swell, and then for a few moments left all very dark. The moon was new, the sky was cloudy, and the swell ran high, for it rolled, unbroken and gathering momentum, from the Antarctic ice. When the lightning was bright, one saw a low cloud that looked like steam, with a white streak beneath that marked the impact of the big rollers on the sandy coast. The crash of breakers came out of the dark, like the rattle of a goods train crossing an iron bridge.

"Four fathoms at spring tides, and a shifting channel!" Brown remarked, quoting from a pilot-book. "The depth, however, varies with the wind, and a stranger must use caution when entering the lagoon." He stopped, and laughed as he resumed: "If this was a sober undertaking I'd steam off and wait for daylight."

"I reckon it would be prudent," said Lister dryly.

"We have nothing to do with prudence," Brown rejoined. "Our job's to work in a sun that knocks a white man down, and stew in the hot malaria damp the land breeze brings off at night. Cartwright's orders are to lose no time and I want to finish before the fever finishes me. Very well! When the moon is new, high-water's at twelve o'clock, and along this coast sunset's about six hours later. If we wait for noon-to-morrow, it will be four or five o'clock before we get on board the wreck—I understand the tide doesn't leave her until about four hours' ebb. If we push across the bar to-night, we'll see her at daybreak and can make our plans for getting to work."

Lister agreed. Expenses were heavy and it was important they should not lose a day. Moreover, Cartwright had hinted that he expected them to run risks, and Lister had promised Barbara to help him out. If Brown touched bottom steaming in, tug and barge would soon break up; but Lister was not going to be daunted.

"I'll go down and raise some extra steam," he said. "You'll need full pressure to shove her through the surf."

He was occupied for some time, but when a plume of steam blew from the escape-pipe he came up to the door and looked about. *Terrier's* languid roll was getting sharper; mast and funnel swung into a wide sweep. Sometimes the dark hull lurched up high above the tug's stern, and sometimes sank in a hollow. The rollers had angry white tops, and a belt of filmy vapor that looked luminous closed the view ahead. Lister knew the vapor was phosphorescent spray, flung up by the turmoil on the bar, through which they must go. If the tug struck and stopped, the white seas would beat her down into the sand. In the meantime, she was using full steam, because, since tide and surf carried her on, one must have speed to steer.

The spray cloud got thick, and wavered with luminous tremblings when the long rollers broke. They came up, spangled with green and gold flashes, from astern, shook their fiery crests about the tug, and vanished ahead, but one heard them crash. Lister thought the tug throbbed to the savage concussion. He could not hear his engines; one heard nothing but the daunting uproar.

By and by he felt a shock; not a violent shock, but as if the boat had touched, and was pushing through, something soft. She slowed and Lister saw the black hulk swing up and ride forward on a giant roller's top. It looked as if she were coming on board the tug, and Lister jumped through and slammed the iron door. Brown would need him now.

He heard the roar of water on deck, there was a crash of broken glass, and a shower fell on his head. A cloud of steam and a loud hissing came from the stokehold, and he knew the sea that swept the tug had covered the gratings. If she stuck, the next sea would swamp her and drown the fires, but she had not altogether stopped. The propeller was beating hard and he opened the throttle wide. He felt her move and tremble, as if she struggled in the grip of the sand, and then lift buoyantly. The water that pressed her down had rolled off the deck and the oncoming comber had picked her up and was carrying her along.

Her progress was obvious. One felt the headlong rush, and Lister thought about a toboggan speeding down an icy slope. The roller would bear her on until it broke, but if she struck the sand she might not lift again. She did not strike; there was another wild leap forward, a savage plunge, and a comber crashed astern. It looked as if she had crossed the shoal and Lister let go the wheel and got his breath. He had used no effort, but he gasped and his hand shook.

The gong signaled *half-speed*, and when he slowed his engines the roar of escaping steam pierced the turmoil of the surf. This was significant, because he could not have heard the steam a few minutes earlier. *Terrier* rolled, but the rolling was not violent and began to get easy. The gong signaled *stand by, stop*; he shut the valve and presently heard the anchor plunge and the rattle of running chain. Then *Terrier* swung languidly and all was quiet but for the monotonous rumble in the background. Lister gave some orders and went to his room.

In the morning, he put a greasy jacket over his pajamas and went on deck. The land breeze had dropped and it was very calm. Vague trees loomed in the fog that hid the beach; there was a belt of dull, heaving water, and then the spray cloud closed the view. The air was heavy, the men on deck moved slackly, and Lister's skin was wet by sweat. He felt dull and shrank from effort, but when he saw Brown in a boat alongside he jumped on board.

The light was getting brighter and the wreck lay about a hundred yards off. The stump of her broken funnel, a bare iron mast, a smashed deckhouse, and a strip of slanted side rose from the languid swell. The rows of plates were red with rust and encrusted by shells. When the smooth undulations sank, long weed swung about in the sandy water. Lister thought the story of the wreck was, on the surface, plain. Steaming out with a heavy load, *Arcturus* had struck the bar. The surf had beaten in her hatches, broken some plates, and afterwards washed her back across the sand. Then, while the captain tried to reach the beach, she had sunk in deeper water. The story was plausible, but, if Cartwright had found the proper clew, it did not account for all.

They rowed round *Arcturus*. She lay with a sharp list and her other side was under water. The tide was beginning to rise and when it crept up her slanted deck they pulled back to the tug.

"We'll moor the hulk alongside and rig the diving pumps. I think that's all to-day," Brown remarked. "When the sun is low I'll go to the factory up the creek and try to hire some native boys. On this coast, a white man who does heavy work soon gets fever."

In the afternoon they took two men and rowed up a muddy creek that flowed into the lagoon, but the factory was farther than they thought and when they landed dusk was falling. The white-washed wooden house stood near the bank, with a stockaded compound between it and the water. It was built on piles and at the top of the outside stairs a veranda ran along the front. The compound was tunneled by land-crabs' holes, and light mist crept about the giant cotton woods behind. There was no movement of air, a sickly smell rose from the creek, and all was very damp.

Lister and Brown went up the stairs and were received by a white man in a big damp room. A lamp hung from a beam and the light touched the patches of mildew on the discolored walls. There was not much furniture; a few canvas chairs, a desk and a table. Flies crawled about the table and hovered in a black swarm round the lamp. The room smelt of palm oil and river mud. The white man was young, but his face was haggard and he looked worn. His rather long hair was wet and his duck jacket was dirty. It was obvious that he did not bother about his clothes.

"Good of you to look me up! I expect you know I'm Montgomery; the house is Montgomery and Raeburn," he said. "However, to begin with, you had better have a drink. I'll call my boy."

A negro came in and got a bottle and some glasses. He was a strongly-built fellow with a blue stripe on his forehead, and muscular arms and chest, but his legs, which stuck out from short cotton trousers, were ridiculously thin. He beat up some frothy liquor in a jug and when he filled the big glasses Lister felt disturbed, for he knew Brown and had noted the quantity of gin the negro used. The captain, however, was cautious and they began to talk. Lister asked Montgomery if he carried on the factory alone.

"I'm doing so for a time. My clerk died two or three weeks since and I haven't got another yet."

"Fever?" said Brown.

"Common malaria. Perhaps this spot is worse than others, because, although we're beginning to kill mosquitos and poison the drains, we can't keep English boys. The last two didn't hold out six months."

Lister got thoughtful. He knew the African coast was unhealthy, but had not imagined it was as bad as this. He said nothing and Montgomery resumed: "I have been forced to lie up and am shaky yet. Malaria gets us all, but as a rule it gets strangers, particularly the young, soonest. Looks as if the microbe liked fresh blood."

"If I was an African merchant, I'd let an agent run my factories," Brown remarked.

Montgomery smiled. "Sometimes it's necessary for me to come out. This factory is perhaps our best, and when Nevis, our agent, died, I started by the first boat. Montgomery's is an old house, but since the big men combined and the Amalgamation built a factory on the next creek, we have had some trouble to pull along. Our capital is small and we can't use up-to-date methods. In fact, I imagine our situation is much like Cartwright's. When he bought the wreck he no doubt felt some strain. But won't you take another drink?"

Brown indicated his glass, which still held some liquor, and Lister refused politely. He noted that Montgomery knew their object and was surprised, since he thought Cartwright had not talked much about the undertaking. Then, although Montgomery was obviously ill, one felt he tried to paint the coast in the darkest colors.

"What do you think about our job?" Brown asked.

"I think it a rash experiment and imagine Cartwright agrees. All the same, the old fellow's a bold gambler and is perhaps willing to speculate on the chance of getting out of his embarrassments. However, this is his business and you'll, no doubt, get your wages, although you won't float the wreck."

"What do you reckon the obstacles?"

"Fever," said Montgomery dryly. "The salvage people lost some men. Surf will wash the sand about her, if the wind comes fresh from the south-east. Then the sharks may give you some trouble. They're nearly as numerous as they are at Lagos Roads." He paused and added carelessly: "I expect you know my father loaded *Arcturus*?"

"I heard something about it," Brown replied. "All the same, Cartwright sent us to lift her and we have got to try. Will you let me hire some of your factory boys?"

"Sorry, but they're Liberian Kroos, engaged on a twelve-months' contract to work in my compound, and I'm accountable for them to the Liberian government."

"Then what about boys from the bush?"

Montgomery smiled. "I can't recommend the bushmen. They're a turbulent lot, but you might send a present to the headman at the native town up river, and it's possible he'll let you go to see him. For all that, some caution's indicated. The fellow's a cunning old rascal."

Brown looked thoughtful, but began to talk about something else and by and by got up. Montgomery went with him and Lister to the steps and when they reached the compound they found the sailors bemused with gin under the veranda. Brown had some trouble to get the men on board, and when they awkwardly pulled away Lister was conscious of relief.

"I agree with the fellow. Caution *is* indicated," Brown observed.

CHAPTER III

A FUEL PROBLEM

A few days after his visit to the factory, Lister sat one morning under a tarpaulin they had stretched across the hulk. The paint on the canvas smelt as if it burned, but the awning gave some shade and one could not front the sun on the open deck. The sea breeze had not sprung up and dazzling reflections played about the oily surface of the swell. In one place, where the shadow of the wreck fell, the water was a cool, dull green.

A row of bubbles slowly crossed the belt of shade, stopped and made a frothy patch, and then lengthened out. A flexible pipe slipped across the edge of the open gangway, and Lister felt the line he held. The line was slack and he knew the diver needed nothing. Two half-naked men, their skins shining with sweat, turned the air-pumps handles, and the rattle of the cranks cut the dull rumble of the surf. Brown, sitting on a tool-box, studied a plan of the wreck Cartwright had given him, and Lister thought it typical Cartwright had got the plan. The old fellow was very keen.

By and by Brown looked up and indicated the panting men.

"We want colored boys for this job and must get a gang. I expect you noted Montgomery declared his lot were Kroos. The Kroos are hefty boys and pretty good sailors, but they come from Liberia and there are regulations about their employment. You must engage them on a contract, hold yourself accountable for their return and so forth. All the same my notion is, Montgomery didn't mean to help."

"Then we had better try the native headman he talked about."

Brown smiled, "I've no use for bushmen, but didn't see much use in telling Montgomery I'd been on the Coast before. For one thing, his boys were not all Kroos. You know the Kroo by his blue forehead-stripe, but I saw two or three with another mark. Thought them Gold Coast Fantis, and a Fanti fisherman is useful on board ship. In a day or two I'm going back to see."

Lister lighted his pipe and weighed the captain's remarks. On the whole, he agreed that it did not look as if Montgomery meant to help. The fellow was hospitable, but hospitality that implied his pressing liquor on the captain and making the sailors drunk had drawbacks. Brown had used control, but Lister doubted if his resolution would stand much strain. Then, although Montgomery's story about the need for his being on the spot was plausible, it was, perhaps, strange the head of a merchant house would stop for some time at a factory where his clerks died. However, now Lister thought about it, Montgomery did not state if he had been there long.

"The fellow was generous with his liquor and his boy can mix a cocktail," he remarked.

Brown grinned. "On the Coast, they're all generous with liquor. Montgomery knows this; but I've a notion you are wondering whether he knows me. I reckon not, but he knows the kind of skipper you generally meet in the palm oil trade. Still the type's going out; now ship-owners pay higher, they get better men. In fact, I'm something of a survival from the old school."

He picked up the plan and Lister thought about Montgomery. The man was ill and highly-strung, but this was not strange. The factory was rather a daunting spot; reeking with foul smells and haunted by a sense of gloom. Lister thought one might get morbid and imaginative if one stopped there long. Yet he rather liked Montgomery; there was something attractive about him. Perhaps if they had met in brighter surroundings, when the other's health and mood were normal, they might have been friends. Now, however, he doubted and saw Brown was not satisfied.

The line he held jerked and he signed to the men at the pump. One kept the cranks turning; the other went to the top of a ladder lashed to the hulk's side. The bubbles moved away from the wreck and broke the surface in a fixed, sparkling patch. The diver was coming up and Lister presently helped him on board. When they had taken off his copper helmet and unfastened his canvas he leaned against the pump and breathed hard.

"Well?" said Brown, after waiting a minute or two for the man to get back his normal breathing.

"She lies with a sharp list; sand's high up her starboard bilge. Engine-room doors jambed, but I found the stokehold grating and got some way down the ladder. Sand's washed down and buried the starboard bunkers. To clear out the stuff will be a long job."

"Packed hard?"

The diver nodded. "Like cement! I reckon the pump won't move it."

Lister understood the captain's frown. Sometimes the sand that enters a sunken vessel solidifies, with the pressure of surf or tide, into a mass that one can hardly dig out. This, however, was not all.

"Starboard bunkers buried?" Brown resumed. "They were pretty full. When she left Forcados she had a list to port, and they trimmed her by using the coal on that side first. Well, it's awkward! I reckoned on getting the fuel!"

"There is some coal on the port side," said Lister.

"If Cartwright's plan and notes are accurate, there's not enough to see us out. The wrecking pump will burn a lot," Brown rejoined and turned to the diver. "Did you see any sharks?"

"One big fellow; he hung about as if he was curious and I didn't like him near my air-pipe, but he left me alone. The pulps you meet in warm seas are worse than sharks. When I was down at the Spanish boat, crawling through the holes in her broken hull was nervous work. Once I saw an arm as thick as mine waving in the dark, and started for the ladder. We blew in that piece of her bilge with dynamite before I went on board again. However, when I've cleared up a bit, I'll take Mr. Lister down."

The diver got into the boat and rowed to the tug, but the others stopped in the shade of the awning. They had brought a spare diving dress, and before they tried to lift the wreck Lister must find out if Cartwright's supposition was correct, because if Cartwright had found the proper clew the job would be easier. For all that, Lister frankly shrank from the preparatory exercise. Diving in shark-haunted water had not much charm.

In the morning they hauled the tug alongside the wreck and at low-water rigged a derrick and opened the fore hatch. The palm kernels had rotted and a horrible pulpy mass, swollen by fermentation, rose nearly to the ledge. It was glutinous and too thick for the pump to lift, since the water that filled the vessel drained away through the broken plates as the tide sank. Brown, kneeling on the hatch-coaming, knitted his brows.

"The stuff's water-borne, forced up by its buoyancy," he said. "We may find it looser as we get down. In the meantime, suction's no use; we have got to break it out by hand. Start your winch and we'll fill the skip."

Lister signaled a man on board the tug, the winch rattled, and a big iron bucket, hanging by a wire rope, dropped into the hold. A gang of men climbed across the ledge and began to cut the slimy mass with spades. The surface heaved beneath them like a treacherous bog and the smell was horrible. Now and then a spade made an opening for the gases to escape and the nauseated men were driven back. For all that, they filled the skip and the swinging derrick carried the load across the deck and tilted it overboard.

The heat was almost unbearable, the reflections from the oily swell and wet deck hurt one's eyes, and Lister noted that the deck did not dry until the sea breeze began to blow. The wind brought a faint coolness and drove back the smell, but the men's efforts presently got slack. The labor was exhausting and one must wear some clothes because the sun burned one's skin. They held out until the rising water drove them from the hatch and when they went back to the tug Brown looked thoughtful.

"The men can't keep it up; the thing's impossible! A week like this would knock out the lot," he said. "We must use native boys and I'm going to get some."

In the morning Lister took his first diving lesson, and when the big copper helmet was screwed on and the air began to swell his canvas clothes, he shrank from the experiment. The load of metal he carried was crushing, he could hardly drag his weighted boots across the deck, and at the top of the ladder he hesitated, watching the bubbles that marked the spot where the diver had vanished. Then he remembered his promise to Barbara and cautiously went down.

The dazzling sunshine vanished, a wave of misty green closed above the helmet glass, hot compressed air blew about his head, and his ear-drums began to throb. Then lead and copper lost their weight; he felt buoyant and clung to the steps. At the bottom he was for a few moments afraid to let go, but an indistinct, monstrous object came out of the strange green gloom and beckoned him on. Lister went, making an effort for balance, because he now felt ridiculously light. Then the reflections were puzzling, for the light came and went with the rise and fall of the swell. Yet he could see and he followed the diver until they stopped opposite the wreck's port bilge. Her side went up like a dark wall, covered by waving weed.

Lister's head ached and his breathing was labored, but not much pressure was needed to keep out the shallow water and the diver had promised to warn him when they had stayed long enough. He forced himself to examine the plate the other indicated. *Arcturus* was a butt-strapped vessel and a number of the straps had burst. Plates were smashed and some of the holes were large, but in places the iron was drilled and in others patches had been bolted on. The salvage company had done part of this work and he thought it possible to make the damage good. If they could stop the remaining holes, the big pump ought to throw out the water; but Cartwright had talked about another opening and this would be awkward to reach.

Signing the diver to go on, he followed him round the vessel's stern. The sand on the other side was high and one could climb on board, but Lister shrank from the dark alleyway that led to the engine-room. For all that, he went in and saw the diver had opened the jambed door. When he reached the ledge a flash from the other's electric lamp pierced the gloom and he tried to forget his throbbing head and looked about.

Sparkling bubbles from his and the diver's helmets floated straight up to the skylights, along which they glided and vanished through a hole in the glass. The water, moving gently with the pulse of the swell, broke the beam of light and objects it touched were distorted and magnified. The top of the big low-pressure cylinder looked gigantic, and the thick columns appeared to bend. Long weed clung to the platforms, from which iron ladders went down, but so far as Lister could distinguish, all below was buried in sand.

He had seen enough. To clear the engines would be a heavy task, and one must work in semi-darkness amidst a maze of ladders, gratings, and machinery. To keep signal-line and air-pipe free from entanglement looked impossible, but perhaps when they had broken the surface the pump would lift the sand. Anyhow, he was getting dizzy and his breath was labored.

He touched the diver and they went back along the alleyway and round the vessel's stern. Lister was desperately anxious to reach the ladder and it cost him an effort to use control. As he went up his dress got heavy and he was conscious of his weighted boots. The pressure on his lungs lessened, he was dazzled by a strong light, and feeling the edge of the hulk's deck, he got his knee on her covering-board and lurched forward. Somebody took off his helmet and lifted the weight from his chest. He shut his eyes and for a few moments lay on the deck.

"Well?" said Brown presently. "You reached the engine-room?"

Lister nodded. "She's badly sanded up. It's plain we shan't get much coal from the starboard bunkers until we can lift her to an even keel."

"That will be long," Brown rejoined and pondered. "We must have coal," he resumed. "If I can't find another plan, you must take the tug to Sierra Leone and bring a load; but we'll let it go just now. The first thing is to hire some negro laborers, and as soon as I can leave the wreck I'll try again."

CHAPTER IV

MONTGOMERY'S OFFER

High-water was near and a trail of smoke, creeping up along the coast, streaked the shining sea. Brown watched the smoke until two masts and a funnel rose out of the vapor and began to get distinct. Then he put down his glasses and lighted his pipe. The steamer was making for the lagoon.

He had not long since gone to the native town up the creek and returned with a gang of laborers. So far, the negroes had worked well, but just now he did not need them and they lay about in the shade, some wearing a short waist-cloth and some a sheet of cotton that hung from their shoulders. The tide had covered the wreck, but the big rotary pump was running and, since the men had loosened the top of the cargo, it lifted the slimy stuff.

A plume of steam that looked faint and diaphanous in the strong light blew away from the noisy machine. A large flexible pipe rose from the submerged hold and another ran from the pump across the hulk's deck. From the end of the pipe a thick, brown flood poured into the water and stained the green lagoon as the flood tide carried it along. The clash and rattle of the engine carried far, for the load was heavy and Lister was using full steam. The boiler was large and the furnace burned more coal than he had thought. Sometimes palm kernels that had not altogether rotted jambed the fans, and he held the valve-wheel, trying to ease the shocks, while the perspiration dripped from his blistered skin. When Brown indicated the steamer he looked up.

"She's coming in; I think I know the hooker," the captain remarked. "Shallow-draught, coasting tank; goes anywhere she'll float for twenty tons of freight. The skipper, no doubt, expects Montgomery's got a few hogsheads of oil, and it's possible he'll sell us some coal. The parcels-vanners are pretty keen to trade."

"We want coal," said Lister and turned abruptly.

The pump jarred and stopped, the swollen suction pipe shrank, and the splash of the discharge died away. For some time Lister was occupied and when he restarted the engine and looked about again the steamer was steering for the hulk. She was a small vessel, going light, with much of her rusty side above water. A big surf-boat hung, ready for lowering, at her rail and a wooden awning covered her bridge-deck. When the throb of her engines slackened two or three white men leaned over her bulwarks and looked down at the hulk with languid curiosity. Their faces were haggard and their poses slack. The stamp of the fever-coast was plain.

The telegraph rang, the engines stopped, and a man on the bridge shouted: "Good morning! You have taken on an awkward job!"

His voice was hollow and strained, and by contrast Brown's sounded full and hearty.

"We're getting ahead all the same. Where are you for?"

"*Sar* Leone, after we call at Montgomery's."

"Then you can fill your bunkers, and our coal's getting short. Can you sell us some?"

The other asked how much Brown wanted and how much he would pay. Then he beckoned a man on the deck to come up, and turned to Brown again.

"We might give you two or three surf-boat loads, but I'll see you when we come back. We must get up the creek and moor her before the tide ebbs."

He seized the telegraph handle, the propeller began to turn, and when the steamer forged ahead Brown looked thoughtful.

"Perhaps I'd better take a trip up the creek in the evening. We want the coal and I don't altogether trust Montgomery," he said.

Lister agreed that it might be prudent for Brown to go, but he was occupied by the pump and they said no more. To lift the cargo when the water covered the wreck's hatches and loosened the pulpy mass was easier and he must keep his engine running full speed. When they stopped he was exhausted by the heat and the strain of watching and did not go with Brown.

The captain did not, as he had promised, come back in the morning, but after a time a smoke-trail streaked the forest and the steamer moved out on the lagoon. Lister sent a boy for the glasses, since he expected Brown was on board, but so far as he could see, the captain was not. The white wave at the bows indicated that the vessel was steaming fast and it did not look as if she was going to stop. In order to reach the channel across the bar, she must pass near the hulk, and Lister waved to the captain.

"What about the coal?" he shouted.

The other leaned out from the rails and Lister, studying him with the glasses, saw a small patch, like sticking plaster, on his forehead. The side of his face was discolored, as if it were bruised, and frowning savagely, he shook his fist.

"You can go to *Sar* Leone or the next hottest spot for your coal!" he roared and began to storm.

Lister had sometimes disputed with Western railroad hands and marine firemen, but he thought the captain's remarks equaled the others' best efforts. In fact, it was some relief when a lump of coal, thrown by a sailor on the hulk, crashed upon the wooden awning, and for a moment the savage skipper paused. For all that, Lister stopped the sailor, who was going to throw another block.

"Hold on! The stuff is valuable!" he said.

The captain began again, but the steamer had forged ahead, and his voice got fainter and was presently drowned by the beat of the screw. Lister went back to the pump. The machine was running unevenly and sometimes the powerful engine jarred. He meant to take it down, but so long as the pump sucked up the kernels he durst not stop. Speed was important; they must finish the job and get away before the heat and malaria wore them out. In the meantime, he was disturbed about Brown, who ought to have returned, and at sunset he started for the factory in the tug's second boat.

Dark came suddenly and when he landed a hot, clammy fog thickened the gloom. Little fires the factory boys had lighted by ancient custom twinkled in the haze and a yellow beam from the veranda windows touched the towering cottonwoods, but all else was dark and the spot was somehow forbidding. One felt the gloom was sinister. A few miles up the creek, the naked bushmen served their savage gods with fantastic rites and the Ju-Ju men and Ghost Leopards ruled the shadowy land. At the factory white men got sick and died.

Lister went up the steps, and entering the big room, saw Montgomery in a Madeira chair. His face was wet by sweat, but although his thin form was covered by a blanket he shook with ague. Brown occupied a rude couch, made from two long boxes in which flintlock guns are shipped. He lay in an ungainly pose, his head had fallen from a cushion, and his face was dark with blood. His eyes were shut and he breathed with a snoring noise.

"What's the matter with the captain?" Lister asked, although he thought he knew.

"He's exhausted by his efforts and the worse for liquor," Montgomery answered with a laugh. "On the whole, I think you had better let him sleep. Perhaps you remarked that some of the glass is broken and two of my chairs are smashed!"

Lister had not remarked this, but he looked about and began to understand. He had seen Brown throw a Spanish landlord out of a Grand Canary wine shop.

"Your captain arrived when the steamboat men were dining with me," Montgomery resumed. "In this country we're a hospitable lot and it's the custom to send West African factories a supply of liquor every three months. Mine arrived not long since, and if you open the cupboard you'll see how much is left. But there are cigarettes in the tin box; they mildew unless they're canned. Make yourself a cocktail. I don't want to get up and my boy's in the compound, playing a drum to keep off the ghosts."

Lister lighted a cigarette and listened. A monotonous, rhythmic throb stole into the room, and he felt there was something about the noise that jarred.

"I'll cut out the cocktail. You're rather generous with your liquor," he remarked dryly. "But how did the trouble Brown made begin?"

"By a dispute about some coal."

"Ah!" said Lister, who looked at Montgomery hard.

He imagined the steamboat captain had meant to give them coal, since the man had agreed with Brown about the price. In fact, it looked as if he had been willing to do so, until he arrived at the factory. Then he refused, and Brown, no doubt, got savage.

Montgomery was not embarrassed and indicated the unconscious skipper.

"If Cartwright's not losing his keenness, it's strange he sent out a man like this, but perhaps he couldn't get a sober captain to go."

"Brown has some talents. For example, he got the boys we wanted, although you refused to help."

"We must see if he can keep them!" Montgomery rejoined, with a meaning smile. "In the meantime, it's not important. Are you making much progress at the wreck?"

Lister admitted that they were not getting on as fast as he had hoped, and when Montgomery gave him a keen glance tried to brace himself. He felt slack and his head ached. He had been getting slack recently, and now, when he imagined he must be alert, to think was a bother.

"You have not been long at the lagoon, but you're beginning to feel the climate," the other remarked. "It's perhaps the unhealthiest spot on an unhealthy coast, and a white man cannot work in the African sun. However, you know why the salvage company threw up their contract. They lost a number of their men and if you stay until the morning you can see their graves. The rest of the gang had had enough and were too sick to keep the pump running."

"You are not encouraging," Lister observed.

"I don't exaggerate. I know the country and the caution one must use, but you see I'm ill."

The thing was obvious. Montgomery's hollow face was wet by sweat, his eyes were dull, and his hands shook. Lister saw he tried to be cool, but thought him highly strung.

"If you're wise, you'll give up your post and get away before fever knocks you out," Montgomery resumed. "In fact, I think I can promise you another berth. The house owns two or three factories and at one we are going to start a big oil-launch running to a native market up river. Then we have bought new machinery for breaking palm nuts and extracting the kernels and have fixed a site for the building at a dry, sandy spot. I don't claim the neighborhood's healthy, but it's healthier than this, and we have inquired about an engineer. Would you like the post?"

"I think not. I'm Cartwright's man. I've taken his pay."

Montgomery smiled ironically. "Let's be frank! I expect you want to force me to make a high bid. You don't know the African coast yet, but you're not a fool and are beginning to understand the job you have undertaken. You can't float the wreck; the fellow Cartwright sent to help you is a drunken brute, and I have grounds for thinking Cartwright, himself, will soon go broke. Well, we need an engineer and I'll admit we have not found good men keen about applying. If you can run the launch and palm-nut plant, we'll give you two hundred pounds bonus for breaking your engagement, besides better wages than Cartwright pays."

Lister knitted his brows and lighted a fresh cigarette. He was not tempted, but he wanted to think and his brain was dull. To begin with, he wondered whether Montgomery did not think him something of a fool, because it was plain the fellow had grounds for offering a bribe. His doing so indicated that he did not want the wreck floated. Anyhow, Montgomery had imagined he would not hesitate to break his engagement for two hundred pounds. He must be cautious and control his anger.

"On the whole, it wouldn't pay me to turn down Cartwright's job," he said. "Two hundred pounds is not a very big wad, and if we can take the boat home I reckon the salvage people would give me a good post. I must wait until I'm satisfied the thing's impossible."

"When you are satisfied I'll have no object for engaging you. We want an engineer now," Montgomery replied.

"Well," said Lister, "I reckon that is so." He paused, and thinking he saw where the other led, resolved to make an experiment. "All the same, since you are willing to buy me off, it looks as if we had a fighting chance to make good. Then, if I am forced to quit, I rather think you'd pay me something not to talk. For example, if I put Cartwright wise—"

Montgomery gave him a scornful smile. "You're keener than I thought, but you can't tell Cartwright much he doesn't believe he knows. I'll risk your talking to somebody else."

"Oh, well," said Lister, "I guess we'll let it go. In the meantime, I'll get off and take the captain along. I allow you have fixed him pretty good but he put his mark on the steamboat man and your furniture."

He called the sailors, and finding the two who had brought Brown to the factory, carried him downstairs and put him on board the boat. The captain snored heavily and did not awake. When they pushed off, and with the other boat in tow drifted down the creek, Lister pondered.

He did not know if he had well played his part, but he had not wanted Montgomery to think his staunchness to his employer must be reckoned on; he would sooner the fellow thought him something of a fool. When Montgomery offered the bribe he probably knew he was rash; his doing so indicated that he was willing to run some risk, and this implied that Cartwright's supposition about the wreck was justified. Montgomery was obviously resolved she should not be floated and might be a troublesome antagonist. For example, he had stopped their getting coal and Lister was persuaded he had made Brown drunk. If the control the captain had so far used broke down, it would be awkward, since Montgomery would no doubt supply him with liquor.

It was plain the fellow meant to bother them as much as possible, but since he had not owned the wrecked steamer his object was hard to see. In the meantime, Lister let it go and concentrated on steering the boat past the mud banks in the creek.

CHAPTER V

MONTGOMERY USES HIS POWER

Some time after Lister went to the factory he woke one night from disturbed sleep. His small room under *Terrier's* bridge was very hot and the door and port were open. A faint draught blew in and the mosquito curtain moved about his bed. The tug rolled languidly and the water splashed against her side. Farther off the gentle swell broke with a dull murmur across the wreck.

This was all, but Lister was persuaded he had, when half awake, heard something else. At dusk a drum had begun to beat across the lagoon and the faint monotonous noise had jarred. It was typically African; the negroes used drums for signaling, although white men had not found out their code. Lister had come to hate all that belonged to the fever coast.

The drum, however, was not beating now, and he rather thought he had heard the splash of a canoe paddle. There was no obvious reason this should bother him, but he was bothered and after a few minutes got up and put on a thin jacket. On deck it was very hot and he felt the warmth of the iron plates through his slippers. In West Africa one puts on slippers as soon as one gets out of bed, for fear of the jigger insect that bores into one's foot. A gentle land breeze blew across the lagoon and the air was hot and damp like steam. Lister smelt river mud and aromatic forest.

There was no moon, but he saw the dark hull rise and fall, and the flash of phosphorescent foam where the swell washed across the deck. In the distance, the surf rumbled and now and then there was a peal of thunder. Lister wondered why he had left his berth. He was tired and needed sleep, for he had been occupied all day at the pump, which was not running well. Recently he had been conscious of a nervous strain and things that were not important annoyed him; then he often woke at night, feeling that some danger threatened.

Walking along the deck he found a white sailor sitting on the windlass drum. The man did not move until Lister touched his arm.

"Did you hear something not very long since, Watson?"

"No, sir," said the other with a start. "Now and then a fish splashed and she got her cable across the stem. Links rattled. That was all."

Lister thought the man had slept, but it was not important, since there was no obvious necessity for keeping anchor watch.

"Did you hear something, sir?" the other inquired.

"I don't know. I imagine I did!"

The sailor laughed, as if he understood. "A queer country; I've been here before! Beautiful, bits of it; shining surf, yellow sands, and palms, but it plays some funny tricks with white men. About half of them at the factories get addled brains if they stay long. Believe in things the bushmen believe, ghosts and magic, and such. Perhaps it's the climate, but on this coast you get fancies you get nowhere else. I'd sooner take look-out on the fo'cas'le in a North Sea gale than keep anchor watch in an African calm."

Lister nodded. He thought the man felt lonely and wanted to talk and he sympathized. There was something insidious and daunting about the African coast. He walked round the deck and then returning to his room presently went to sleep.

At daybreak he heard angry voices and going out found Brown storming about the deck. Two white sailors had come back in the boat from the hulk, with the news that the negroes berthed on board her had vanished in the night, except for three or four whom the sailors had brought to the tug. When Brown got cooler he went up to the men who squatted tranquilly on the hatch. They were big muscular fellows and wore, instead of the usual piece of cotton, ragged duck clothes.

"Where's the rest of the gang?" Brown asked.

"No savvy, sah," said one. "Some fella put them t'ing Ju-Ju on him and he lib for bush."

"What's a Ju-Ju?" Lister inquired.

"Hocus-pocus, magic of a sort," the captain growled. "When a white man knows much about Ju-Ju his proper place is an asylum." He turned to the boys. "How did them other fellows go?"

"No savvy, sah. We done hear not'ing."

"I expect they were afraid to meddle," Brown remarked, and resumed: "Why did you lib for stop?"

"We Accra boy; white man's boy. Them bushman him d—n fool too much. Run in bush like monkey, without him clo'es."

Brown knitted his brows and then made a sign of resignation. "I reckon it's all we'll know! Well, the tide's falling and we must shift for some kernels before the sun is hot. Better start your pump."

The pump was soon at work, and Lister, watching the engine, mused. He wondered how much the Accra boys knew, or if it was possible the others had stolen away without waking them. Watson, the look-out, had heard nothing, and Lister remembered Brown's remarks about the Ju-Ju and thought the boys did know something but were afraid to tell. Watson had said the country was queer, and if he meant fantastic, Lister agreed. There was something about it that re-acted strangely on one's imagination. In the North American wilds, one was, so to speak, a materialist and conquered savage Nature by using well-known rules. In Africa one did not know the rules and felt the power of the supernatural. It looked as if there was a mysterious, malignant force. But the pump was running badly and Lister saw he must not philosophize.

When the sun got hot he stopped for breakfast and afterwards he and Brown smoked for a few minutes under the awning.

"I'm bothered about the boys' going," the captain declared. "There's not much doubt Montgomery got somebody to put Ju-Ju on them; bribed a magician to frighten them by a trick. Since they're a superstitious lot, I reckon we can't hire another gang in this neighborhood. However, now he's stopped our coal, you'll have to go to *Sar* Leone, and may pick up some British Kroos about the port."

"Then I'd better go soon," said Lister. "The braces I bolted on the pump won't hold long; she rocks and strains the shaft when she's running hard. I must get a proper casting made at a foundry. Besides, the engine crosshead's worn and jumps about. I must try to find a forge and machine-shop."

"They've got something of the kind at *Sar* Leone; I don't know about a foundry," Brown replied. "Take Learmont to navigate, and start when you like. We'll shift the hulk to leeward of the wreck and she ought to ride out a south-east breeze."

Lister sailed a few days afterwards, and reaching Sierra Leone found nobody could make the articles he required. For all that, they must be got, and he resolved to push on for Grand Canary. The distance was long, he had not men enough for an ocean voyage, and would be lucky if he got back to the lagoon in three or four weeks, but if he could not mend the pump, the salvage work must stop. Lister knew when to run a risk was justified.

After he passed the Gambier, wind and sea were ahead, his crew was short, and he was hard pressed to keep the engine going and watch the furnaces. He slept when he could, in snatches, with his clothes on, and now and then used an exhausted fireman's shovel On the steamy African coast the labor and watchfulness would have worn him out, but the cool Trade breeze was bracing. Although he was thin, and got thinner, the lassitude he had felt at the lagoon vanished, and the fatigue he fought against was not the fatigue that kills.

In the meantime, *Terrier* pushed stubbornly north across the long, foam-tipped seas that broke in clouds of spray against her thrusting bows. She was swept by the sparkling showers, but the showers were warm, and the combers were not often steep enough to flood her deck. For all that, their impact slowed her speed. She must be driven through their tumbling crests, full steam was needed to overcome the shock, and the worn-out men moved down coal from the stack on deck to feed the hungry fires.

Lister's eyes ached from the glare of smoky lamps that threw puzzling lights about the machinery. After long balancing on slanted platforms, his back and legs were sore; his brows were knit in a steady frown, and his mouth was always firm. When the strain was over, he sometimes wondered what he thought about in the long, exhausting watches, but remembered nothing except his obstinate concentration on his task. The strange thing was, he did not think much about Barbara, although he was vaguely conscious that, for her sake, he must hold out. He meant to hold out. Perhaps his talents were not numerous, but he could handle engines, and when it was necessary he could keep awake.

At length, Learmont called him one morning to the bridge, and he leaned slackly against the rails. His eyes were dull, and for some hours he had breathed the fumes of burning tallow. A slide had given him trouble; he could keep the metal cool. On the bridge, however, the air was keen and sweet, and he felt the contrast. *Terrier* plunged and threw the spray about, but the seas were short, as if something ahead broke the wind. By and by Learmont indicated a lofty bank of mist.

"Teneriffe!" he said. "I was half-asleep when I took the sun, but my reckoning was not very far out."

Lister looked up. In the distance a sharp white cone, rising from fleecy vapor, cut the sky, and Lister, with dull satisfaction, knew the famous peak. Nearer the tug was another bank of mist, that looked strangely solid but ragged, as if it were wrapped about something with a broken outline. Some minutes afterwards a high, dark object like a mountain-top, loomed in the haze.

"Grand Canary!" Learmont remarked. "The range behind Las Palmas town. I expect the smudge ahead is the Isleta hill."

"We've made it!" Lister said hoarsely, and braced himself. Now the strain was gone, he felt very slack.

The sun rose out of the water, the mist began to melt, and rolling back, uncovered a line of surf and a belt of rough hillside. Then volcanic cliffs, a sandy isthmus, and a cluster of masts and funnels got distinct, and Lister fixed the glasses on a white stripe across a cinder hill. His hand shook, but he steadied the glasses and saw the stripe was a row of huge letters.

"... *ary Engineering Co* ..." he read.

His heart beat when he went below. Luck had given him a hard job, but he had put it across. Soon after *Terrier* arrived he went to the engineering company's office and the manager looked at him curiously. Then he gave Lister some wine and, after studying his drawings and patterns, said he could make the things required. Lister drove to the town, and going to a Spanish barber's, started when he saw his reflection in a glass. He had not shaved for long, and fresh water was scarce on board the tug. His face was haggard, the engine grime had got into his skin, and his eyes were red. He was forced to wait, and while the barber attended to other customers, he fell asleep in his chair. When he left the shop he went to a hotel and slept for twelve hours.

CHAPTER VI

LISTER MEETS AN OLD ANTAGONIST

The hotel Catalina, half-way between Las Palmas harbor and the town, was not crowded, and a number of the quests had gone to a ball at the neighboring Metropole. Barbara, going out some time after dinner, found the veranda unoccupied and sat down. Mrs. Cartwright was getting better and did not need her, and Barbara was satisfied to be alone. Her thoughts were disturbing, and trying to banish them for a few minutes, she looked about.

The veranda was long, and the lights from the hotel threw the shadow of the wooden pillars across the dusty grass. Barbara's figure was outlined in a dark silhouette. She did not wear a hat and, since the night was warm, had put nothing over her thin dinner dress. She looked slender and very young.

A strip of parched garden, where a few dusty palms grew, ran down to the road, across which the square block of the Metropole cut the shining sea. Steamers' lights swung gently against the dark background of the Isleta hill. Beyond the Metropole a white belt of surf ran back to the cluster of lights at the foot of the mountain that marked Las Palmas. One heard the languid rollers break upon the beach and the measured crash of surges on the reefs across the isthmus. Sometimes, when the throb of the surf sank, music came from the Metropole. A distant rattle indicated a steam-tram going to the port.

The long line across the harbor was the mole, and Barbara had thought the small steamer, lying near its end, like *Terrier*. There was nothing in the soft blue dark behind the mole until one came to the African coast. Then Barbara firmly turned her glance. In a sense, she had sent Lister to Africa, but she was not going to think about him yet. She must not think about him until she had weighed something else.

A few hours since she had got a jar. Walking in the town she saw a man whose figure and step she thought she knew. He was some distance off, and she entered a shop and bought a Spanish fan she did not want. Perhaps her disturbance was ridiculous, but the man was very like Shillito, and their meeting at the busy port was not impossible. Las Palmas was something like an important railway junction. Numerous steamers called, and passengers from all quarters, particularly South America and the West Indies, changed boats. Then Barbara understood that a fugitive from justice was safer in South and Central America than anywhere else. She wondered with keen anxiety whether the man had seen her.

She knew now she had not loved Shillito. He had cunningly worked upon her ignorance, discontent, and longing for romance. Illumination had come on board the train, but although she had found him out and escaped, she had afterwards felt herself humiliated and set apart from happy girls who had nothing to hide. The humiliation was not altogether earned, and the people who knew about her adventure were not numerous, but they were all the people for whom she cared. When she thought about it, she hated Louis Shillito.

The steam-tram stopped at the Metropole and went on to the port, trailing a cloud of dust. When the rattle it made began to die away, Barbara roused herself with a start from her moody thoughts. A man was coming up the path, and when he reached the steps she shrank back against the wall. The light from the hotel touched his face and she saw it was Shillito.

Anger conquered her shrinking, for Barbara had pluck and her temper was hot. When Shillito, lifting his hat, advanced, she got up and stood by a pillar. Her skin had gone very white, but her eyes sparkled and her hands were clenched. Shillito bowed and smiled.

"It looks as if I was lucky!" he remarked, and Barbara imagined his not finding Mrs. Cartwright about accounted for his satisfaction.

"I suppose you saw me in the *calle mayor*?" she said.

He nodded. "You went into a shop. Your object was pretty obvious. I allow it hurt."

Barbara gave him a scornful glance. "The statement's ridiculous! Do you imagine you can cheat me now, as you cheated me in Canada?"

"In one way, I did not cheat you. When I said I loved you, I was honest."

"I doubt it! All was dishonest from the beginning. You taught me deceit and made me ashamed for my shabbiness. For your sake I tricked people who loved and trusted me; but to you I was rashly sincere. I trusted you and was willing to give up much in order to marry you."

"You mean you thought you were willing, until you knew the cost?" Shillito rejoined. "Then you saw you couldn't make good and resolved to turn me down."

The blood came to Barbara's skin, but she fronted him steadily.

"I had *found you out*. Had you been something of the man I thought, I might have gone with you and helped to baffle the police; but you were not. You were very dull and played a stupid part. When you thought you had won and I was in your power, I knew you for a brute."

Shillito colored, but forced a smile. "Perhaps I was dull; I was desperate. You had kept me hanging round the summer camp when I knew the police were on my track; and I had been put wise they might hold up the train. A man hitting the trail for liberty doesn't use the manners of a highbrow carpet-knight. I reckoned you were human and your blood was red."

"Ah," said Barbara, "I was very human! Although I was afraid, I felt all the passion hate can rouse. You declared I must stay with you, because I durst not go back; I had broken rules and my fastidious relations would have no more to do with me. Something like that! In a sense, it wasn't true; but you said it with brutal coarseness. When I struck you I meant to hurt; I looked for something that would hurt—"

She stopped and struggled for calm. To indulge her anger was some relief, but she felt the man was dangerous and she must be cool. There was not much use in leaving him and going to her mother, because he would, no doubt, follow and disturb Mrs. Cartwright. It was unlucky her step-father had not arrived; he was coming out, but his boat was not expected for a day or two.

"Oh, well," said Shillito, "let's talk about something else. I didn't calculate to meet you at Las Palmas, but when I saw you in the *calle*, I hoped you might, after all, be kind for old times' sake. However, it's obvious you have no use for me, and if you are willing to make it easier, I'll pull out and leave you alone."

Barbara gave him a keen glance. She had known he wanted something.

"How can I make it easier for you to go?"

"You don't see? Well, I've had some adventures since you left me on board the train. I had money, but I'd waited too long to negotiate some of the bonds and my partner robbed me. I made San Francisco and found nothing doing there. Went down the coast to Chile and got fixed for a time at a casino, in which I invested the most part of my wad. One night a Chileno pulled his knife on another who cleaned him out, and when the police got busy the casino shut down. I pushed across for Argentina, but my luck wasn't good, and I made Las Palmas not long since on board an Italian boat. On the whole, I like the dagos, and reckoned I might try Cuba, or perhaps the Philippines—"

"A Lopez boat sails for Havana in two or three days," Barbara interrupted.

"That is so," Shillito agreed, smiling because he noted her relief. "The trouble is, I haven't much money. Five hundred pounds would help me along."

"You thought I would give you five hundred pounds?"

"Sure," said Shillito, coolly. "You're rich; anyhow, Mrs. Cartwright is rich, and I reckoned you would see my staying about the town has drawbacks. For one thing, the English tourists are a gossiping lot. It ought to pay you and your mother to help me get off."

Barbara tried to think. The drawbacks Shillito indicated were plain, and as long as he stayed at Las Palmas she would know no ease of mind, but she had not five hundred pounds, and Mrs. Cartwright must not be disturbed. Moreover, one could not trust the fellow. He might take the money and then use his power again. He had power to humiliate her, but unless she was willing to meet all his claims, she must resist some time.

"I imagine you put your importance too high," she said. "You can stay, if you like. I certainly will not bribe you to go away."

He studied her for a few moments; Barbara looked resolute, but he thought her resolution forced.

"Very well! Since I can't start for Cuba without money, I must find an occupation at Las Palmas, and I have a plan. You see, I know some Spanish and something about running a gambling joint. The people here are sports, and one or two are willing to put up the money to start a club that ought to attract the English tourists. If I found the thing didn't pay before you went back, I could quit and get after you."

"I think not," said Barbara, desperately. "If you came to England, a cablegram to the Canadian police—"

Shillito laughed. "You wouldn't send a cablegram! If I was caught I could tell a romantic story about the girl who helped me get off. No; I'm not going to bother about your putting the police on my trail!"

He turned his head and Barbara clenched her hand, for a rattle of wheels in the road broke off, as if a *tartana* had stopped at the gate. If the passengers from the vehicle were coming to the hotel she must get rid of Shillito before they arrived.

"You waste your arguments," she declared. "I will not give you money. If you come back, I will tell the *mayordomo* you are annoying me and he must not let you in."

"The plan's not very clever," Shillito rejoined. "If I made trouble for the hotel porters, the guests would wonder, and when people have nothing to do but loaf, they like to talk. I expect you'd find their curiosity awkward—" He paused and laughed when he resumed: "You're embarrassed now because somebody will see us!"

Barbara was embarrassed. A man was coming up the path, and she knew her figure and Shillito's cut against the light. When the stranger reached the veranda he would see she was disturbed; but to move back into the gloom, where Shillito would follow her, would be significant. She thought he meant to excite the other's curiosity.

The man stopped for a moment at the bottom of the steps and Barbara turned her head, since she imagined he would think she was quarreling with her lover. Then he ran up the steps, and when he stopped in front of Shillito her heart beat fast. It was Lister, and she knew he had remarked her strained look, for his face was very stern.

"Hallo!" he said. "Are you bothering Miss Hyslop again?" He glanced at Barbara. "I expect the fellow is bothering you?"

For a moment Barbara hesitated, but she had borne a heavy strain and her control was going. Besides, one could trust Lister and he knew ... She signed agreement and he touched Shillito.

"Get off the veranda!"

Shillito did not move. His pose was tense and he looked malevolent.

"You won't help Miss Hyslop by butting in like a clumsy fool. The thing's too delicate for you to meddle—"

"Get off the veranda!" Lister shouted, and threw Shillito back.

He was highly strung, and worn by want of sleep and exhausting labor, but he had some notion of all Barbara had borne on Shillito's account. Although perhaps caution and tact were indicated, he was going to use force. When Shillito struck him he seized the fellow, and rocking in a savage grapple, they fell with a crash against the rails. Lister felt the other's hand at his throat, and straining back, jerked his head away while he tried to lift his antagonist off the ground. He pulled him from the rails and they reeled across the veranda and struck the wall.

A neighboring window rattled with the shock, the heavy tramp of their feet shook the boards, and Barbara knew the noise would soon bring a group of curious servants to the door; besides, all the guests had not gone to the Metropole. Yet she could not meddle. The men's passions were unloosed; they fought like savage animals, driven by an instinctive fury that would not vanish until one was beaten. She looked on, trembling and helpless, while they wrestled, with swaying bodies and hands that felt for a firmer hold.

Her face was very white and she got her breath in painful gasps. There was something horribly primitive about the struggle, but it fascinated.

In the meantime, Lister was conscious that he had been rash. Shillito was muscular and fresh, but he was tired. It was plain he could not keep it up for long. Moreover, unless the fight soon ended, people would come to see what the disturbance was about. This would be awkward for Barbara; he wanted to tell her to go away, but could not. He was breathless and Shillito was trying to choke him.

Afterwards he knew he was lucky. They had got near the steps and he threw Shillito against the post at the top. The jar shook the other, his grasp got slack, and Lister saw that for a moment the advantage was his. Using a desperate effort he pushed his antagonist back and struck him a smashing blow. Shillito vanished and a crash in the gloom indicated that he had fallen on an aloe in a tub by the path. Lister leaned against the rail and laughed, because he knew aloe spikes are sharp.

Then he heard steps and voices in the hotel, and turned to Barbara. His face was cut, his hat was gone, and his white jacket was torn. He looked strangely savage and disheveled, but Barbara went to him and her eyes shone. Lister stopped her.

"Don't know if I've helped much, but you must get off!" he gasped. "People are coming. Go in by another door!"

He turned and plunged down the stairs, and Barbara, seeing that Shillito had vanished, ran along the veranda. A few moments afterwards she stood by the window of her room and saw a group of curious servants and one or two tourists in the path at the bottom of the steps. It looked as if they were puzzled, and the *mayordomo* gravely examined Lister's battered hat.

Barbara went from the window and sat down. She was horribly overstrained and wanted to cry, but she began to laugh, and for some minutes could not stop. She must get relief from the tension and, after all, in a sense, the thing was humorous.

CHAPTER VII

BARBARA'S REFUSAL

In the morning Barbara went to the Catalina mole. The short lava pier was not far off, and one got the breeze, although the hotel garden was hot. Besides, she did not want to meet people and talk about the strange disturbance on the veranda. On the whole, she thought nobody imagined she could satisfy the general curiosity. Finding a block of lava in the shade, she sat down and looked about.

A boat crossed the harbor mouth, swinging up on the smooth swell and vanishing when the undulations rolled by. A tug towed a row of barges to an anchored steamer, and the rattle of winches came down the wind. In the background, clouds of dust blew about the coaling wharfs, and a string of flags fluttered from the staff on the Isleta hill. Barbara beckoned a port-guard and inquired what the signal meant.

The Spaniard said an African mail-boat from England was coming in, and Barbara was conscious of some relief. Cartwright was on board and would arrive sooner than she had thought; the boat had obviously not called at Madeira, the time-bills stated. Cartwright would know how to deal with Shillito if he bothered her again. In the meantime she mused about Lister. She had thrilled when he ran up the steps at the hotel, but, in a sense, his arrival just then was awkward.

She turned her head, for the sunshine on the water dazzled her eyes, and the port was not attractive. The limekilns, coal-wharfs, and shabby lava houses had for a background volcanic rocks, bare cinder slopes and tossing dust. Besides, she wanted to think. She would see Lister soon; she wanted to see him, but she shrank. For one thing, the line she ought to take was hard.

By and by she heard a rattle of oars thrown on board a boat behind the neighboring wall; somebody shouted, and Lister came up. His white clothes were clean but crumpled, and Barbara smiled when she saw his hat was new. Crossing the lava pavement, he stopped opposite her and she noted a piece of sticking-plaster on his cheek.

"May I join you for a few minutes?" he asked.

"Of course," she said graciously.

Lister sat down. The sailors had gone off, and except for an officer of the *Commandancia*, nobody was about.

"I was going to the hotel to look for you. For one thing, I reckoned I ought to apologize. When I came into the veranda and saw Shillito—"

"I think you stopped for a moment at the bottom of the steps!" Barbara remarked.

He colored, but gave her a steady look. "That is so. I admit the thing's ridiculous; but at first I felt I'd better pull out. Then I noted something about your pose; you looked angry."

"Ah," said Barbara. "It was a relief to see I was angry? You were satisfied then?"

"I was really satisfied before. It was impossible you should engage a brute like that in friendly talk. Anyhow, I took the wrong line and might have made things awkward. In fact, the situation needed a lighter touch than mine. All the same, when I saw the fellow was bullying you—"

"You butted in?" Barbara suggested, smiling, although her heart beat.

"Like a bull moose," said Lister with a frown. "I ought to have kept cool, used caution, and frozen him off by a few short arguments. You can picture Cartwright's putting across the job! After all, however, I don't know the arguments I could have used, and I remembered how the fellow had injured you—"

He saw Barbara's color rise, and stopped for a moment. It looked as if he had not used much caution now.

"Since I thought you in Africa, I don't understand how you arrived," she began.

"The thing's not very strange," said Lister. "I saw your name in a visitors' list and meant to ask for you in the morning. Then I ran up against Shillito, who didn't know me, and when he got on board the steam tram, I hired a *tartana*. Thought he might mean trouble and I'd better come along—"

"Well," he resumed, "I'm sorry I handled the job clumsily, since I might have hurt you worse; but I hated the fellow on my own account and saw red. Perhaps it was lucky I was able to throw him down the steps, because I expect neither of us meant to quit until the other was knocked out." He paused and added, with a laugh: "Now I'm cool, I think the chances were I got knocked out. Last time we met he threw me off the car; I reckon my luck has turned!"

Barbara studied him and was moved by pity and some other emotions. He was very thin and his face was pinched. He looked as if he were exhausted by the work she had sent him to do. Barbara admitted that she had sent him. Before Cartwright planned the salvage undertaking she had declared he would find Lister the man for an awkward job.

"You ran some risk for my sake, and I must acknowledge a fresh debt," she said. "I would sooner be your debtor than another's, but sometimes I'm embarrassed. You see, I owe you so much."

"You have paid all by letting me know you," Lister declared.

She was quiet for a few moments, and then asked: "Are you making much progress at the wreck?"

"Our progress is slow, but we are getting there," Lister replied, and seeing her interest, narrated his and Brown's struggles, and his long voyage with a short crew on board the tug.

The story was moving and Barbara's eyes sparkled. Lister had borne much and done all that flesh and blood could do. He was the man she had thought, and she knew it was for her sake that he had labored.

"It's a splendid fight!" she said.

"We haven't won yet," he replied, and was quiet for a few moments. Then his look got very resolute and he went on: "All the same, if the thing is anyhow possible, I'm going to win. You see, I've got to win! When Cartwright engaged me I was engineer on board a cattle boat; a man of no importance, without friends or money, and with no particular chance of making good. Now I've got my chance. If we put across the job a big salvage company turned down, I'll make my mark. Somebody will give me a good post; I'll have got my foot on the ladder that leads to the top."

"I wish you luck," said Barbara. "I expect you will get near the top."

"If you are willing, you can help."

"Ah," said Barbara, with forced quietness, "I think not—"

He stopped her. "I didn't expect to find you willing. My business is to persuade you, and I mean to try. Well, I wasn't boasting, and my drawbacks are plain, but if I make good in Africa, some will be cut out and you can help me remove the others. I've long wanted you, and now my luck's turning. I was going to Catalina to tell you so. If Brown and I float *Arcturus*, will you marry me?"

Barbara's color came and went, but she said quietly: "When you came to the hotel in the evening you met Shillito!"

"I did," said Lister, with incautious passion. "If I had killed the brute I'd have been justified! However, I threw him on to the aloe tub and ran off. The thing was grotesquely humorous. A boy's fool trick!"

"You ran off for my sake," said Barbara. "I liked you for it. I like you for many things, but I will not marry you."

He saw she was resolute. Her mouth was firm and her hand was tightly closed. He thought he knew the grounds for her refusal, and his heart sank. Barbara was stubborn and very proud. Moreover, the situation was awkward, but the awkwardness must be fronted.

"Let's be frank; perhaps you owe me this," he urged. "Since you allow you do like me, what's to stop our marrying?"

"For one thing, my adventure in Canada," she replied and turned her head.

Lister put his hand on her arm and forced her to look up. "Now you're clean ridiculous! Shillito cheated you; he's a plausible wastrel, but you found him out. It doesn't count at all! Besides, nobody but your relations know."

"You know," said Barbara, and, getting up started along the mole.

Lister tried to brace himself, for he saw she could not be moved. Yet there was something to be said.

"You are the girl I mean to marry," he declared. "Some day, perhaps, you'll see you're indulging a blamed extravagant illusion and I'm going to wait. When you're logical I'll try again."

Barbara forced a smile. "Sometimes I am logical; I feel I'm logical now. But I have left my mother alone rather long and you must let me go."

Lister went with her to the road and got on a tram going to the town. He was hurt and angry, but not altogether daunted. Barbara's ridiculous pride might break and she was worth waiting for. When he returned on board, a small African liner had anchored not far off, and while he watched the boats that swarmed about the ship, one left the others and came towards the tug. The Spanish crew were pulling hard and a passenger occupied the stern. Learmont, lounging near, turned his glasses on the boat.

"I'm not sorry you are boss," he said. "The Old Man is coming!"

A few minutes afterwards Cartwright got over the tug's rail. His face was red, and he looked very stern.

"Why have you left the wreck?" he asked Lister.

"I came for some castings I couldn't get at Sierra Leone. The pump and engine needed mending."

"Then where's Brown?"

"He's busy at the lagoon, sir. There's enough to keep him occupied, unless the pump plays out before I get back."

Cartwright looked relieved, but asked meaningly: "Did you know Mrs. Cartwright and Miss Hyslop were at Las Palmas?"

"I did not know until yesterday evening, twenty-four hours after I arrived; but we'll talk about this again. I expect you want to know how we are getting on at the wreck?"

Cartwright nodded. "I think my curiosity is natural! Let's get out of the sun, and if you have liquor on board, order me a drink. When the mail-boat steamed round the mole and I saw *Terrier*, I got a nasty jolt."

Lister took him to the captain's room and gave him some sour red Canary wine. Cartwright drained his glass and looked up with an ironical smile.

"If you use stuff like this. Brown ought not to be tempted much! However, you can tell me what you have done at the lagoon, and the difficulties you have met. You needn't bother to smooth down Brown's extravagances, I knew the captain before I knew you."

Lister told his story, and when he stopped Cartwright filled his glass, raised it to his lips and put it back with a frown.

"Send somebody along the mole to Garcia's shop for two or three bottles of his Amontillado and white Muscatel. Charge the stuff to ship's victualing. When you got Brown out of the factory, did you think it possible he had a private stock of liquor?"

"I'm satisfied he had not. Montgomery gave him the liquor, and I imagine meant to give him too, much."

"It looks like that," Cartwright agreed. "If we take something I suspect for granted, Montgomery's opposition would be logical. I imagine you know part of the cargo was worth much? Expensive stuff in small bulk, you see!"

"I have studied the cargo-lists and plans of the holds, sir."

Cartwright nodded. "We'll find out presently if my notion how the boat was lost is accurate," The cargo's another thing. There may have been conspiracy between merchant and ship-owner; I don't know yet, but if it was conspiracy, this would account for much. Some of the gum shipped was very costly, and African alluvial gold, washed by the negroes, has been found mixed with brass filings."

"Montgomery frankly stated his father loaded the vessel."

"His frankness may have been calculated," Cartwright rejoined and knitted his brows. "Yet I'll admit the young fellow's name is good at Liverpool, and all he sells is up to sample. His father was another sort, but he died, and the house is now well run. However, in the meantime we'll let it go."

He looked up, for a fireman, carrying a basket, came in. Cartwright took the basket and opened a bottle of white wine.

"Take some of this," he said. "I understand you have seen Mrs. Cartwright?"

"Not yet, sir," said Lister, quietly. "I met Miss Hyslop soon before your boat arrived. Perhaps I ought to tell you I asked her if she would marry me if we floated the wreck."

"Ah!" said Cartwright. "But why did you add the stipulation?"

"It ought to be obvious. If we put the undertaking over, I expect to get a post that will enable me to support a wife, although she might be forced to go without things I'd like to give her."

"I see!" said Cartwright, with some dryness. "Well, I don't know if Barbara is extravagant, but she has not used much economy. Was she willing to take the plunge?"

"She was not, sir."

"Then I suppose she stated her grounds for refusing?"

"That is so," said Lister. "Perhaps Miss Hyslop will tell you what they are. I will not."

Cartwright looked at him hard. "All the same, I imagine you did not agree?"

"I did not agree. If I make good at the wreck, I will try again."

"Barbara is pretty obstinate," Cartwright remarked with a smile, and then filled Lister's glass. "I must go; but come to the hotel in the morning. We must talk about the salvage plans."

He went off, but when the boat crossed the harbor he looked back at the tug with twinkling eyes. Lister was honest and had not asked Barbara to marry him until he saw some chance of his supporting a wife. Since Barbara was rich, the thing was amusing. All the same, it was possible the young fellow must wait. Barbara exaggerated and indulged her imagination, but she was firm.

CHAPTER VIII

CARTWRIGHT GETS TO WORK

The morning was hot and Barbara, sitting on the hotel veranda, struggled against a flat reaction. The glitter of the sea hurt her eyes, and the dust that blew in clouds from the road smeared her white dress. Her mouth dropped and her pose was languid. To refuse Lister had cost her much, and although she had done so because she felt she ought, the sense of having carried out a duty was not remarkably soothing. It was a relief to know she need not pretend to Cartwright, who occupied a basket-chair opposite. One could not cheat her step-father by false cheerfulness.

"When you disappointed Lister you took the prudent line," he said. "The young fellow has some talent, but he has not yet made his mark. I approve your caution, and expect your mother will agree."

"I wasn't cautious; I didn't argue at all like that," Barbara declared. "Besides, I haven't told mother. She mustn't be disturbed."

Cartwright looked thoughtful. To some extent he was sympathetic, and to some extent amused.

"Then I don't altogether understand why you did refuse!"

"Oh, well," said Barbara, and the blood came to her skin, "for one thing, Mr. Lister waited for some time, and then asked me to marry him, after Shillito arrived." She paused and her look got hard when she resumed: "Perhaps he thought he ought; sometimes he's chivalrous."

Cartwright imagined Barbara was badly hurt, and this accounted for her frankness.

"Your reasoning isn't very obvious, but I think I see a light," he said. "It's possible, however, he asked you because he wanted you, and there is an explanation for his waiting. I understand he hesitated because he doubted if he could support a wife. It looks as if Mr. Lister didn't know you were rich."

"He doesn't know; I think I didn't want him to know," Barbara admitted with some embarrassment.

"Shillito knew, but one learns caution," Cartwright remarked. "Well, Shillito became somewhat of a nuisance, and I don't imagine you want him to look us up again. I rather think I must get to work."

"I hate him!" said Barbara, passionately. "Until your boat was signaled I was horribly alarmed, but then the trouble went. I felt I needn't bother after you arrived." Her voice softened as she added: "You are a clever old dear! One feels safe while you're about!"

"Thank you," said Cartwright. "I am old, but I have some useful talents. Well, is there something else about which you want to talk?"

Barbara hesitated. There was something for which she meant to ask, although her object was not very plain. Perhaps Shillito's demand for money had made her feel its power; moreover, she was independent and liked to control her affairs.

"My birthday was not long since, and I'm entitled to use some of the money that is mine."

"That is so," Cartwright agreed with a twinkle. "All the same, you're not entitled to use much until you marry, and you have just sent off one lover. Would you like me to send you out a sum?"

"I think I'd like a check book, and then I needn't bother people."

Cartwright nodded. Barbara was not extravagant. "Very well. I expect we can trust you, and the money is yours. I can probably arrange for a business house to meet your drafts. I'll see about it when I'm in the town."

He started for Las Palmas presently, and after some inquiries stopped at a Spanish hotel, where he found Shillito. The latter frowned when he saw Cartwright, but went with him to the courtyard and they sat down in the shade.

"Have you bought your ticket for Havana?" Cartwright asked.

"I have not," said Shillito. "So far I haven't decided to leave Las Palmas."

"Then I imagine you had better decide *now*. If money is a difficulty, I might lend you enough for a second-class passage, but that is all."

Shillito smiled. "If you want to get rid of me, you'll have to go higher. I reckon it's worth while!"

"I think not," said Cartwright, dryly. "In fact, since I can get rid of you for nothing, I doubt if it's worth the price of a cheap berth on board the Lopez boat. However, I'll risk this, in order to save bothering."

"Bluff! You can cut it out and get to business!"

"Very well. Your call at the Catalina didn't help you much, and if you come again you will not be received by Miss Hyslop, but by me. I have met and beaten fellows like you before. My offer's a second-class berth. You had better take it!"

"Not at all," said Shillito. "Before long you'll want to raise your bid."

Cartwright got up and crossed the flags; the other frowned and hesitated, but let him go. When he reached the street Cartwright called his *tartana* and told the driver to take him to the British Vice-Consul's. The Vice-Consul was a merchant who sometimes supplied the Cartwright boats with stores, and he gave his visitor a cigar. Cartwright told him as much about Shillito as he thought useful, and the Vice-Consul weighed his remarks.

"The extradition of a criminal is a long and troublesome business," he observed. "In the meantime the fellow must not be allowed to annoy you, and I imagine my duty is to inform the Spanish *justicia.* Don Ramon is tactful, and I think will handle the situation discreetly. Suppose we go to see him?"

He took Cartwright to an old Spanish house, with the royal arms above the door, and a very dignified gentleman received them politely. He allowed the Vice-Consul to tell Cartwright's story in Castilian, and then smiled.

"Señor Graham has our thanks for the warning he has brought," he said. "In this island we are sportsmen. We have our cockpits and casinos, but our aim is to develop our commerce and not make the town a Monte Carlo. Then the play at the casinos must be honest. Our way with cardsharpers is stern."

The Vice-Consul's eyes twinkled. He knew Don Ramon, who resumed: "Señor Cartwright's duty is to inform the British police. No doubt he will do so, but until they apply to our *justicia* in the proper form, I cannot put in prison a British subject for a robbery he did not commit on Spanish soil. Perhaps, however, this is not necessary?"

"On the whole, I don't think it is necessary," Cartwright remarked. "The fellow is a dangerous scoundrel, but I don't know that it is my duty to give you the bother extradition formalities would imply. Still you may find him a nuisance if he stays long."

Don Ramon smiled. "I imagine he will not stay long! My post gives me power to deal with troublesome foreigners. Well, I thank you, and can promise you will not be disturbed again."

He let them go, and when they went out the Vice-Consul laughed.

"You can trust Don Ramon. For one thing, he knows I have some claim; in this country a merchant finds it pays to acknowledge fair treatment by the men who rule. For all that, Don Ramon is just and uses prudently a power we do not give British officials. The Spanish know the advantages of firm control, and I admit their plan works well."

Shillito did not return to the Catalina. When he was playing cards for high stakes one evening, two *guardias civiles* entered the gambling house and one touched Shillito's arm.

"You will come with us, señor," he said politely.

Shillito pushed back his chair and looked about. The man carried a pistol, and the civil guards have power to shoot. His comrade watched the door.

"What is your authority for bothering me?" he asked.

"It is possible Don Ramon will tell you. He is waiting," said the other. He took Shillito to the house with the coat of arms, and Don Ramon, sending off the guards, indicated a chair.

"We have heard something about you, and do not think you ought to remain at Las Palmas," he remarked. "In fact, since we understand you meant to go to Cuba, we expect you to start by the Lopez boat."

"I don't mean to go to Cuba," Shillito rejoined.

Don Ramon shrugged. "Well, we do not mind if you sail for another country. Numerous steamers touch here and the choice is yours. So long as you leave Las Palmas—"

Shillito looked at him hard. "I am a British subject and stay where I like!"

"You are obstinate, señor, but I think your statement's rash," Don Ramon observed. "A British subject is governed by British laws, but we will not talk about this."

He paused and studied Shillito, who began to look disturbed. "One would sooner be polite and take the easy line," Don Ramon resumed. "So far this is possible, because you are not on the list sent our Government by the British police, but we have power to examine foreigners about whom we are not satisfied. Well, I doubt if you could satisfy us that you ought to remain, and when we begin to investigate, a demand for your extradition might arrive. If you forced us to inquire about you, a cablegram would soon reach London."

Shillito saw he was beaten and got up.

"I'll buy my ticket for Havana in the morning," he replied.

The Lopez liner was some days late, and in the meantime Lister haunted the office of the engineering company. At length the articles he needed were ready, and one afternoon Cartwright hired a boat to take him and

Barbara across the harbor. *Terrier* lay with full steam up at the end of the long mole, and when her winch began to rattle, Cartwright told the Spanish *peons* to stop rowing. The tug's mooring ropes splashed, her propeller throbbed, and she swung away from the wall.

She was rusty and dingy; the screens along her bridge were cracked and burned by the sun. The boat at her rail was blackened by soot, and when she rolled the weed streamed down from her water-line. She looked very small and overloaded by the stack of coal on deck. The wash round her stern got whiter, ripples ran back from her bows, and when she steamed near Cartwright's boat, her whistle shrieked. Cartwright stood up and waved; Learmont, on the bridge, touched his cap, but for a few moments Barbara fixed her eyes on *Terrier's* deckhouse. Then she blushed and her heart beat, for she saw Lister at the door of the engine-room. He saw her and smiled.

The tug's whistle was drowned by a deeper blast. A big liner, painted black from water-line to funnel-top, was coming out, and Cartwright's boat lay between her and the tug. Barbara gave the great ship a careless glance and then started, for she read the name at the bow. This was the Havana boat.

Studying the groups of passengers at the rails, she thought she saw a face she knew. The face got distinct, and when the liner's lofty side towered above the boat, Shillito, looking down, lifted his cap and bowed with ironical politeness. Barbara turned her head and tried for calm while she watched the tug.

Lister had not gone. Barbara knew he would not go so long as he could see the boat, and standing up, with her hand on Cartwright's shoulder, she waved her handkerchief. Lister's hand went to his cap, but he was getting indistinct and *Terrier* had begun to plunge on the long swell outside the wall. She steered for open sea, the big black liner followed the coast, and presently Cartwright signed the men to pull. Then he looked at Barbara and smiled, for he knew she had seen Shillito.

"Things do sometimes happen like that!" he said. "I think the fellow has gone for good, but the other will come back."

CHAPTER IX

LISTER MAKES GOOD

Arcturus' holds were empty and a long row of oil puncheons occupied the beach, but the men who had dragged the goods from the water were exhausted by heavy toil in the scorching sun, and some were sick. The divers had bolted on plates to cover the holes in the vessel's bilge before one fell ill and his mate's nerve went. The heat and poisonous vapors from the swamps had broken his health, and he got a bad jar one day his air-pipe entangled and the pump-gang dragged him, unconscious, to the top.

Afterwards, for the most part, Lister undertook the diving, but for long his efforts to reach the floor of the engine-room were baffled. To crawl across slanted gratings and down weedy ladders, while air-pipe and signal-line trailed about the machinery, was horribly dangerous, but he kept it up, although he got slacker and felt his pluck was breaking. Then one afternoon he knew he could not go down again, and he stayed under water long.

Brown, standing by the air-pumps, looked at his watch and waited anxiously. The bubbles broke the surface above the wreck and the signal-line was slack, but Lister had been down longer than he ought. He wars not a diver, and the others who knew their job, had come up sooner. Then Brown had other grounds for anxiety. If Lister were beaten, their chance of floating the wreck was small.

At length, the bubbles began to move towards the hulk, the ladder shook, and a dull, red reflection shone through the water. Then the copper helmet broke the surface, rose a few inches, and stopped, and Brown ran to the gangway. Lister was exhausted and his worn-out body could not meet the change of pressure. They dragged him on board and took off his helmet and canvas dress. For some minutes he lay like a log, and then opened his eyes and looked at Brown.

"Cartwright was on the track!" he gasped. "We can go ahead—"

The sun was low, but the pitch in the seams was liquid and smeared the hot planks, and Brown pulled Lister into the shade. For a time he was quiet, but by and by he said, "When the tide falls we'll start the pump and let her go all night. I must get up and tell Jones to clean the fire."

"I'll tell him. You stay there until we get some food," Brown replied.

The cook served the meal on deck, but they had hardly begun when he lighted a storm-lamp. As soon as the red sun dipped thick vapor floated off from the swamps, the water got oily black, and dark clouds rolled across the sky. Flickering lightning illumined the tumbling surf and sandy beach, but there was no thunder and the night was calm. The hulk and tug were moored at opposite sides of the wreck, forward of her engine room, and thick wire ropes that ran between them had been dragged back under the vessel for some distance from her bow. The ropes, however, were not yet hauled tight. When the cook took away the plates Brown made a rough calculation.

"We have caulked all hatches and gratings forward, and stopped the ventilators," he said. "I reckon the water will leave the deck long enough for the pump to give her fore-end some buoyancy. If she rises with the flood tide, well heave the cables aft, until we can get a hold that will lift her bow from the ground. Then you can pump out the fore hold and we'll make a fresh start aft. We'll soon know if Cartwright's notion is correct."

"We know *now*; I'll satisfy you in the morning," Lister rejoined and his confidence was not exaggerated.

A steamer's hull below her load-line is pierced in places to admit water for the condensers and ballast tanks. Lister had found some inlets open, but now they were shut.

"I'll own old Cartwright's a great man," Brown said thoughtfully. "When he takes on a job he studies things all round. The salvage folks, no doubt, reckoned on the possibility that the valves were open, but they couldn't get at the controls and didn't know all Cartwright knew—" He paused and added with a laugh: "I wonder how much the other fellows got for the job! But it's time we started."

Lister got up with an effort and went to the pump, which presently began to throb. The mended engine ran well and the regular splash of water, flung out from the big discharge pipe, drowned the languid rumble of the surf. The hull shook; shadowy figures crossed the beam of light from the furnace, and vanished in the dark. Twinkling lamps threw broken reflections on the water that looked like black silk, lightning flashed in the background, and when the swell broke with phosphorescent sparkles about the wreck Lister marked the height the pale illumination crept up her plates. She would not lift that tide, but the pump was clearing the hold, and he hoped much water was not coming in. If the leakage was not excessive, her bow ought to rise when the next tide flowed.

For some hours he kept his watch, dragging himself wearily about the engine and pump. He had helpers, but control was his, and to an engineer a machine is not a dead mass of metal. Lister, so to speak, felt the pump had individuality and temperament, like a spirited horse. Sometimes it must be humored and sometimes urged; it would run faster for a man whose touch was firm but light than for another. Perhaps he was fanciful, and he was certainly over-strung, but he imagined the big, rattling machine knew his hand.

At length when he looked at the gauge glass he found he could not see the line that marked the water-level. His head swam and his legs shook, and calling a fireman to keep watch, he sat down in the coal. He wanted to get to the awning, out of the dew, but could not, and leaning against the rough blocks, he went to sleep.

In the morning, he knew the fever that bothered him now and then had returned. For all that, he must hold out and he began his labor in the burning sun. When the flood tide rippled about the wreck it was obvious the pump was getting the water down. The bows lifted, and starting the winches, they hauled aft the ropes. If they could keep it, before long they might heave her from the sand.

It was a time of stubborn effort and crushing strain. Some of the men were sick and all had lost their vigor. The fierce sun had not burned but bleached their skin; their blood was poisoned by the miasma the land breeze blew off at night. For all that, Cartwright's promise was they should share his reward and somehow they held on.

At length, in the scorching heat one afternoon when the flood tide began to run, they hauled the hulk and tug abaft the wreck's engine-room and made the great ropes fast. If Lister's calculations were accurate, the pump had thrown out enough water, and the buoyancy of the other craft would lift the wreck's stern. If not—but he refused to think about this.

The sea breeze had dropped and the smoke of the engine went straight up. There was not a line on the glittering lagoon. The sea looked like melted silver; one felt it give out light and heat. The men's eyes ached and the intolerable sun pierced their double hats and dulled their brains. When all was ready, they waited and watched the sandy water creep up *Arcturus'* plates until the ropes stretched and groaned and the hulk began to list. On the wreck's other side, the tug's mast and funnel slanted.

Arcturus was not yet afloat, and the big wire-ropes, running beneath her bilge, held down the helping craft. The ends were made fast by hemp lashings and somebody had put an ax beside the post. For all that, Lister did not think Brown would give the order to cut; he himself would not. If they did not float Arcturus now, she must remain in the sand for good. He would hold on until the rising tide flowed across the tug.

In the meantime, he watched the pump. The engine carried a dangerous load and the spouting discharge pipe was swollen. Throbbing and rattling, she fought the water that held *Arcturus* down. A greaser touched the crosshead-slides with a tallow swab, and a panting fireman thrust a bar through the furnace door. Their skin was blackened by sweat and coal dust; soaked singlets, tight like gloves, clung to their lean bodies. Nobody else, however, was actively occupied. The negroes lay on the deck and the white men lounged in the shade of the awning. They had done all that flesh and blood could do, in a climate that breaks the white man's strength, and now the tide ought to finish their labor. But they did not know, and some doubted.

The ropes cracked and the hulk's list got sharp. On one side, her deck was very near the water. She was broad, but if *Arcturus* did not lift, it was obvious she must soon capsize. Lister opened the engine throttle until the valve-wheel would not turn. The cylinders shook, a gland blew steam, and the pump clashed and rocked. All the same, he knew himself ridiculous. The extra water the pump lifted would not help much now. They had a few minutes, and then, if nobody cut the ropes, the hulk would go down.

The massive oak mooring-post groaned and the deck-seams opened with the strain; the wire-ropes were rigid; one could see no hint of curve. The water touched the hulk's deck and began to creep up. Then it stopped, the hulk shook, and the wreck's long side slowly got upright.

"She's off!" said Brown hoarsely. Somebody blew the tug's whistle, and one or two shouted, but this was all. They had won a very stubborn fight, but winning had cost them much, and Lister felt their triumph was strangely flat. He smiled and owned he would be satisfied to lie down and sleep.

Brown gave an order; *Terrier's* propeller splashed noisily, and *Arcturus* began to move. Somehow it looked impossible, but she was moving. They took her slowly and cautiously across the lagoon, and when the tide was full put her on the sand. There was much to do yet and Lister wondered whether he could hold out until all was done.

In the evening Montgomery came off on board a boat pulled by four sturdy Kroos. He was very thin and haggard, but the fever had left him. When his boat got near, Brown, frowning savagely, went to the rail.

"What d'you want?" he asked.

"Let me come on board. If we can't, agree, I'll go back in a few minutes," Montgomery replied, and climbing the bulwarks, went to the awning and lighted a cigarette.

"You have floated her, but the job's not finished," he said. "I expect you mean to bring off the cargo you landed and you'll need a fresh gang of native boys. Well, I can help."

"You imply you can bother us if we don't agree?" Brown remarked.

"Something like that! I can certainly make things awkward. However, all I want is to go with you when you open the lazaret where the boxes of gold were stored."

"Ah!" said Brown. "I expect you see what your wanting to go indicates? Looks as if you knew something about the wreck."

"I imagine I do know something," Montgomery admitted quietly. "At the beginning, I reckoned you would not float her, but in order to run no risk, I meant to hinder you as much as possible. Now I'm beaten, I'm going to be frank—"

He paused and resumed in a low voice: "When I was left control of a respected business house I was young and ambitious. It was plain the house had weathered a bad storm, but our fortunes were mending and I thought they could be built up again. Well, I think I was honest, and when one of *Arcturus'* crew demanded money I got a jar. Since my father loaded the ship, I expect you see where the fellow's threats led?"

"I see the line Cartwright might take," Brown remarked dryly. "If the boxes don't hold gold, he could break you! We have found out enough already to give him a strong pull on the boat's last owners. They're in his power."

"He won't use his power. Cartwright is not that sort! Besides, the company is bankrupt."

"You are not bankrupt. Do you know what sort Lister and I are?"

Montgomery smiled. "It's not important. If there is no gold in the boxes, I don't want to carry on the house's business. You can do what you like—"

He stopped for a few moments and Lister began to feel some sympathy. The man was desperate and had obviously borne much.

"My staying at the factory was a strain," Montgomery continued. "I was ill and when at length I saw you might succeed, the suspense was horrible. You see, I risked the honor of the house, my marriage, my fortune. All I had and cared about!"

"Were you to be married?" Lister asked.

Montgomery signed agreement. "The wedding was put off. While it looked as if my mended fortune was built on fraud and I had known, and agreed to, the trick, I could not marry a high-principled girl."

Brown knitted his brows and was quiet for some moments. Then he said, "You are now willing to get us the boys we want and help us where you can?"

"That is so," Montgomery agreed.

"Very well!" said Brown. "We expect to open the lazaret at daybreak and you can come with us. You had better send off your boat and stop on board."

CHAPTER X

BARBARA TAKES CONTROL

The sun was rising and the mist rolled back from the lagoon. The tide was low and *Arcturus'* rusty side rose high above the smooth green water. Damp weed hung from the beams in her poop cabin and a dull light came down through the broken glass. A sailor, kneeling on the slimy planks, tried to force a corroded ring-bolt from its niche; another trimmed a smoky lantern. Lister, Brown and Montgomery waited. In the half-light, their faces looked gray and worn. The sun had given them a dull pallor, and on the West African coast nobody sleeps much.

After a few minutes the sailor opened the swollen trap-door and then went down, Brown carrying the lantern. As a rule a ship's lazaret is a small, dark strong-room, used for stowing liquor and articles of value. *Arcturus* was wet and smelt of salt. A row of shelves crossed the bulkhead and some water lay in the angle where the slanted floor met the side sheathing. A thin jacket and an officer's peaked cap were in the water. Brown indicated the objects.

"Looks as if somebody had stripped before he got to work, and then left without bothering about his clothes," he said. "I don't know if I expected this, but we'll examine the thing later." He lifted the lantern and the flickering beam touched five or six small, thick boxes. "Well, there's some of the gold!"

Lister seized a box and tried to lift it up, but stopped.

"It feels like gold," he said and signed to a sailor. "Help me get the stuff on deck, Watson."

They carried the boxes up the ladder and Brown brought the cap and jacket.

"Second-mate's clothes," he said, indicating the bands round the cuffs and cap. The imitation gold-lace had gone green but clung to the rotten material.

"Something in the pocket," he added and taking out a small wet book put it in the sun. "We'll look at this again, and now for the first box! I may want you to state you saw me break the seals."

Sitting in the shade of the poop, they opened the box, which was filled with fine dull-yellow grains. Then Lister sent a man to the boat for some things he had brought, and when the fellow came back hung a small steel cup from a spring-balance.

"The scale's pretty accurate; I use it on board," he said. "Well, I got the specific gravity of gold, zinc and copper from my pocket-tables, and made a few experiments with some bearing metals. They're all brasses; alloys of copper and zinc, with a little lead and tin in some. I weighed and measured two or three small ingots and afterwards calculated what they'd weigh, if their cubic size was the capacity of the cup. I'll give you the figures."

He did so and then filled the cup with the yellow grains and held up the balance. Montgomery, leaning forward, looked over his shoulder.

"Weighs more than your heaviest bearing metal! It's gold!" he exclaimed hoarsely.

"Yes," said Lister, "it's obviously gold. Perhaps we needn't open the other boxes. When we get on board well weigh them against this lot. So far as I can reckon after heaving them up the ladder, well not find much difference."

Montgomery sat down, as if he were too limp to stand. "But these are not all the boxes that were shipped—"

Brown went for the pocket-book he had put to dry and took out some papers. "This thing belonged to Gordon Herries, second officer."

"Mr. Herries?" exclaimed the sailor Watson. "The second-mate as was drowned when the surf-boat capsized!"

"What do you know about it?" Brown asked.

"I know something, sir," said Watson, but Montgomery stopped him and turned to the others.

"It seems the second mate tried to *save* the stuff."

"Looks like that," Brown agreed and signed to the sailor. "Now tell us all you do know."

"We was lying in Forcados river, shifting cargo to the Lagos boat alongside. Barret, my townie, was on board her; he'd made a run in *Arcturus*, and told me about the wreck. When she struck, Mr. Herries swung out number two surf-boat and Barret was her bowman. He went to the lazaret with Herries and they got up some bags of special gum and some heavy boxes. Barret thought they were gold, but hadn't seen them put on board. Then a big comber hit the poop, smashed the skylights, and flooded the lazaret. They reckoned she was going over and had some bother to get out. Well, they got the surf-boat off her side; she was pretty full with a load of Kroo boys and three or four white men. In the surf, the steering oar broke, she yawed across a sea, and turned out the lot. Some held on to her, but she rolled over and Barret made for the beach. They all landed but Mr. Herries; Barret thought the boat hit him. Gum and boxes went down in the surf."

"Very good," said Brown. "Now get off and send somebody to help heave the boxes on board."

Montgomery turned his head and leaned against the poop. Lister saw he trembled as if the reaction from the strain was keen. After a few moments he braced himself.

"It's done with! I think all the boxes held gold, but they're gone."

Brown indicated the cloud of spray that tossed above the advancing lines of foam. The long rollers had crashed on the bar from the beginning and would never stop.

"All the surf gets it keeps," he said. "If there is a secret, I reckon the secret's safe! However, we have to talk about something else. You can get us some native boys?"

"I'll send you a fresh gang. If my new agent arrives soon, I'll go with you as far as Sierra Leone. Since you're short-handed, I might perhaps help, and I've had enough of the factory."

The others agreed and soon afterwards got to work. When the negroes Montgomery sent arrived all the cargo worth salving was re-stowed, and he bought the hulk for a floating store. Then, one night when the moon and tide were full, *Terrier* steamed slowly across the lagoon. Two massive ropes trailed across her stern and *Arcturus'* high dark bow towered above her phosphorescent wake. The land breeze blew behind her and the surf had not the fury the sea breeze gives by day, but when *Terrier* plunged into the turmoil Brown watched the tow ropes with anxious eyes.

Arcturus rolled and sheered about, putting a horrible strain on the hawsers, and sometimes for a minute or two it looked as if she went astern. Flame blew from the tug's funnel, lighting the black trail of smoke; steam roared at her escape-pipe, and the engines throbbed hard. The ebb tide, however, was beginning to run and helped her across the shoals. The leadsman got deeper water, the rollers got smooth, and presently the swell was long and regular and the spray cloud melted astern. In the morning, a faint dark line to starboard was all that indicated the African coast. Next day Brown steered for the land and called Montgomery to the bridge.

"I reckon to make an anchorage before dark," he said. "We'll give the boys the rest they need and send *Terrier* to *Sar* Leone for coal. Learmont will land you."

"Then you're not going to take *Arcturus* into port?" Montgomery remarked with some surprise.

"I am not. Cartwright expects me to save him as much as possible and there are British officers and Board of Trade rules at *Sar* Leone. You don't imagine they'd let me start for Las Palmas? Surveys, reports, repairs and sending for another tug, might cost two or three thousand pounds. Then half my crew are sick and some are helpless, though I reckon they'll pick up sooner at sea than in an African hospital."

"It's a big risk. After all, I owe you much and know something about curing malarial fever. Besides, I'm a yachtsman and can steer and use the lead. If you'll take me, I'll go all the way. However, you ought to send Lister off. He can't hold out."

"He claims he can," Brown said dryly. "We have argued about his going to Grand Canary by a mail-boat, but he's obstinate. Means to finish the job; that's his sort! Anyhow, it's possible the Trade breeze will brace him up, and if he did go, the chances of my taking *Arcturus* to Liverpool are not good."

Montgomery stayed on board and when the tug returned with coal they hove anchor and began the long run to Las Palmas. For a time, Lister kept the engines going and superintended the pump on board the wreck, but he could not sleep and in the morning it was hard to drag himself from his bunk and start another laborious day. The strain was horrible and he was weakening fast, but it would be cooler soon and perhaps he might hold out until they met the invigorating Northeast breeze.

In the meantime, Cartwright went back to Liverpool, Mrs. Cartwright got better, and Barbara waited for news. She had refused Lister, but to refuse had cost her more than she had thought. After a time Cartwright wrote and stated that the tug and Arcturus had started home. No fresh news arrived and Barbara tried to hide her suspense, until one morning a small African liner steamed into port. Some passengers landed and when they lunched at the hotel one talked about his going off with the first officer to a ship that signaled for help.

"It was a moving picture," he said. "The rusty, weed-coated steamer rolling on the blue combers, and the little, battered tug, holding her head-to-sea. The breeze was strong and for some days they had not made three knots an hour. Well, I know something about fever, but they were *all sick;* the engineer delirious and very weak—"

Barbara, sitting near the passenger, made an effort for calm. Her heart beat and her breath came fast. Nobody remarked her abrupt movement and the other went on:

"Coal, food and fresh water were running out; their medicine chest was empty. Everything was foul with soot, coal-dust and salt. I expect it was long since they were able to clean decks. The skipper was in a hammock under the bridge-awning and could not get up. An African trader, Montgomery of a Liverpool house, seemed to have control. His skin was yellow, like a mulatto's."

A young American doctor to whom Barbara had been talking looked up.

"Jaundice after malaria!" he remarked. "I don't know West Africa, but I was at Panama! Was malaria all the rest had got?"

"It was not," the passenger replied meaningly. "However, if you know Panama—"

"Did you try to tow the ship?" Barbara interrupted.

"The mate thought it impossible. She was big and foul with weed, our boat is small, and we could not delay much because of the mails. We sent a surf-boat across with water and food, and then steamed on."

Barbara looked about the table. Mrs. Cartwright was at the other end and Barbara thought she had not heard. She touched the young doctor.

"Will you help me on board the African steamer? I must see the captain."

"Why, certainly! We'll look for a boat," the other replied and they went off.

Barbara saw the captain and when she stated that the owner of *Arcturus* was her step-father he sent for the chief mate, who narrated his visit to the wreck.

"You took the ship's doctor," said Barbara. "Is he now on board?"

The mate said he imagined the doctor had not landed and Barbara turned to Wheeler.

"Go and find him! Find out all you can!"

For some time afterwards she talked to the ship's officers, and when Wheeler returned went back to her boat. While the *peons* rowed them to the mole she asked Wheeler for his pocket-book and wrote an address.

"Don Luis Sarmiento is the best doctor in the town and had something to do with a fever hospital in Cuba," she said. "If you tell him I sent you, he will help. Take all the medicine he can give you and then go to Leopard Trading Company and buy whatever you think sick men would need. Bring me the bills."

"If I get all that would be useful, it will cost you high," said Wheeler and helped her up the steps at the mole.

"That is not important. Get the things!"

"Very well. But the ship is six hundred miles off. How are you going to put the truck on board?"

"I'm going to see about that next," Barbara replied and indicated a cloud of dust rolling along the road. "There's the steam tram. Don't talk; hustle!"

Wheeler lifted his cap and running along the mole jumped on board the tram.

When he had gone Barbara went to the office of an important English merchant house and asked for the junior partner. She was strangely calm, although she knew that when the strain was over she would pay. In the meantime, she needed help and admitted it was lucky young men liked her; she had not hesitated to use her charm on the American. The junior partner was keen to help, and going with her to a coaling office, offered to charter a powerful Spanish tug the company had recently bought. The manager agreed and Barbara made a calculation.

"If you can get the boat ready to sail in the morning, I'll send you a check when she starts," she said.

They went out and the merchant gave Barbara an approving smile. "I imagine they haven't at the moment much use for the tug, which accounts for their being willing to take a moderate sum. All the same, you handled the situation like a good business man. Had they known much about your plans before we agreed, they would have sent the tug and claimed a large reward for salvage. In fact, it looks as if you had saved Mr. Cartwright—"

"It's possible," Barbara broke in impatiently. "Still they don't know where *Arcturus* is and that her crew are ill. Now, however, we must engage fresh men to relieve the others. I don't mind if you pay them something over the usual rate."

The merchant engaged the crew of a Spanish fishing schooner that was being laid up, and Barbara returning to the hotel found Wheeler in the garden.

"I've got all the medicine and truck I reckon would be useful," he said. "If the steamboat man didn't exaggerate, you want a doctor next."

Barbara gave him a level glance and smiled. "If you like, you may go! A fast tug sails in the morning."

"Why," he said, "I'd be delighted! You can call it fixed. I came along for a holiday, but soon found that loafing made me tired—"

"Thank you," said Barbara and was gone.

The doctor laughed and joining an English friend in the hotel ordered a drink.

"I reckon I've been rushed," he remarked. "You folks look slow, but I allow when you do get started some of you can move. Since lunch I've been helping an English girl fix some things and she hit a pace that left me out of breath."

"Miss Hyslop?" said the other. "Perhaps if she'd had a job for me I might have used an effort to get up speed. A charming girl, and I think she's resolute."

"She's surely resolute!" Wheeler agreed. "Miss Hyslop sees where she wants to go and gets there by the shortest road."

When dusk fell Barbara thought all was ready and sitting down by Mrs. Cartwright narrated what she had done. After she stopped Mrs. Cartwright put her hand gently on the girl's arm.

"It's lucky you came out with me," she said. "I would not have known what to do, and I doubt if Mortimer—"

Barbara laughed. "Mortimer would have calculated, weighed one thing against another, and studied his plans for a week. Mine are rude, but in the morning they'll begin to work. After all, in a sense, I have not done much. I have sent others, when I want to go myself."

"It's impossible, my dear," said Mrs. Cartwright, firmly.

"Well, I expect I must be resigned. One is forced to pay for breaking rules! I have paid; but we'll talk about something else."

"The tug and supplies have, no doubt, cost much," Mrs. Cartwright remarked. "You must let me give you a check."

"No," said Barbara in a resolute voice. "I will take no money until mine's all gone. Father's a dear, I owe him much, and now I can help I'm going to help. I have sent a cablegram he had better come out but in the meantime he needn't be anxious because I have taken control."

Mrs. Cartwright let her go presently and Barbara went to her room. She had borne a heavy strain, but the reaction had begun, and throwing herself on a couch she covered her face with her hands and cried.

CHAPTER XI

LISTER'S REWARD

Signal flags fluttered in the breeze at the top of the Isleta and a smoke cloud stained the blue horizon. For a few minutes the cloud vanished, and then rolled up again, thicker than before. Cartwright studied it carefully and gave the glasses to Barbara, who stood near him on the Catalina mole.

"Is that *one* trail of smoke?" he asked.

"I think I see two. Sometimes they melt, but they're getting distinct now. There *are* two!"

"Ah!" said Cartwright. "Then it's *Arcturus*. I expect your tug has saved the situation."

"Lister saved *Arcturus* before I meddled," Barbara declared with a blush. "However, I'm glad I could help. You have often helped me."

Cartwright's eyes twinkled. "All I gave I have got back, but I'm not persuaded you didn't mean to help another. Well, perhaps, the other deserves your interest. Brown's a useful man, but he has some drawbacks and I doubt if he could have carried through the undertaking."

"If you'll wait in the shade, I'll get a jacket," Barbara replied. "There's a fresh breeze, the launch splashes, and I'm going with you to meet *Arcturus*."

When the first flag blew out from the Isleta staff, she had called Cartwright, and they had hurried to the neighboring mole. Cartwright had arrived two days before and they had watched the signals until the longed for message came: *Steamer in tow from the South.*

"I think you'll wait," said Cartwright quietly. "You don't know much about fever and the men I sent are not altogether making a triumphant return."

The blood came to Barbara's skin. She had meant to go and hated to be baffled, but Cartwright gave her a steady glance and she knew there was no use in arguing when he looked like that.

"Did you or your mother tell me Mrs. Seaton arrived by a recent boat?" he resumed.

Barbara was surprised, but said Mrs. Seaton was at the Metropole. Cartwright looked at the tugs' smoke.

"Then, I ought to have time to see her before they tow *Arcturus* in. Some sea is running and they can't steam fast."

He started for the Catalina and when he stopped by Mrs. Cartwright's chair his face was hot and he trembled. Hurry and muscular effort upset him, but time was valuable.

"I have not yet asked you for money, Clara," he said.

"That is so," Mrs. Cartwright agreed. "Sometimes I was hurt because you did not. You ought to know all that's mine is yours."

Cartwright smiled. "You are a good sort and I'm going to borrow now because I can pay back. I want you to telegraph your bank to meet my check."

"I'll write you a check."

"No," said Cartwright, "I think the other plan is better. Well, the sum is rather large—"

He stated the sum and Mrs. Cartwright said, "I'm not very curious, but why do you want the money?"

"I'm going to buy Mrs. Seaton's shares."

"Ah," said Mrs. Cartwright with a disturbed look, "she tried to force you to buy before."

Cartwright knew his placid, good-humored wife hated Mrs. Seaton.

"You're puzzled?" he remarked. "Well, I'd have bought the shares long since, but I wasn't rich enough and didn't think my borrowing was justified. All the same, the block she holds gives her a dangerous power, and if I can get them I'll baffle the opposition at the company's meeting. But I must be quick."

"If you want to baffle Ellen Seaton, you can use all the money I have got!" Mrs. Cartwright declared. "Tell me what I must telegraph the bank."

Cartwright did so and made for the Metropole as fast as possible, because the tugs' smoke was not far off. When he reached the big square hotel he gave a page his card and frowned while he waited in the glass-roofed patio. Time was valuable and he hoped Mrs. Seaton would not be long. On the whole, he did not think he was going to be shabby, but perhaps shabbiness was justified. Ellen had not forgotten she had thought him her lover, and although it was long since she would not forget. She hated his wife and had tried to injure him. Cartwright imagined she would try again, and so long as she kept her shares her antagonism was dangerous.

She entered the patio with two young tourists, whom she sent off, and beckoned Cartwright to a bench behind a palm. The sun that pierced the glass roof was strong and he reflected with dry amusement that Ellen looked better by electric light in the evening. Although she smiled, her glance was keen and not friendly.

"I arrived some days since and met Barbara in the street, but she has not been to see me yet," she said. "However, now you have come I ought to be satisfied! Since you were able to get away from the office, I expect shipping is languid."

Cartwright thought she meant to be nasty. For one thing, Barbara had not gone to see her and perhaps had not urged her calling at the hotel. Ellen did not like the girl, but she wanted to know people and Mrs. Cartwright had stopped at Las Palmas for some time. As a rule, Clara's friends were good. This, however, was not important. He must buy Ellen's shares before *Arcturus* arrived and the news of her salvage got about.

"Oh, well," he said, "although I think I see signs of improvement, things are not very promising yet."

"If you are not hopeful, the outlook must be black," Mrs. Seaton remarked meaningly. "Perhaps I ought to sympathize, but the effort's too much. My investments have all gone wrong and my luck at the Grand National was remarkably bad. In fact, if nobody will buy my shares in your line, I may be forced to agree with the people who want to wind up the company."

Cartwright thought his luck was good. Ellen was extravagant and a gambler. No doubt, she needed money, but he knew she was willing to hurt him and could do so. All the same, if she could force him to buy the shares she thought worth nothing, her greed would conquer her spitefulness. Well, he was going to indulge her.

"If you did join my antagonists, I might pull through, but I'll admit it would be awkward," he replied. "In order to avoid the fight, I'll buy your shares for ten shillings."

Mrs. Seaton hesitated. She did not want to lose her power, but she wanted money. Nominally, the shares were worth a much larger sum, but she had found out that nobody else was willing to buy the block. For all that, Cartwright was cunning and she wondered whether he knew something she did not. She asked for a higher price, but Cartwright refused. He was cool and humorous, although he knew *Arcturus* was steadily nearing the harbor. Perhaps in a few minutes the look-out on the Isleta would read her flags. At length he pulled out his watch.

"I have an engagement, but I rather want the shares. My getting them would help me at the meeting," he said. "Shall we say twelve-and-sixpence? This is the limit."

"Very well," said Mrs. Seaton and smiled with a sense of triumph. "It looks very greedy, but when can I have a check? You see, I'm nearly bankrupt."

"Now," said Cartwright, and taking out his fountain pen, rang a bell. "Send a page for some notepaper and write an undertaking to deliver me the shares."

Mrs. Seaton did so and Cartwright wrote the check. Then she signed to one of the young men she had sent off. "Since you are very business-like, you had better have a witness! I'm relieved to get the check, particularly since I expected you would be forced to ask Clara for the money."

Cartwright had to smile. The sneer was Ellen's Parthian shot. She was retiring from the field, but he owned that she might have beaten him by a bold attack and he had been afraid.

He went to the bar and ordered a drink, and then going out saw fresh signals blow from the Isleta staff. *Arcturus'* hull was visible in the tugs' thick smoke; the look-out on the hill with his big telescope had read her flags and was signaling her name and number to the town. Cartwright had won by a few minutes and was satisfied, although he had given Mrs. Seaton twelve-and-sixpence for her shares, when perhaps he need not. This was now about their just value, and, for old time's sake, he had not meant to cheat her. In the meantime a launch was waiting to take him on board *Arcturus* and he hurried to the mole.

Barbara saw the launch start, with mixed emotions. She was something of a rebel and had anybody but Cartwright ordered her to stop she would not have obeyed. She waited in the shade, fixing her eyes on the laboring tugs. Sometimes she felt a thrill of triumph because Lister had conquered; sometimes she was tortured by suspense. She did not know if he stood at the levers in the engine-room, or lay, unconscious, in his bunk. Well, she would soon know and she shrank.

She rubbed the glasses and looked again. There were two towropes; *Terrier* plunged across the rollers on *Arcturus'* starboard bow, the Spanish tug to port. It looked as if the wreck's steering-gear did not work. Spray blew about the boats and the crested seas broke in foaming turmoil against the towed vessel's side until she drew in behind the Isleta. A few minutes afterwards she swung round the mole and Barbara thought the picture moving.

The tugs looked very small; the half-loaded hull they towed to an anchorage floated high above her proper water-line. Rolling on the languid swell at the harbor mouth, she looked huge. Her rusty side was like a warehouse wall. When she lifted her plates from the water one saw the wet weed shine; higher up it clung, parched and dry, to the red iron, although there were clean belts where the stuff was scraped away. Barbara pictured the exhausted men scraping feebly when the sea was calm and the sun did not touch the vessel's side.

All the same, the men had won a triumph. It looked impossible that the handful of bemused ruffians she had seen start at Liverpool could have dragged the big vessel from the bottom of the lagoon, but the thing was done. *Arcturus*, battered and rusty, with sagging masts and broken funnel, was coming into harbor. A big pump throbbed on board, throwing water down her side; she flew a small, bright red ensign aft and a new house-flag at the masthead. Barbara thought the flag flaunted proudly and the thing was significant. Cartwright had weathered the storm, but she had helped.

The tugs' engines stopped and Barbara's heart beat, for a yellow flag went up. She hated the ominous signal, and turning the glasses, followed the doctor's launch. The boat ran alongside *Terrier*, a man went on board, returned and climbed a ladder to *Arcturus'* deck. He did not come back for some time and Barbara looked for Lister, but could not see him. Then the yellow flag was hauled down and *Arcturus* moved slowly up the harbor.

A fleet of shore-boats followed and when the anchor dropped crowded about the ship. Barbara braced herself and waited. Half the voyage was over and when the engines were cleaned and mended *Arcturus* would steam to England. The salvors had won, but sometimes victory cost much, and Barbara knew she might have to pay.

A launch with an awning steamed to the mole and vanished behind the wall. Barbara stopped in the shade; somehow she durst not go to the steps. Cartwright came up, but seeing his grave look, she let him pass. Then the American doctor reached the top and called to somebody below. Three or four men awkwardly lifted a stretcher to the pavement, and Cartwright signed to the driver of a carriage waiting in the road. Wheeler stopped him.

"It's not far. Carrying will be smoother."

"Very well, I'll see all's ready," said Cartwright and got into the carriage.

Then Barbara went to the stretcher, which was covered by green canvas. She thought she knew who lay behind the screens, and her look was strained.

"Is Mr. Lister very ill?" she asked.

Wheeler gave her a sympathetic glance. "He is pretty sick; he was nearly all in when I boarded the ship. Now it's possible he'll get better."

Barbara turned her head, but after a few moments looked up. "Thank you for going! Where are the others?"

"We have sent some to the Spanish hospital, landed them at the coaling wharf. They're not very sick. The rest are on board."

"*All* the rest?"

"Three short," said the doctor quietly. "They have made their last voyage. But the boys are waiting to get off with the stretcher."

Barbara let him go and followed. He looked very tired and she did not want to talk. She saw the stretcher carried up the hotel steps and along a passage, and then went to her room. A Spanish doctor and nurse were waiting and she knew she would be sent away. To feel she could not help was hard, but she tried to be resigned and stopped in the quiet room, listening for steps. Somebody might bring a message that Lister wanted her.

The message did not come and she was conscious of some relief, although she was tormented by regretful thoughts. Lister loved her and she had refused him, because she was proud. Perhaps her refusal was justified, but she was honest, and admitted that she had known he would not let her go, and had afterwards wondered how she would reply when he asked her again. Now she knew. The strain had broken her resolution. She had indulged her ridiculous pride and saw it might cost her much. Her lover was very ill; Wheeler doubted if he would get better.

In the evening Montgomery joined Cartwright in a corner of the smoking-room.

"I expect Captain Brown told you about the bother I gave him," he remarked.

"That is so," said Cartwright. "He, however, stated you gave him some help."

"All the same, at the beginning, I held up the job. When Brown could not work, your expenses ran on and I feel I ought to pay."

"It's just. Coming home, when my men were sick and Brown was in his bunk, you undertook the duties of doctor and navigator, and Wheeler admits your cures were good. Since you have a counter-claim, suppose we say we're quits?"

Montgomery felt some relief. It looked as if Cartwright did not mean to use his advantage; the old fellow was generous. Montgomery hesitated for a moment and then resumed: "I understand you bought the wreck?"

"I used the shareholders' money; at all events, I used as much as I durst. She's the company's ship."

"But the cargo?"

"The cargo's mine. That is, I get an allowance, agreed upon with the underwriters for all I have salved. I rather think the sum will be large."

"Then you're satisfied? Although you didn't get all the gold and lost the valuable gum in the lazaret?"

Cartwright's eyes twinkled. "I've some grounds for satisfaction, and I know when to stop! But perhaps I'd better be as frank as is needful. Very well! I get salvage on some of the gold. The rest is under the surf and nobody will open the boxes now. The thing's done with."

Montgomery was moved, but he saw there was no more to be said and asked quietly: "Will you tell me what you think about the prospects of the line?"

"On the whole, I imagine the prospects are good. We have got a useful boat for a very small sum, and the last report was *Oreana* could probably be floated without much damage when the St. Lawrence ice breaks. Well, I calculate next year's trading will earn us a small dividend, and since business is improving, we ought to prosper before very long."

"Thank you," said Montgomery. "I know something about the line and imagine the directors may need support. Just now I have some money that does not earn much. Would it help if I bought a number of your shares?"

"I think not," said Cartwright. "The plan has drawbacks. People are sometimes uncharitable and I have antagonists who might hint at a bribe. Besides, I don't need support. My luck has turned and I rather think I can break the opposition." He smiled and getting up, put his hand on Montgomery's arm. "All the same, when I send a boat to Africa you can load her up. Now I'm going to find the nurse and ask about Lister."

Lister was delirious, and for two or three days the doctors doubted his recovery. Then, one morning, they said his temperature had fallen and there was hope. Next morning they admitted that he was slowly making progress. Barbara did not leave the hotel, lest she miss the latest news from the sick-room. She was not allowed to go in, and when evening came she knew she could not sleep. She had not slept much since they carried Lister up the steps.

When all was quiet and the guests had gone to bed she went to the veranda and leaned against the rails. She was highly strung and rebellious. Lister had sent her a message, but she was not allowed to see him yet. She wanted to see him and was persuaded that for him to see her would not hurt. She knew he wanted her.

The moon was bright, but the shadow of the hotel stretched across the garden. Somebody was moving about in the gloom and Barbara started when she saw it was the nurse. The tired woman had gone out to rest for a few minutes in the cool night air and Barbara saw her opportunity.

Stealing across the veranda, she went along a passage and up some stairs. The landing at the top was dark, but she knew Lister's door, and turning the handle quietly, looked in. Bright moonlight shone through the open window and a curtain moved in the gentle breeze. Mosquito gauze wavered about the bed where a quiet figure lay. Barbara stole across the floor and pulled back the guard. The rings rattled and Lister opened his eyes. He smiled, and Barbara, kneeling by the bed, put her arm round his neck.

"My dear! You know me?"

"Of course! I wanted you. Since I got my senses back, I've tried to call you."

"You called not long since. I cheated the nurse and came; but if you ought to be quiet, I mustn't talk. The doctors said—"

"They don't understand," said Lister. "Now I have seen you, I'm going to get well."

Barbara lifted her head and studied him. His face was pinched, his skin was very white and wet. Her eyes filled and she was moved by tender pity.

"Oh, my dear!" she said. "It was for my sake you went!"

Lister took her hand, and she felt his was thin and hot. "I'm paid for all! But, Barbara, I think you're *logical* When I'm better—?"

She kissed him. "Of course. I'll marry you when you like. In the meantime you're weak and tired and must go to sleep."

"I am tired," he admitted. "Besides, the nurse will come."

Barbara gently touched his wet hair and moved his pillow. "The nurse is not important, but you mustn't talk."

She gave him her hand again and he went to sleep. Some time afterwards the nurse returned and started when she saw the white figure kneeling by the bed. Then she began to talk angrily in a low voice. Barbara was getting cramped, but without moving her body, she looked at the nurse and her eyes sparkled with rebellious fire.

"Be quiet; he mustn't wake!" she said. "There's no use in arguing. I mean to stay!"

CPSIA information can be obtained
at www.ICGtesting.com
Printed in the USA
LVHW032054310323
743149LV00005B/543

9 789356 891074